Learning to See

Learning to See

A Memoir of Southern Africa

RICHARD CHRISTENSEN

RESOURCE *Publications* · Eugene, Oregon

LEARNING TO SEE
A Memoir of Southern Africa

Resource Publications
An Imprint of Wipf and Stock Publishers
199 W. 8th Ave., Suite 3
Eugene, OR 97401

www.wipfandstock.com

PAPERBACK ISBN: 978-1-6667-3144-6
HARDCOVER ISBN: 978-1-6667-2394-6
EBOOK ISBN: 978-1-6667-2395-3

02/22/22

This book is dedicated with affection
to Sherry, whose courage and love have
always inspired me.

Jesus said to the man, "What do you want me to do for you?" He replied, "Lord, I want to see."

—LUKE 18:41

Contents

Preface | ix

Acknowledgments | xi

1   The Face of a New World | 1

2   Starting Over | 5

3   If You Want to Go Quickly, Go Alone; If You Want to Go Far, Go Together | 10

4   Teacher Training and Travel | 16

5   Settling in and Making Friends | 23

6   Keep Your Eyes on Your Destination and Not Where You Stumbled | 30

7   If You Want to Teach Someone, Don't Beat Around the Bush | 37

8   Death of a President | 53

9   Students and Teachers | 60

10   Doubling the Size of Our World | 71

11   Scripture Union and a First Retreat | 79

12   Life in Maun | 83

13   Believing Is Seeing | 95

14   Wisdom Is Like a Baobab Tree: A Single Person's Hand Cannot Embrace It | 110

15 Christmas Travel Adventures | 120

16 Transitions, Troubles, and Death in a New Year | 127

17 If You Never Raise Your Eyes, You Think That
    You Are the Highest Point | 138

18 Games, Stories, and Celebrations | 146

19 Teaching Teachers | 159

20 The One Who Has Many Friends Is Not Caught
    by Darkness on the Road | 167

21 The One Who Has Many Friends . . . (II) | 171

22 The Circle of Life | 179

23 The One Who Stumbles, Falls Forward | 184

24 Beauty Will Save the World | 189

25 The Road to Freedom Is Full of Thorns and Fire,
    Yet Happy Is the One Who Follows It | 201

26 The Light Shines in the Darkness . . . | 209

27 . . . And the Darkness Will Not Overcome It | 231

28 Too Many Bends on a Footpath Do Not Prevent
    One from Reaching One's Destination | 243

29 Farewells and a Final Adventure | 251

30 The One Who Never Leaves Home Thinks
    Mother Is the Best Cook | 257

Bibliography | 263

Preface

IN THE HISTORY OF Christian missions, examples abound of European and North American mission personnel arriving in a foreign culture and immediately misinterpreting local customs and mannerisms. Early missionaries in many African countries often rejected local customs and beliefs out of hand, disparaging them as inferior, immoral, or even meaningless. The missionaries frequently insisted that any convert to Christianity abandon any vestiges of African culture or religion. Such cultural imperialism divided tribes and disrupted communities. Other mission programs later recognized the need for dialogue and understanding, a much more valuable approach involving respect rather than disparagement.

When my wife Elaine and I went to Botswana, the invitation had come from the United Congregational Church of Southern Africa, the major Protestant denomination in the country. We arrived to carry out work that they requested, and to do it under their direction, not to impose our own ways. Entering a new world with a double sense of newness—I married Elaine six weeks before we and her ten-year-old daughter Sherry made the trip—we encountered a life of discovery beyond our imagining. This book is an account of that discovery through my eyes.

Leaving home and becoming immersed in a new cultural setting can be surprising, even shocking, as well as a source of unexpected learning. Surprised and often inspired by clever and creative uses of limited

resources available, we were introduced to life in a tribal, communal society where people did not hesitate to cooperate and help one another, a
community where consensus building could be patiently achieved only
after long hours of discussion and debate at the kgotla, the tribal meeting ground. A different sense of time as fluid and not rigid pervaded the
culture. On an official visit, one Ministry of Education official remarked
to me late one morning, "You and I will talk about your work in Religious
Education this afternoon." She then smiled and added, "That's an African
appointment." She meant that we would meet sometime between noon
and 4:30, whenever we had a chance.

We came to a place where the Christian church already had a strong
presence—approximately half of the people were Christians—but needed
more personnel to carry out important tasks. Independent only fourteen
years when we arrived in 1980, the developing nation built schools quickly but lacked enough teachers to staff them. Thus I had been recruited as
a teacher of Religious Education, a required subject in the curriculum.

The vast cultural differences between communal and individualistic
societies caused me to re-think our dependence on one another. While
the gospel rightly proclaims that God has set us free, God has not made
us independent. We are dependent on, and responsible to, one another.
Writing in the midst of the COVID pandemic has highlighted this all
the more. Learning and growing together as a family in the communal
setting of African culture, we came to understand more clearly the real
meaning of love and support for one another. In the cultural immersion
as well as in the process of writing this book, I discovered not only a
greatly enriched sense of the joys and struggles of African people but also
a deeper understanding of my own life and work. The African experience
has had a profound impact on my ministry and teaching ever since.

Acknowledgments

My sincere thanks go to Myka Kennedy Stephens, librarian at Lancaster Theological Seminary, and to librarians Abby Collier and Robin Sinn of the Milton S. Eisenhower Library at Johns Hopkins University, who each provided me with helpful guidance on issues of fair use and copyright permissions. Hearty thanks to Lucretia Crawford, friend and former colleague, who provided very helpful feedback and suggestions along the way. An especially warm thanks also to my friend Signe Jorgenson, a creative and patient teaching of writing who opened my eyes to the possibility of writing this memoir and always provided helpful advice and prodding. Any errors or shortcomings in my writing are obviously my own.

My greatest thanks and appreciation I give to Elaine, whose companionship and compassion have always lifted me up.

1

The Face of a New World

SUNDAY MORNING IN A NEW LAND

African Worship

"STOP! STOP!" THE CHURCH deacon leading worship interrupted the hymn singing, scolding the congregation for not singing more vigorously. He insisted that they begin the hymn again at a faster tempo. People responded by holding their personal Setswana language hymnals higher as they began to sing again, this time with more volume and greater enthusiasm.

Early in our time in Maun, at the edge of the Okavango Delta in northern Botswana, Jack Purves took Elaine, our ten-year-old Sherry, and me to worship with the local congregation of the United Congregational Church of Southern Africa. Our partner church with the United Church of Christ, the UCCSA helped sponsor Maun Secondary School, where Jack served as principal and we were assigned for a three-year term. The church's roots lay in the nineteenth-century work of the London Missionary Society, the group that sent missionaries Robert Moffatt and his son-in-law David Livingstone to Botswana. Old-timers still referred to the church as the "LMS church." The pastor, Rev. Peter Mudiwa of the majority Shona tribe in Zimbabawe, had fled the violence of Zimbabwe's civil war two years before. He served as pastor of the church and also taught some of the religious education classes at our school, work that I would share with him and Jack's wife Christine.

On entering the church building, we mingled with people of all ages as we found a place in a pew midway down the center aisle. Much chatter surrounded us as people settled in to their places. People around us greeted us with shy but warm smiles. We watched as little children wandered the building at will. Dogs roamed around the back of the sanctuary and up and down the side aisles, but the more than 150 people filling the building didn't seem to mind. Several elderly women sat on the floor, legs stretched straight out in front of them as they customarily sat on the ground at home. On the front wall hung a simple wooden cross. We noticed many of the women dressed in what appeared to be a kind of uniform: white cap and blouse with a black skirt. Many men wore white t-shirts with the words "Soldiers of Christ" printed on the front. We later learned that each of the churches in Maun (and around the country) had distinctive uniforms, many quite colorful and festive. Walking through the village on our way to worship, we had spotted a group of women with sky blue sashes worn diagonally across one shoulder over white blouses. Each sash had a bright yellow star sewn on it. We soon learned to identify which church someone attended by the style and color of the uniform.

In a setting quite different from our Pennsylvania experience, Elaine and I soon became caught up in the enthusiastic spirit of joy that poured forth in the worship. Her shyness overcoming her, introverted Sherry seemed hesitant and uncertain about participating, clinging close to her mother. Rev. Mudiwa baptized a small baby and welcomed two new converts into the life of the church. A deacon helped to lead worship, calling on several elderly men in the congregation to pray on behalf of the church, a common custom in African church life. Each man rose, sometimes slowly and in obvious pain, to offer a lengthy prayer. As different as the setting seemed to us, we experienced almost immediately the warmth and fellowship of the church universal. Barriers of culture and distance broke down as people welcomed us, loaning us hymnals and helping us find the right page as we joined in singing hymns. People carried their own personal hymnals to worship, so none lay available in the pews. One tune seemed quite familiar at first, but I could not place it because of the Setswana language. Then it dawned on me: "Bringing in the Sheaves."

Rev. Mudiwa had been ordered from Zimbabwe to Maun by his Methodist bishop after being threatened by one of the rival liberation movements fighting to overthrow the White minority government of the nation once known as Rhodesia. As Peter had not yet mastered Setswana, one of the deacons translated his sermon from English into the local language. From the sermon and by simply looking around at the congregation gathered there, we had our eyes opened to the circumstances faced by many people at the time. In a congregation of more than a hundred people, the offering that day totaled a little more than the equivalent of fifteen US dollars. Most people had little or no cash, depending upon raising cattle and a couple of crops for their living. Even so, moved to contribute more than they already had, a few people came up front toward the end of the worship to drop more coins in the offering plate. Strange and mystifying to us, a widespread belief in witchcraft and magic spells in the entire region generated fear in the hearts of many. Peter spoke to this fear in his sermon by declaring that fear could be overcome only by trusting in something stronger than fear: the love of God that binds us together.

Looking around the room, I also noticed a larger issue of love and reconciliation evident in the congregation. Some members of the Herero tribe mixed in with the others in the crowd. The Herero had fled east from Namibia into Botswana many years before, and Botswana people often regarded them with disdain. But there they were, the Herero women in their colorful patchwork skirts worn at ankle-length and cloth headdresses shaped like cattle horns. Defying common divisions of tribe and clan, a sign of the power of real reconciliation shone brightly.

A Powerful Witness

Mr. Motsamai Mpho, the national leader of the Botswana Independence Party and a former presidential candidate, sat in the congregation. People generally had a high respect for Mr. Mpho, both for his political activity and for his deep Christian faith. In the early 1950s, he had studied in South Africa and joined the African National Congress, actively working in the ANC's nonviolent political activities. In December 1956 the government arrested him as one of a group of 156 political and trade union leaders charged with high treason. The police assigned each prisoner a number, designating Mr. Mpho as accused no. forty-eight and Mr. Nelson Mandela as accused no. thirty-two. Charges were soon dismissed. But in March 1960, the apartheid government declared a state of emergency and arrested a large group again, jailing Mr. Mpho in Pretoria. After detaining him for four months, the government released him, giving him seven days to leave South Africa to return home to Botswana, then called Bechuanaland. Some months later, he and two other men founded a political party initially known as the Bechuanaland Peoples' Party.

Only a month before we arrived in Maun, Mr. Mpho had stood up in worship one Sunday and confessed that he realized that he hated Ian Smith, the White leader of the minority government in Rhodesia/Zimbabwe. Saying that he knew he could not be a Christian if he held this hate within himself, he then stated that both Botswana and the newly liberated Zimbabwe now welcomed Ian Smith. Upon hearing this remarkable story of his life and commitment, a feeling arose in me that would come often that first year. In southern Africa, it seemed, I would learn far more than I ever taught.

2

Starting Over

AN END AND A BEGINNING

Wilderness Wanderings

I CAME TO SOUTHERN Africa as a result of a broken marriage and an over-powering desire to take up a challenge unlike anything I had ever done. In 1979, the year I turned thirty-four, the need for a change grew strong in me. Two years before, serving as a parish minister in central Pennsylvania, I suffered the pain of an unwanted divorce. As a result, a powerful urge began to grow in me to see the world in a new way. Always being one who sought more information, more understanding, seeking the right questions, always looking for ways to open the eyes of others to new worlds and greater possibilities, I grew up with a strong desire to learn, to understand, and to help others to see meaning. Attending theological school and becoming a pastor helped me to get a grasp of the depth and seriousness of life. I learned to be fully present with people struggling with grief, pain and aimlessness. Those two years up through 1979 had been spent in an agony of thrashing my way through the disenchanted forest of the painful divorce, a time filled with agony and uncertainty. I longed to see something new, yearned to see the real beauty in the midst of the ugliness of the world.

An introvert in the extravert profession of parish pastor, I struggled with a strong desire to understand and explain the *whys* of life. I wanted to interpret ideas and experiences so that people would grasp something of the rich tapestry of this world we inhabit. I longed to see the world with new eyes, as a child does when seeing sights for the first time. The word *religion* itself has roots in a Latin verb which means to reconnect, to put things back together, to make meaning, to see the world whole. Wherever people lose connection, they fail to see one another, blocking the relationships that make life truly human. When the connections in life are broken, we find it much easier to dismiss others, pay no attention to them, and even harm them. For me, becoming a minister became a matter of fostering relationships, making meaning in the light of Christ. In 1979, to my surprise and delight, intriguing opportunities came to my attention through the world mission agency of the United Church of Christ: chaplaincy positions in Indonesia, France, and the southern African nation of Botswana.

My refuge in loneliness became prayer and dear friends. For more than a year I wandered through a wide range of emotions, doubting my own worth. Emotions ranged from "It can't be real," to a despairing, "What will I do now?" and then finally, "Maybe I'll be okay, even if I'm alone." Slowly I came to see that I still had a life, a gift always greater than we imagine. Gradually the conclusion formed in my mind that my own worth as a person did not depend upon being married. Even more importantly for my self-understanding, I began to recognize what had been my own lack of sensitivity in the marriage, reluctantly concluding that placing the fault for a failed marriage completely outside of myself involved simple self-righteousness and denial. I found it no easy task to work through the slow process of honest self-examination and admit the truth to myself. I had paid much too little attention to her needs for affirmation and support.

Elaine Enters

In the midst of the application process for overseas ministry, I met Elaine, a woman of deep sensitivity, strong faith, and keen wit. Coincidentally, in the same time period of 1977–79, Elaine had endured a similar experience of a difficult divorce. Her husband had left after almost ten years of marriage. Both Elaine and I had entered a first marriage fully confident of lifelong commitment, so each of us felt bereft when our respective spouses no longer wished to be married. My own parents had lived a long love affair through four years of dating and what eventually became sixty-one years of marriage. It never entered my mind that anything different would be true for me. The feeling stuck with me of having been roughly thrown off a merry-go-round of wishful illusions of a perfect marriage.

We met in October at a Christian singles group meeting. In later years, she would smile and tease me about being too slow to approach her. Several weeks after meeting me, she realized that if she wanted more attention from me, the first move would have to be hers. One evening in mid-November, she telephoned to ask me for a date.

Our first date, over sundaes at an ice cream parlor, resulted in a remarkable two-hour conversation overflowing with the joyous discovery of one another and an openness neither of us had encountered in what seemed a very long time. We discovered in one another genuine compassion and a passion for life that had not been shut down by the agony of the previous several years. When we said goodbye outside in the cold and windy night, I shivered, but not from the cold. Something inside had broken loose, an outpouring of longing and emotion too long bottled up. We met frequently thereafter, talking for long stretches, praying together, and continually discovering how much we shared in common, in attitudes, in faith, and in our quest to offer ourselves fully to another in love and real openness. I had emerged from the disenchanted forest.

Elaine and her ten-year-old daughter Sherry lived in a mobile home that she owned on a two-acre tract of land near the little town of Rebersburg, twenty miles east of State College. Her mother lived a short distance down the road and could look after Sherry when necessary. One of her two sisters also lived nearby. With no rent or mortgage to pay, along with the help of her family, Elaine managed to live on her paycheck from her job as an assistant bookkeeper at a local bank. Her take-home pay amounted to $210 every two weeks. I began to see something of her faith and character when I discovered that each pay period she wrote a check for $21 to her church, one-tenth of her income.

Her strength of mind and heart showed itself to me often through that winter. One evening she came to my house and told me of a conversation with Sherry. The first time I had visited their home to meet Sherry had been one evening the week before. After I left that night, Elaine, eager for a positive evaluation, asked Sherry, "Well, what do you think of him?" The ten-year-old responded by wiggling her hand in the commonly understood gesture indicating definite ambivalence, commenting, "Ehh." Needless to say, not exactly the ringing endorsement Elaine had hoped! The next morning, Sherry had a gloomy look about her. Elaine asked, "Are you afraid that if I love Rich, I won't love you any more, or at least not as much?" Sherry nodded her head yes. Her mother said, "Sher, you are very special to me and that will never change. Nothing else will change that." This proved to be the first of many times Elaine's wisdom and strength of character would be revealed to me.

Decisions Made

Elaine knew sometime before I recognized it that she could not let me go off to another part of the world without her. On a wintry evening in mid-January, I arrived at the same conclusion and proposed marriage. Teasing about our brief courtship and my slow recognition of reality, Elaine announced one day that she planned to write a book about her experience. Tongue in cheek, she proposed the title *How to Get Rich Quick*.

Upon interviewing her, the mission board quickly recognized Elaine's intelligence and ability. They approved her for the assignment. As part of our preparation, the board sent us to a career counselor for several days of tests and interviews. We both took psychological tests, intelligence tests, and vocational and aptitude indicators, all to determine more precisely our strengths and skills. Elaine measured very strong in intelligence, detail work, and inclination to the caring professions.

After examining my scores and results, the counselor posed a question to me: "Have you published anything?" Surprised by the question, I answered, "No." He quickly came back to me with, "Why not?" I had no answer. He said I reminded him of an enormous steam locomotive at a railroad yard, sitting on a side track, switched off, not using its power. The question jolted me. Failing to exercise my gifts seemed to stem from a foolish sense of false humility. His observation gave me a courage unknown before, a real sense of being able to accomplish more than I had imagined.

We drove to New York for a final interview to determine our destination. The southern African nation of Botswana became our choice, and we prepared for a wedding and an assignment at a secondary school that would bring challenge and rich reward.

Elaine's sisters, Jeanne and Kay, hearing of her plans, had a completely understandable reaction: they thought she had lost her mind. Marrying just a few months after meeting me and taking her ten-year-old daughter eight thousand miles away to a strange culture struck them as nothing remotely resembling common sense. But it became the best decision Elaine and I ever made. Being both tenderhearted and wise, Elaine became not only my partner, lover, and best friend, but the one I trusted to challenge me when I became too set in my opinions. Flying off to southern Africa took a great deal of love and courage on her part. To this day, I still marvel at her willingness to take such a risky leap of faith.

3

If You Want to Go Quickly, Go Alone; If You Want to Go Far, Go Together

—TSWANA PROVERB

A NEW LIFE BECKONS

The Journey Begins

WE MARRIED MARCH 8, 1980, in front of a large crowd of family and friends at St. John's United Church of Christ in the little town of Boalsburg, with good friend Rev. Bill Rader presiding and Sherry as our only attendant and flower girl. Bill and his wife Clara had provided a warm and welcome refuge during the most painful times in the immediate six months after my first wife had left me. Any time I called them to ask for help, they would always say, "Why don't you come over here and have a cup of tea?" Their empathy and wisdom filled many of my evenings. So it became a joy to celebrate the wedding at the church Bill served as pastor.

The mission board originally intended for us to attend a training conference in Toronto during the month of July, and then make the trip to Botswana. But to our surprise, the New York office telephoned us less than two weeks after our wedding to say that the school in Botswana wanted us there before the end of April. I needed to attend a scheduled training conference for teachers. With a frenzied and hectic short few weeks ahead of us, we had a brief moment of panic. But we agreed and began to do a quick and frantic job of packing.

The weekend before departure, doing our last-minute packing, we kept reducing what we put in our suitcases, trying to pack as lightly as possible. Because we were packing for three years, this proved to be a daunting task. Eventually we sent four trunks by air freight and carried six suitcases with us on the airplanes. Clara Rader kindly offered to drive us to the Philadelphia airport in her roomy station wagon. We departed Pennsylvania on a beautiful April spring day, each of us filled with nervous anticipation, hopes, and not a little anxiety. Heading into an extraordinary phase of our lives, we faced the challenge of being a new family in a cultural context quite foreign to our experience. Would we be "innocents abroad," in Mark Twain's famous phrase,[1] or would we be alert to new insights and understanding? We had no idea how much we would learn or what kind of family we would establish.

Sherry may not have been very sure about me, but that first day of travel I began to learn to have real admiration for her. As part of our preparation for the journey, we had all been given typhoid shots the morning before we left. Sherry developed a 102-degree fever, which she endured without complaint through the entire two-and-a-half-day trip. I could see that she had picked up some of her mother's self-confidence, self-reliance, and ability to endure. These traits showed up even more clearly when she played a key role in getting us through a serious obstacle in the London airport.

South African Airways

Our journey took us from Philadelphia to Boston, Boston overnight to London, then a fourteen-hour flight to Johannesburg. But at the South African Airways security portal in London, a totally unexpected snag arose. Going away for three years, we held only one-way plane tickets. The airline official checking our passports and tickets informed us that we had to show him a document confirming that I had a job waiting for me in Botswana. If not, we would not be allowed on the flight. We had not been informed of this. I had no such document. The South African government did not want anyone entering their country without a guaranteed means of support.

"Do you have a letter inviting you to your job?"

No, I did not.

1. Twain, *Innocents Abroad*.

"Then you must show me that you have enough money with you to purchase return tickets to London."

It meant that we had to show him we had over two thousand dollars in cash or travelers' checks with us. This presented a challenge, as we knew very well that we had no more than $800 in travelers' checks, divided among several suitcases to be sure that we had money available if some of our luggage failed to reach Botswana. I realized that we had one option: bluff our way through. After I nodded to Elaine to help, the two of us began looking through our suitcases to find the travelers' checks. Kneeling down and opening the suitcases, we moved slowly, deliberately, searching the bags carefully. We took clothing out, unfolding and folding it again, replacing it in the suitcase, trying to drag out the process as much as possible. Gathering the travelers' checks a few at a time, we finally reached the $800 amount. Then we acted as though we were searching for more. Turning to Sherry, I asked her to search her suitcases. Catching on immediately to our bluffing and appearing completely unintimidated by the stern-faced South African Airways official, she began to search slowly through her bags. Finally, the airline official's forbearance ran out. With a brusque impatience, he said, "Very well, I can see that you have quite enough. Put your bags through the security checkpoint." Struggling mightily to hide my enormous relief, I realized that together we had met our first real challenge.

South Africa in the early 1980s, still in the grip of the racial oppression of the apartheid system, had an iron-fisted security apparatus that took no chances. Because we traveled long before the 9/11 terror attacks, we had never seen a security checkpoint as rigorous as the one for South African Airways. Four security people examined every inch of the x-ray of each piece of luggage, peering intently at the screen like radiologists viewing an x-ray for signs of the tiniest tumor. They took what seemed an inordinate amount of time, checking for any bombs or anything with the slightest possibility of being a weapon. This intensive surveillance—long before 2001—seemed almost comical to us. But the security people were deadly serious, determined that no threat would escape their view. The x-ray revealed three pairs of scissors, which Elaine had packed for sewing. The security people confiscated those. They had us sign a paper stating that we had transferred the scissors to their custody, promising to return the scissors when we exited the plane in Johannesburg. At the time, this all seemed rather silly to us, but it definitely reinforced our impression of the fear and paranoia of an especially repressive government.

We boarded the plane, passing two Afrikaner stewardesses, blonde hair shiny and smooth, makeup perfectly in place. Sitting on the flight, I glanced through the information brochures about South Africa and the airline. The map of our flight path visually portrayed the widespread condemnation of South Africa: the route took us in a huge half circle completely around the west coast of the entire African continent. In other words, the flight took fourteen hours because no other African nation permitted South African Airways to use their airspace. Other reading material described the business climate and the natural beauty of the nation, with no hint whatsoever of the reality of the apartheid system, where five and a half million White Afrikaners held complete control of a government which shut out the participation of approximately twenty-eight million other people of color. On the plane itself, the entire crew and all the passengers were Caucasian. Observing this, Sherry asked, "I thought there were a lot of Black people in South Africa. Why are there all White people on this plane?"

Arriving in Johannesburg, we walked through the airport to change planes for a one-hour flight to Gaborone, Botswana's capital. As we walked, Sherry kept looking around, again letting nothing escape her attention. She asked, "Why are there so many policemen here?" A striking sight, to be sure: police were everywhere. The obvious air of fear made us ill at ease and eager to be on our way. We would encounter that fear again when we visited South Africa two years later.

Welcome to Botswana

Arriving in Botswana a few hours later, we found an entirely different atmosphere. We were whisked through the customs area with no hesitation because of the presence of Christine Purves, a religious education teacher from Maun Secondary School. Christine very simply explained to the customs official who we were, and we passed quickly through customs without even opening our suitcases.

Chris Purves became our guide to all of our new circumstances. A Mennonite with a keen sense of humor and a gentle, good-natured way of dealing with people, her cheerful kindness put us at ease. From explaining government procedures to regaling us with African proverbs and stories of the secondary school, Chris proved to be invaluable in introducing us to the new world we were about to inhabit.

Weeks before we arrived, she had sent us a long letter with suggestions on what to pack for our African sojourn. One item surprised us: long underwear. We thought at first that this seemed laughable in a country largely covered by the Kalahari Desert with summer temperatures often reaching more than 120 °F. But as we discovered later, the winter months of June through August, with average daytime degree readings at 75 °F, featured nights with lows down to 40 °F—and no heat in the houses.

Accompanying Chris at the airport came Nancy Sales, another UCC missionary also serving long-term in Africa with her husband Dick. Nancy and Chris proved to be excellent companions and guides those first couple of days in the country. The two women spoke to Sherry as an equal, without condescension, putting her at ease and making her feel as welcome as Elaine and I felt. Our first day in Botswana ended at the home of Jennifer Potter, a British woman working for the United Congregational Church of Southern Africa. A short, spritely woman with red hair, she served us a leisurely, simple supper of bread, jelly, cheese, and fruit as we sat in comfort marveling at the pleasant evening air.

Elaine observed that life in this new world seemed far more relaxed than back home. No one, not even the missionaries—very busy people— gave the impression of being under time pressures. The next day Christine and I went to the Ministry of Education to obtain a letter exempting me from a normal work permit, necessary because I lacked a formal teaching certificate. Fortunately, my master's degree in theology made the exemption possible. A Ministry official met us and walked us to the Immigration Office to help me get the letter. He waited with us for about twenty minutes while officials processed the exemption, then walked leisurely back with us to his own office. Long lunch breaks were the norm, and no one seemed in a hurry. An additional bonus came when we found that in Botswana, people scrupulously observed the British practice of mid-morning and 4:00 pm tea. Neither Elaine nor I had ever been coffee drinkers, so we felt even more at home.

Nancy and Chris took us to stay in the President Hotel, a modern facility in the Gaborone Mall, a shopping mall not unlike those back home. Stark contrasts between affluence and poverty existed in many African nations, Botswana being no exception. Western-style buildings and full indoor plumbing systems sat only a short distance from villages of thatched-roof huts built with mud, dung, and wood. We stayed in the hotel for a couple of nights, celebrating my thirty-fifth birthday on our second day there. Nancy went home after our first day, while Chris remained in Gaborone so she could take us a few miles south to the town of Moeding to attend the weekend teaching conference with me.

The warmth and hospitality of our welcome to Botswana had put me at ease, happy that Sherry and Elaine experienced similar feelings. This hospitality continued with our living quarters for the weekend, provided by Derek and Carole Lindfield, British missionaries assigned to the secondary school in Moeding. As one of the workshop leaders, Derek had experience as a religious education teacher and pastor in the United Reformed Church in the south of England. We found the warm hospitality with them that we would enjoy from many people in southern Africa in the next several years. The Lindfields hosted us with grace and generosity. We awoke each morning to the sight of Carole at our bedroom door holding a tray with cups of hot tea for us. Leaving for the conference with me the first morning, Derek told Elaine to make full use of the kitchen for her and Sherry, adding, "There's some mince in the refrigerator." Ah, but what is mince, Elaine thought. She had no idea. Not until that evening did she discover that in British English, "mince" meant ground beef. Thus we began to encounter the truth of Winston Churchill's wry observation that the British and the Americans are two people divided by a common language. Along with learning to drive on the wrong side of the road, it seemed that we would also need to learn an unexpected new language. Little did we know that eventually we would also learn to recognize the distinctive accents of English, Scottish, Irish, Australian, and South African speakers of English.

4

Teacher Training and Travel

TEACHERS' WORKSHOP

Learning a New Curriculum

AT THE CONFERENCE, TWO matters impressed me almost immediately. First, the dedication of the RE (religious education) teachers stood out. They all had strong commitments to teaching, especially notable since the severe shortage of teachers (in most subjects) meant that everyone had large numbers in their classes. In my first term, beginning May 13, I would have a total of 280 students, a typical number for many teachers. It seemed daunting at first, but it pleased and gratified me to arrive in a situation where the need outstripped the number of teachers available. The second matter concerned the government's strong backing of the workshop. An official of the government's Ministry of Education formally opened the workshop, stressing the concern the government had that religious and moral education be an important part of the school curriculum. Christians comprised about half of the population, so the fact that the new curriculum being introduced featured a Christian framework demonstrated the prominent place of Christian faith in the culture.

The workshop introduced us to a new RE curriculum that had been produced in Africa, written in large part by Africans, not missionaries from Europe or the United States. More significantly, the authors had based the curriculum on African traditions and personal experiences, making use of those traditions and experiences to teach the Bible. When a vocal minority in Botswana had objected to teaching Christianity as something Western that did not belong in the school curriculum, the authors of the course made it clear that the teaching affirmed and valued African traditions. They placed a big emphasis on the fact that Christianity had flourished in Africa in the several hundred years before the seventh century, long before it had much strength or sometimes even existed in Western Europe or the Americas. They rightly insisted that Christianity could not be labeled a religion of White people only. Leaders of the workshop explained that the RE course dealt with life experience and how the Bible intersected with that experience. Scattered throughout the material were many African proverbs showing wisdom I thought would be valuable for Western people. One example: *The child who does not cry out will die on its mother's back*, a Tswana proverb which comments imaginatively on our dependence on others for life.

A short explanation of terms would help the reader here. *Tswana* is the name of the culture. A *Motswana* is one person from the culture. The plural of Motswana is *Batswana*. The prefix *mo-* indicates singular, the prefix *ba-* means plural. *Setswana* is the language, *Botswana* is the name of the nation.

The method and procedure of the curriculum seemed to me to be the best Christian education material that I had ever seen. In summary, it worked this way:

1. My personal experience

2. Our (collective) African experience

3. The Bible experience (how the Bible speaks to us in our circumstances)

4. Synthesis (what is asked of me now?)

Reflecting on all this, I thought that North Americans often lack the opportunity to discover the richness of other cultures largely unknown to them. Beginning to learn this new curriculum invigorated me and made me eager to get started. A typical quote from the curriculum regarding African values showed the contrast with Western culture:

> In today's more individualistic societies, people are evaluated more than valued. In the best tribal societies, people were valued

not for what they could achieve but because they were there. It was their presence, not their achievement, which was appreciated.[1]

I began to see why elders in Africa were viewed with such reverence and respect. One of the other African teachers mentioned an African proverb that heartened me: *The one who stumbles falls forward.* Although certainly anticipating stumbles, I had the feeling that my own life would be genuinely enriched.

Teachers attending the weekend came from many different back-grounds: experienced teachers and clergy from Britain, missionaries like me, Roman Catholic nuns from Australia, Ireland, and the Netherlands with long experience in Africa, and Batswana teachers, some experienced and some recent university graduates. For a long time, a standard Bible Knowledge curriculum from Great Britain had been the norm in all the schools. It involved mostly the memorization of Bible verses and stories. Students simply repeated on exams what the teachers had given in lectures. The government had determined to phase out that curriculum. The new material being introduced especially delighted those who had been teaching in the old system. Confronted with a fresh approach and the obvious relevance to students, teachers were enthused about the fact that the course method began with the student's own experience and integrated African traditions with the biblical story. The method of the course seemed less didactic and much more interactive than the old curriculum. Lessons included units on friendship and relationships with others, the meaning of community life, understanding one's life vocation, issues of justice, and more, always relating to African lifestyles, history, and traditions.

It energized me to be able to learn from and with all these people from varied backgrounds. I especially appreciated the emphasis that the workshop leaders put on Religious Education as a means to keep people open to other traditions and not disparage them. My own lack of African experience did not stop me from seeing the potential benefit and impact the change in method could have on students. They would, I thought, be engaged and stimulated by these lessons. My confidence in my ability to do my work well grew considerably in the two-day workshop.

But something else boosted my positive attitude about my new teaching task. For several weeks before we arrived in Botswana, Christine Purves had been informing every Maun student she encountered

1. Mbiti et al., *Christian Living Today*, 118.

that a new RE teacher would arrive soon. She made sure to emphasize that I had a master's degree in bible and theology. Students perked up considerably at this news. Accustomed to many poorly-trained or incompetent teachers in the primary schools, students were thrilled to think of studying with someone with advanced credentials. Christine told me that almost everyone she informed reacted by saying, "Ah, we will be sure to pay close attention to our RE class now!"

A LONG ROAD TO TRAVEL

Train Ride

As we prepared to leave the workshop on Sunday for our journey northward to Maun, one of the other workshop participants approached us, offering to take most of our luggage with him in his car to his home up north. A British teacher named Tony Jones, he lived with his American wife Betsy in Francistown, second-largest city in Botswana. The two of them had met while teaching in Uganda. His kind offer relieved us of the burden of dragging all those suitcases on the all-night train trip northeastward from Gaborone to Francistown. He promised to meet us there, where Christine had left the school's van. We would then make the three-hundred-mile drive west across northern Botswana to our new home in Maun. Gratefully, we accepted his offer and put four of the suitcases in his car.

After getting a lift from the Moeding staff to the Gaborone railway station, we watched the train arrive. The National Railways of Zimbabwe ran from South Africa through Botswana into Zimbabwe. We had never seen a train or a boarding procedure quite like it. Tickets had to be purchased in advance, after which passengers found their way to the place along the platform corresponding to the class of ticket obtained (first through fourth class). When the train stopped, a White Zimbabwean conductor in neatly pressed black uniform, white shirt, and black cap, descended from the train, clipboard in hand. A quite disorderly and chaotic scene ensued, the passengers crowding around him on all sides, like moths to a lamp, pushing their way closer and calling out their names. He consulted his list on the clipboard, informing each person of his or her assigned compartment. Upon boarding with our second-class tickets, we were surprised to find that the railway cars had old-fashioned private compartments with beautifully finished, polished wooden walls and fixtures. Sleeping berths folded down out of the wall on each side of the compartment. Under the window, a small basin and water spigot folded out. It reminded us of trains in old films about the nineteenth-century American West. Given the fancy nature of our second-class accommodations, we wondered what first-class might be like. Then a porter surprised us newcomers by coming to make up our beds. With the swaying railroad cars rocking us to sleep, we had a good night's rest, waking soon before our 7:30 am arrival in Francistown after eleven hours on the train.

At that point we felt rather pampered. But we faced a long drive to Maun through the northern Kalahari Desert. Christine picked up the secondary school's seven-passenger van she had left near the train station, discovering that Tony Jones awaited us there with our transported luggage. After we thanked Tony profusely for saving us the strain of carting all those suitcases, Christine searched the area and found Peace Corps volunteer Larry Kies, an agriculture teacher arriving from the Botswana village of Serowe to be re-assigned to Maun Secondary School. A smart, affable, guitar-playing Iowa farm boy in his late twenties, Larry would become a valuable colleague and close friend to us all. He cracked corny jokes, had an easy smile, and brought with him valuable experience from his time at another school.

Crossing the Desert

Maun lay 300 miles from Francistown, the nearest large town. Most government officials and teachers regarded the village as difficult to reach—and an especially undesirable post, given its distance from any urban setting. On a good day, the trip by car from Francistown took a full eight hours, largely because two-thirds of the trip took drivers over a rough, bumpy road of sand, dirt, and stones. At times that day I could barely determine where the road actually ran. I kept wondering along the way how Christine could tell where the road lay through the stark beauty of the wide open spaces. The land did feature some scattered trees and scrub brush, all on flat landscape. Seven-foot ostriches ran alongside the van occasionally. At one point we passed a herd of more than a hundred zebra on the right and some wildebeest on the other side, grazing not very far from the road. With no air conditioning, the windows stayed open for the journey, filling our hair and clothing with sand from the roadway.

At one point, a vast area of pure white appeared to our left, stretching endlessly into the distant horizon. Thousands of years ago, shallow lakes had covered the area, eventually drying up leaving vast salt deposits on the flat earth. On these Makgadikgadi salt pans, as they were named, very little life or growth could be seen—only a vast stretch of white noth-ingness, like a visual portrayal of infinity.

About half-way to Maun, we stopped to rest at an enormous baobab tree. The baobab is a strange looking growth, a white tree with branches pointing awkwardly from the top in odd, random disorder so that the whole tree appears to be inserted into the ground upside down, its roots sticking up to the sky. This particular tree obviously served as a common rest stop for travelers, as empty soda cans and other trash littered the area around the huge base. Its size required more than a dozen people, arms outstretched and linking hands, to completely surround the tree. As we rested a while by the huge tree, Larry pulled out a container of dried mo-phane worms to offer them as a snack. He encouraged us, with a smile, to taste them. "They have lots of protein," he claimed. But so early in our African experience, we weren't ready to try this offering when we saw the distinctly unappetizing appearance of the worms, each one multi-colored red, green, and white.

Christine then pointed to a giant mound about twenty yards away, saying to me, "Go take a closer look at that." A wide, rounded base eight feet in diameter rose up to a pointed top over six feet high. When I touched my palm to the side, the rough, sandy surface felt rock-hard. "So what is it?" I asked. She put a big grin on her face and said, "A termite mound." "This big??" I said, quickly taking several steps backward. "Yes, they're made of soil, termite saliva, and dung. Out in the hot sun like this, they harden quite fast. Actually, even though it feels so solid and hard, it's quite porous to allow air in all through the structure." We had found one of the many fascinating—and totally unexpected—phenomena in this new world we had entered.

OUR NEW HOME

Arriving in Maun just in time for a beautiful sunset, we took a look at our new surroundings. Located close to the Okavango swamp and not barren at all, the area featured a variety of trees, shrubs, and other plants. As al-most everywhere in the country, sandy soil predominated. Vehicles could easily get stuck in the deeper spots. Christine showed us our temporary quarters, a three-bedroom house with a stone fireplace and a solar water heater. Alongside the house grew two banana trees, mango trees, and one peach tree. A bright red flowering bougainvillea sat in the middle of the front yard. If this represented what being a missionary meant, Elaine and I joked, many more people would sign up!

For the first month, we shared that house with Marion Gilmour, a science teacher from Northern Ireland who had recently taught at a girls' secondary school in South Africa. Raised in the rigidly conservative Reformed Presbyterian Church of Northern Ireland, she explained that many Protestants in her homeland held the strong belief that they were called to defend Protestantism on behalf of the whole world against the Roman Catholic Church. Tragic violence shook Northern Ireland at that time, a frequent and devastating reminder of the ugliness of prejudice. Marion told us, however, that actually the narrow-mindedness of the people kept her from living back home, not so much the violence. "It's just more than I can stand," she said with a touch of sadness tinged with bitterness.

Another smaller house opened up soon, more suitable for us. For the next three years our home would be a simple cinder-block faculty house at the school. The little white house featured gorgeous bougain-villea clinging to the outside wall in a bright red half-circle around the kitchen window. Fruit trees in the yard produced abundant, delicious sweet mangoes and papayas, mulberries, finger-sized bananas, limes, and lemons the size of softballs. We had a living room/dining room area with a fireplace, a screened-in porch facing the river, two small bedrooms, a bathroom, and a tiny, narrow kitchen. Thanks to a gas water heater, we had hot and cold running water. The river provided water, treated with chlorine, but it could not be used for drinking because it often came from the spigot dirty. The house equipment included two large, heavy plastic containers which we filled at one of the village's boreholes, wells the government had drilled and put spigots on the surface for the public's use. Good clean water came fresh, untreated, and quite drinkable from deep in the ground. Because malaria-bearing mosquitoes threatened, we each needed to take a chloroquine pill once a week as a preventive measure, so that became part of our regular routine. Living only a few steps from the main administration building (which included Elaine's office) and the morning assembly ground, where the school day began for me, both of us had a short commute to work. In that house we became a family. We read, cooked, entertained, and played games. Elaine and I continued to grow closer, and Sherry and I learned to know one another.

5

Settling in and Making Friends

BOTSWANA LIFE AND CULTURE

At the Edge of the Kalahari

BOTSWANA IS A LANDLOCKED country about the size of Texas, almost entirely flat and 3300 feet above sea level. It is desert, barrenness, hundreds of zebra crossing a road in front of your car, magnificently-horned antelope grazing but always on the lookout for preying hyena, gangly ostriches sometimes running alongside vehicles on the road. It can also be a land of stark beauty, hospitality, and surprises. Elaine and I quickly discovered how language can provide significant insight into a culture. "*Dumela*," the first word of greeting upon seeing or meeting another person, translates literally as "I believe," which seemed a rather odd way of greeting. One day the school's boarding master (who oversaw the school's male boarders) explained it to me: "When you say *Dumela*, it is actually shorthand for: I believe there is peace between you and me." The Batswana, over several hundred years, had kept traveling farther inland from the coast of Africa to avoid enemy tribes and the colonial powers. Out of pragmatism, not cowardice, they tried to avoid conflict. When people stepped onto a public bus, they sometimes greeted the entire busload of passengers with "*Dumelang ditsala*," or, "Greetings, friends." Their common greeting indicates a sense of connectedness and community, a deeply significant sign of the strength and meaning of relationships. A

Setswana proverb states this well: *A person is a person because of (or by means of) others.*

Situated in the region called Ngamiland at the northern edge of the vast Kalahari Desert which covered most of the country, Maun at that time had almost ten thousand people. It lay at the edge of the Okavango Delta, the only inland delta in the world. Rain-swollen rivers from Angola brought water from the north, creating large areas of swamp and numerous streams through the desert, providing life for a huge variety of plants, birds, fish, and animals. Eventually, the water simply disappeared into the sandy desert soil, leaving behind pools and streams nourishing the plants and wildlife. Maun served as the stopping-off point for travelers going into the delta for safaris.

One great advantage to life in Maun proved to be the Thamalakane River, the one river in the country with flowing water all year round. The river ran alongside the school grounds, just a hundred yards down the hill from our row of faculty houses. It meant that the school could support a large garden, irrigated by river water, where the students could learn new and efficient agricultural methods from our new friend, Larry Kies. Larry had come to replace Loyd Schaad, a long-time Methodist missionary who had spent years in Angola before arriving in Maun to set up the school garden. Over a period of almost ten years, Loyd had fashioned a near-miraculous result in the hot, dry climate, rigging up an irrigation system enabling the growth of a wide variety of nourishing food. The garden produced grapefruit, lemons, oranges, tomatoes, tangerines, papaya, mangoes, and numerous vegetables. Chickens provided a steady supply of eggs. Staff members could place an order and pay for a box full of fruit, eggs, and vegetables, delivered to the administration building for us once a week. It took little time for me to conclude that fresh mangoes and papaya just picked from the trees must surely be the most delicious fruit on earth. After wrongly thinking we would have trouble finding the right foods to eat, all this served as a delightful introduction to our new life in Maun.

Pula and Life

The river running alongside the school grounds served as a great boon to all of us. Water has always been a precious commodity in Botswana. Unlike North American culture, where rain is often regarded as a nuisance which ruins someone's day, southern Africans hold a very different view expressed in the Setswana word "pula." The literal translation is "rain," but it served as an expression of good luck, congratulations, or celebration. People shouted *"Pula, Botswana"* on the nation's independence day. Visitors, upon departing someone's home, heard the hosts bid farewell and good luck with the words *"Tsamaya ka pula"* ("travel with rain"). A light blue background on the Botswana flag represented Pula. The nation had even named the monetary currency the Pula. At the time, one Pula equaled slightly more than one US dollar.

Traditional life in the country always meant keeping cattle. Cattle-rich but poor by most other measures, Botswana traditional life centered around their livestock. Families had a home in the village, another at the cattle post, and a third at what they termed "the lands" where they grew crops. Cattle served as a person's social security, pension fund, symbol and source of wealth, as well as food and drink. A common saying in the culture, very offensive to our ears, stated: "You can take my wife, but not my cattle." The Batswana teachers at our school often spent part of their monthly paycheck to purchase more cattle, a literal investment in stock for the future. In December, January, and February, the rains came swiftly, sometimes violently in short, hard bursts, sometimes long and soaking, creating rivers in the desert and nourishing the grass, plants, and trees that kept the animals alive. If the rains did not come, the grass died. When the grass died, the cattle died. Security no longer existed. *"Pula Botswana"* indeed.

Threats to Livestock

At the time we arrived in Botswana, the cattle faced another threat. Foot-and-mouth disease had been ravaging the nation's herds. The government, forced to respond vigorously to such a potentially devastating threat, had set up stations along the main roads throughout the country to cleanse the wheels of vehicles and the shoes of all travelers passing by. Twice on the road from Francistown to Maun we had been stopped by officials who instructed us to exit our van and walk through a shallow ditch containing a milky white watery mix designed to kill any traces of the disease we might have carried on our shoes. Each time, the officials watched carefully to be sure that we all set our shoe bottoms completely into the water. Then Chris had to drive the vehicle through the ten-foot ditch so that the entire surface of all four wheels passed through the water. It impressed us that the government went to such lengths to combat the spread of the disease. The care and extent of their vigilance indicated to me something of the government's real and effective commitment to democracy.

SHERRY'S NEW LIFE

Situation: Uncertain

Having no children from my first marriage, I confess to being a bit un-nerved at becoming a stepfather with such little advance preparation. I felt somewhat like the school kid who had been absent the day the instructions for an assignment had been handed out. To say that I felt unsure how to act would be a vast understatement. But certainly the circumstances she had entered were harder on Sherry than they were on me. After all, because of me she had been placed into a situation of great uncertainty regarding all sorts of matters in her life. Education, friends, contact with others in a foreign culture—so much of her life would be different from what she had known in rural Pennsylvania. It hardly seemed possible that she would not be distressed, anxious, and unhappy. Sherry could have decided to shut me out and carry resentment toward me for taking her 8000 miles away from her father, her other relatives, and her school friends. But she never displayed such resentment to me. I found this remarkable for one so young, marveling that she showed such resiliency in the new world in which she dwelt.

Not wishing to exercise undue and perhaps unwelcome authority over her, I decided to work slowly at earning her trust, initially leaving directions and discipline to her mother. One mistake (not the only one!) came when I foolishly began triangulating relationships in our household by approaching Elaine as a referee in misunderstandings between Sherry and me. After a few go-rounds at this, Elaine finally said to me, "I'm no longer serving as go-between for the two of you. You're on your own. Talk to each other. I'm out." As often happened in our life together, Elaine's wisdom proved both decisive and prudent.

One evening a few months into that first year, Sherry had gone to bed and I stopped at her door to wish her good night. "Good night, Sher. I love you." With a quiet, halting, not-quite-sure-I-mean-it voice, she replied, "I love you, too." I thought, *Ah, it's a beginning.*

Making Friends

For our first several months in Maun, Sherry bore no burden of school work. Elaine had researched the matter and discovered the Calvert School, a private school in Baltimore, Maryland, with a long history of offering education to Americans posted in distant countries. But the sixth grade school materials we had ordered did not come in the mail until October, almost six months after our arrival. Those first months in Maun Sherry spent a great deal of time reading, sometimes borrowing from the school library. But in addition, during that time, several members of the staff befriended her, including our initial contact Christine Purves. Christine would joke with her and encourage her to open up. Mary Beth Gilbertson, an English teacher and UCC missionary, made an effort to spend some time with her. A young woman in her twenties who had spent part of her childhood with missionary parents in Japan, Mary Beth had a bright smile, a gentle manner, and an obvious compassionate nature which made her one of several excellent role models for Sherry. A Danish couple, Sven and Elinor Sveidahl, invited Sherry for lunch a couple of times before they left Botswana for home when their contract ended. Carol Schaad, who had grown up in Angola with her American Methodist missionary parents Loyd and Margaret, also went out of her way to befriend Sherry. A woman of great confidence, fluent in Portuguese and possessing thorough knowledge of Africa, Carol seemed to have a knack for coping with almost any difficult situation. Picking up on Sherry's discontent and uncertainty, Carol knew from long experience the difficulties of a child facing a foreign culture. Newly assigned to our school as a domestic science teacher, Carol took Sherry under her wing, walking with her, giving her tennis lessons on the school's court just across the path from our yard, and helping to put her more at ease in the new life we had entered. Susan Shopland, another missionary child whose parents had been Presbyterian workers in Egypt, served with the Peace Corps in Maun with her science teacher husband Mark. Yet another self-confident and capable woman, Susan also spent time with Sherry, giving her more tennis practice and extra pointers for her game. One afternoon in early July, I went out to the tennis court to play a game with Sherry, discovering to my great surprise that she had developed a rather nasty backhand.

Christine Purves frequently took Sherry into the village with her when she drove the school van for errands. Christine, the older woman, along with Carol, Mary Beth, and Susan, smart and lively young women in their twenties, became important people in Sherry's first year in Africa. Elaine and I have always been filled with gratitude for these good friends.

Discomfort and Acceptance

When we first arrived at the school, the new term had not yet started, so no students were in residence. Two weeks later, when the new term began, our shy and introverted ten-year-old became overwhelmed by attention from the returning students. At times, four or five girls would appear at our kitchen door asking to see Sherry, curious about the new American girl on campus. Intimidated, very shy, and being so greatly outnumbered, Sherry felt quite reluctant to be subjected to scrutiny by the students and wouldn't come to the door. It took some time for her to overcome her shyness and begin to interact more with other students.

Numerous aspects of our living situation seemed odd and at times uncomfortable to Sherry. We had a lady from the village who worked for us, washing dishes, sweeping the house, and washing clothing. Lettie had been employed by one of the former teachers who had departed, so we hired her for the standard wage rate so she did not go jobless. Sherry thought it quite strange that we had a cleaning lady, that we had no automatic washer or dryer, and that we might or might not have hot water. She soon discovered why we had no need for a dryer. Wet clothing hung outside dried almost instantaneously in the heat and complete absence of any humidity. Just as Lettie finished hanging all the clothes on the line in the bright sunshine, she would start back at the beginning of the line taking them down.

So much seemed strange to Sherry. That strangeness and the feeling of being wrenched from her small town Pennsylvania life made her first few months in Botswana a time of trial and uneasiness. If not for the companionship and attention from the several women on campus, she could have become thoroughly discouraged. After only a few months in Maun, a Dutch family named Langendijk arrived at the school. Jack and Goke had five children. They moved into the big house we had been assigned at first. Sherry became a frequent guest in their home, becoming fast friends with Neeltje, their oldest child. The Langendijks had Sherry over to their house for dinner numerous times, and when Neeltje came to visit our house, Elaine and I could hear frequent laughter coming from Sherry's room.

It became obvious by September that first year that Sherry had grown in her understanding and outlook on life in Botswana. Within a one-week period that month, she had several of her possessions stolen. Two shirts, including her favorite yellow-gold top, disappeared from the clothesline one day. Soon after, someone stole her skateboard. At dinner sometime after those thefts, she surprised us with the statement, "I guess I'm really not so upset with this happening, because I see the children here with not many things, and I know they have a lot less than I do." For a child not yet eleven years old, I found this quite heart-warming and admirable. To be able to see the world from other people's point of view seemed to me not only a sign of increasing maturity but also a mark of her greater acceptance of our new life in Africa.

6

Keep Your Eyes on Your Destination and Not Where You Stumbled

—African Proverb

ELAINE'S TRIALS

We had been set down in the midst of a vastly different world, strangers in the culture living in a village 300 miles from the nearest big town. Those first months in Botswana our days were filled with unexpected discoveries, the dawning of new perspectives, and quick immersion into our new tasks, I as teacher and chaplain, and Elaine as the school's treasurer.

Learning by Doing

I had little doubt from the beginning that Elaine had the tougher job. She took over the financial position from Margaret Schaad, who with her husband Loyd were in the midst of preparing for retiring to the United States after forty years as Methodist missionaries in Angola and Botswana. Ten years before we arrived, the Schaads and their children had fled Angola because the war for liberation from the Portuguese colonialists had made the situation too dangerous. In those years in Maun, Loyd had masterminded the development of the school garden, designating a four-by-eight-foot plot of the garden for every two students. Margaret had served as treasurer and helped in the school's small health clinic. A no-nonsense woman who gave Elaine strong encouragement and expressed confidence in Elaine's ability, Margaret introduced her to the basics of the school's finances, showing her how to deal with paying bills, accepting school fees, and administering a 750,000 Pula annual budget—almost one million US dollars. Elaine found the task daunting, but she determined to master it. After discovering that the school clinic had a highly capable nurse in an Angolan refugee, Mr. Freitas, Elaine found that she could put all her effort into the financial work.

Conscientious, smart, and capable in whatever she took on, Elaine had an admirable ability to adapt to a complicated situation. I surely had a heavy task in front of me, with fellow teachers and pastors close by who could aid me in the struggles of teaching and pastoral care in our African setting. But once Margaret left, Elaine had no one to consult about her financial duties. I discovered very early on that the woman I married carried within her a much greater strength of will and ability than I had previously recognized. In our first year, she found it necessary to teach herself more advanced accounting procedures than she had ever handled in her small town bank position in Pennsylvania. When outside auditors came at the end of our second year to examine the school's financial books for the first time, one of them remarked to Elaine, "These records are really excellent! Where did you do your accounting training?" Elaine replied, "Right here in this chair." Unsurprisingly, the auditors were at first startled, and then greatly impressed—quite appropriately, I thought!

Planning Ahead

A few weeks after she had begun work, Elaine found a small pile of letters deep in one drawer of her desk. It surprised her to discover that they were applications for the treasurer's position from people in the surrounding area. She quickly realized that the school had been advertising the position, but when the school's Board of Governors heard the news of the impending arrival of a missionary with banking experience, they had placed all the applications in the drawer and interviewed no one. By the first of December Elaine had thought it over and decided that she would tender her resignation toward the end of our second year of service. She would try to persuade the Board to search for and hire a local person for the job. She had to give a deadline, otherwise the Board of Governors may have dragged their feet and hesitated to search for a new treasurer as long as they knew that Elaine would be available. Resigning at the end of the second year of our service would give Elaine a full year (our third and final year in Botswana) to train the new person and run through an entire year's cycle of duties. She understood full well that having White foreigners always in charge of the money smacked of colonialism and perpetuated the false narrative of White superiority. It would clearly be best to leave the country at the end of our three years with a Motswana replacing her. Both Elaine and I felt strongly that we would do our work most faithfully and effectively by having native people replace us by the time our three-year term ended. It seemed to us the only proper way to do our jobs.

Job Stress

The responsibility weighed more heavily on her than I realized. One evening in late September, Elaine began trembling, a fearful, panic-stricken look on her face. Turning to me, she said in a half-whisper, "Rich, I can't breathe." It scared me, scared both of us. I needed to act fast. Glancing out the dining room window, I saw Carol Schaad walking by and called to her for help. She helped me put Elaine into a car, jumped in beside her, and we dropped Sherry off at another teacher's house. Then we sped off to the small hospital in Maun, where two Danish doctors worked on contract with the government. An aide ran to get one of them. Rubbing her eyes and pushing hair out of her face as though she'd been napping, the doctor came out, sat down, immediately giving Elaine her full attention.

After examining Elaine, the doctor said gently, "You're not physically sick. Are you worried about something? You seem to be having an acute attack of stress." It certainly had become obvious that in her work as treasurer, the ever-conscientious Elaine had become increasingly worried about having enough money to pay the school's bills. But I obviously had not been paying enough attention to her anxiety. The government money did not always arrive at the proper times, and she took the problem on herself in a personal way. This resulted in an anxiety attack. My insides were churning also as I sat hoping for some answers from the doctor.

The doctor spoke to her a bit more in a calming voice. "It's important that you not hold things inside yourself. You need to let go and let everything out." She sat with Elaine a while longer as she calmed down and began to breathe normally. After a few more minutes of us sitting calmly, the doctor suggested we go home and get some rest. Relieved and grateful, we thanked the doctor warmly and drove Elaine back home. Carol kindly helped her into the house and then went down the lane to her house after I expressed my great gratitude to her. Elaine and I drank some tea and went to bed for the night. I promised myself to be more attentive to her struggles and do what I could to encourage Elaine to let her feelings show. As I write this, years later, Elaine has no memory whatsoever of that incident in our first year in Africa.

Accusation

A troubling incident Elaine could not forget occurred later that same month. One Friday afternoon as she stood at the window in the door of the treasurer's office, a tall senior student approached. A wooden panel immediately under the window swung outward to take in school fees and other transactions. The powerfully built student leaned too heavily on the wooden panel—and broke it in two. When Elaine scolded him for being careless, he quickly retorted, "You're just yelling at me because I'm Black!" Surprised and pained at such an accusation, she responded, "I yell at Sherry and Rich at times! I'm scolding you because you broke this panel. This can't be left open for the weekend. Someone could get into the office and steal something. You need to go find a maintenance man to come fix this right away." He went off, grumbling, as Elaine stood rather unnerved by this distressing encounter. Neither before nor afterward did anything like it occur. Recalling the incident much later, I suspected that it must have reinforced her determination to have a Motswana replace her in the job before we left Africa.

BEGINNING A NEW ROLE

Education in Botswana

For ten years I had been a pastor of churches, being pulled in many directions at once because of the variety of tasks pastors normally face. Now I entered the role of full-time teacher, twenty-four periods a week teaching courses in Religious Education. Each school day I conducted four or five class sessions of forty students each, struggling to find helpful ways to present new information in a manner that would involve them in the process. Students sat in five rows of eight desks each. Each classroom had a blackboard across the front wall and a teacher's desk in the left front corner. Usually no more than two pieces of chalk and one or two erasers lay at the base of the blackboard. No other equipment or pictures were present.

Taken from its history as a British protectorate, Botswana's educational system consisted of primary school with seven grades, or Standards, and a possible five years of secondary school, labeled Forms One through Five. Everyone took a national exam at the end of Standard Seven. Only if pupils scored well on that test would they be admitted to the first year of secondary school. At the end of Form Three, the national Junior Certificate (JC) exams in eight subjects determined if they could go on to Form Four. It often happened that a family would keep a child at home to work, not allowing a child to go to school until he or she turned ten or twelve years of age. In a male-dominated society, given a choice between a son or a daughter, most often the son would first be sent to school. Even so, we did have numerous male students as old as their mid-to-late twenties in years four and five.

In the 1980s, the government spent at least a third of its entire budget on education. Even with this commitment, limited places existed in secondary schools because of a serious shortage of schools and far too few teachers to staff them. Each year the government refused admittance to many students with low but passing grades on the Standard Seven exams. Immediately prior to the beginning of the school year, parents of these students formed long lines outside the principal's office pleading with him to admit their child. More than once a mother barged into the office, sat down on the floor, and declared that she would not leave until the school admitted her son or daughter. Over and over, the principal had the painful duty of explaining that the government made the lists of who would be accepted for each school, and he had no control over that. Parents always refused to accept any explanation. Eventually they would leave, angry and terribly frustrated at their child being denied this opportunity. At the time, only 40 percent of students who finished seven years of primary school could be admitted to a secondary school simply because of lack of space.

Unaccustomed to such scarce resources, it grieved me to see the hurt so many parents suffered having their children denied any educational opportunity beyond primary school. Elaine experienced it firsthand even more than the rest of the school staff, watching the distressed, disconsolate parents walk by her office down the hall from the principal. But we were helpless, completely unable to change it. We knew the government built schools as quickly as possible, but it would take more years of development before the opportunity for education opened for all. Many of our students were the first in their families to attend any school, and this fact put great pressure on the students to succeed.

The Same, Yet Different

On May 12, the day before classes began for the new term, I attended my first staff meeting with all the teachers and the principal. Several foreign teachers had recently departed, their contracts with the government fulfilled. Constant turnover of faculty, I mused, could not be a healthy situation for either the students or the administration. Smiling inwardly, I felt oddly comforted observing that cultural differences did not prevent people from wasting time arguing about trivial issues in meetings. I found it quite reminiscent of numerous church meetings back home. Years later in my teaching career, strikingly similar trivia often dominated college faculty meetings. Some behaviors are simply universal.

Observing the other teachers, I began to learn more of the customs of the culture. One of the senior teachers, Thomas Tau, came in to the meeting with his head shaved. Someone else whispered an explanation to me: "Among the Batswana, a father shaves his head when one of his children dies." At first this seemed strange, but I later remembered the Old Testament account of Job shaving his head when his children were killed. As time went on, I found that Old Testament stories and customs often guided African Christians in their actions. As one common example: some Africans refused to eat pork because of the Jewish dietary restrictions in the Bible.

Christine Introduces the New Teacher

When the new school term began, I spent my first several days with Christine Purves. Scheduled to take over her classes because she and Jack were preparing to leave Maun for another assignment, I watched as she taught the classes and introduced me as the new *moruti* (Setswana for either "teacher" or "pastor"). In the first couple of days, Christine called on the students in each class to stand up one at a time and say, "Rev. Christensen, my name is . . ." Then I responded by greeting each of them by name. They had as much trouble pronouncing my name as I did theirs. Not long into the term, students settled on calling me, "Mr. Chris."

Happy to meet the students at last, I observed their eagerness to learn and their struggles with English. They had some difficulty in expressing what they wanted to communicate, both in speaking and in writing, resulting in non-specific answers to questions. (Why did God pick Joshua as leader? "Because he was a good man.") I began to realize that it would be a challenge to have them learn more complete and appropriate answers for the Junior Certificate examination. Christine explained to me that that the third-year students became terribly tense and anxious in the time leading up to the JC exams in the third term of the year. The exams had such an impact on their future that churning stomachs and stress headaches plagued many at that time. With students so obviously eager to learn and wanting to do well, I looked forward to putting my best effort into teaching them.

7

If You Want to Teach Someone, Don't Beat Around the Bush

—ZAMBIAN PROVERB

MY TASKS

Teaching in a New World

I CAME TO BOTSWANA because the government had put out urgent requests to churches and governments for qualified teachers, recruiting them from Europe, Asia, North America, and other parts of Africa. In a vivid memory from those first weeks of teaching, I recall a paradoxical feeling of both awkwardness and satisfaction standing in front of the forty African young people sitting in each class section. Students at times looked at me as though viewing a visitor from another planet, with my full head of blond hair and my Norwegian-heritage fair skin. I stood in front of them, an affluent Westerner in a country where 90 percent of the people lived in thatched roof houses built primarily with mud, wood, dung, and sand. It would have been easy to feel quite out of place in a region of the world where European colonialism had been so poisonously demeaning to Black Africans. But, surprisingly to me, I didn't have that feeling, being welcomed and valued for my contribution to what the people termed "the building of our country." Certainly some students quite likely viewed me as a representative of that tragic colonial history. But in a country where less than half of the children had the opportunity to go beyond Standard Seven, people prized education highly. Very rarely did I experience discipline problems in class.

Students were, for the most part, alert and respectful. They all knew that passing the exams at the end of year three and obtaining a Junior Certificate gave them a far greater chance of paid employment. Botswana had become an independent nation in 1966, only fourteen years before we arrived, so students felt a sense of pride in being able to contribute to the development of their nation. Earlier at that first teachers' workshop in Gaborone, one of the African teachers had told me a popular saying in the newly independent African nations at the time: *To be a human being is to know that by carrying one brick you can contribute to the building of the world.* Students knew that what they accomplished would be a direct reflection on their families. Motivation did not seem to be a problem, an attitude quite clearly demonstrated in a remarkable phenomenon whenever I gave a test in class. Writing furiously, almost without pause, for the entire test period, students seemed utterly determined to record everything they could possibly remember. They sat with furrowed brows, thinking hard, trying to be sure to omit nothing. Sitting silently at the front, I marveled at their powers of concentration.

Twenty-four class periods a week with a variety of different classes proved overwhelming at first. An added difficulty came in learning names, so strange-sounding and difficult for me to pronounce: *Goit-seone, Uahangana, Kwenagape, Nchunga.* In turn, as I noted before, students could not seem to figure out how to pronounce *Christensen.* Thus *Mr. Chris.* A school year based on the British system had three terms of twelve weeks each. I loved the schedule; exactly at the time of the first and second terms when teachers and students alike became tired of school, we all had a one-month vacation. At the end of November, after the third and final term each year came a seven-week summer break. To me it seemed an ideal setup.

As my class sections could total over 300 students in a single term, learning to pronounce all their names properly took time. Given that many students, reading the same test answers repeatedly for hours on end could be exasperating. But from the beginning, I loved teaching, and not only because of performing a welcome service. My education in history and theology meant that people valued my contribution. I also loved it because the students were so eager and determined. Most of all, I loved it because of the welcome sense of relief of being able to focus primarily on the one task of teaching rather than being responsible for numerous other tasks. It brought on the satisfying feeling of having found my place in the vocation I truly longed for. At age thirty-five, it all felt right. In the midst of the fascination of learning to see a new world, I taught and learned, challenged and became challenged.

To my great good fortune there were few other distractions or options for entertainment to take a teacher away from the task at hand. No television, no telephone, no movie theaters, no McDonald's, and no shopping malls existed within hundreds of miles in any direction. A short time after our arrival, it dawned on me that I had not spoken on a telephone nor watched television in more than two weeks. It did not feel like a loss. It surprised me how much the absence of those ordinary pieces of every-day American activity made life seem so much simpler.

Another benefit of living in Botswana came with the discovery that committee meetings occurred at 5:00 pm on a weekday. For example, the school's board of governors always met at that time, each participant leaving a job immediately after his or her daily work. This happily resulted in being able to go home for supper after the meeting, thus not having to rush away from an evening meal. Eliminating evening meetings struck me as a remarkably clever idea. Elaine, Sherry, and I could spend supper time relaxing, talking, without interruptions and no place to go for the evening. My outside-the-classroom hours were filled with little but course planning, grading, eating, sleeping—and good times with Elaine and Sherry bonding as our own recently-formed family.

Boundary Challenges

Crossing cultural boundaries and learning to see the world through the students' eyes, necessary for my teaching to be effective, proved to be a difficult feat. The cliché is true: being cast into a very different culture actually is like the proverbial fish out of water. Thrown onto the shore of a new experience, one suddenly realizes for the first time what water is. A new world confronted me. With life experiences and worldview differing radically from my own, most students had lived their entire lives in small villages far from larger villages or towns. Non-boarding students from the surrounding area went home every school day to chores, gathering firewood, cleaning house, or helping care for the cattle. Only late in the evening could they settle down to study, usually under the light of dim paraffin lamps, a hardship on the eyes. Most had never seen indications of the great diversity of humanity.

Visiting the family of one of my students in the village one afternoon, the mother invited me into one of the huts in the family compound, where I confronted a surprising sight. A large, beautifully polished dark wood chest of drawers stood up against the rough wooden supports and dried mud of the back wall. At first it seemed to me to be out of place. But then I thought, no, beauty can find a place anywhere. You just have to look for it. I had quite wrongly assumed that such beauty would be absent from something as simple as a mud hut, a conceit of my affluent American upbringing. My African education proceeded.

Initially, my qualifications for the job foolishly caused a sense of superiority to overtake me. But I quickly recognized myself as something of a fraud, knowing next to nothing about African cultures and having minimal teaching experience. My life experience had never involved great suffering or being excluded because of my skin color. Yes, I had certainly suffered anguish and grief through the time of my divorce, but my life had been a mostly comfortable one. I could not parade a deeply troubled life of fear and suffering before any of these African youth. They knew far better how short life could be and how ugly the world could be. Thus the RE curriculum and the students themselves became my teachers.

Standing before my classes, I tried in vain to imagine the differences between their lives and my life as a middle-class American White. The difficulties they faced were so far removed from my experience: taking care of cattle and protecting them from wild animals, walking miles to collect firewood to bring home for cooking, suffering hunger in times of drought, more walking to water holes carrying large, heavy water containers on their heads. I had little grasp of what that must be like. In turn, I had a bit of fun early in the first months trying to explain the phenomenon of winter snow to these youth who had never seen such a thing. It astonished them when I described snow at least three feet deep back home in Pennsylvania the year before. "No!" several of them said at once. "How can that be?" It seemed so impossible to them that they steadfastly refused to believe me.

Soon after the beginning of one school year, a first-year student named Lovy remarked in class, with an expression of wonder on his face, "Mr. Chris, I want to tell you that before I came to secondary school and saw White people, I thought there was only one tribe in the whole world!" Startling to me, but he had been startled even more by differences he never knew existed, boundaries that were being overcome before his eyes. My first reaction had been a tolerant smile, thinking that he had learned to see something new, something important which enlarged his world. But maybe I had learned something also, thinking that perhaps he had initially been more profoundly right than either of us had first realized.

Students Persecuted

A portion of our student population came out of situations of violence, persecution, or civil war. They had fled to Botswana from Angola, Zimbabwe, or South Africa. Soon before I first arrived in the country, the terrible seven-year civil war in Zimbabwe—formerly White-ruled Rhodesia—between the Black liberation movements and the White minority government finally drew to a close. In 1979 near the end of hostilities, the brave mother of one Black Zimbabwean boy sneaked into Zimbabwe from exile in Botswana to help her son escape forcible induction into the Rhodesian military. Fleeing the security police, the two were captured near the Botswana border. Their captors dragged them to a police station, attached electric cords to their legs, repeatedly sending electric shocks through their bodies for most of one afternoon. How they endured it I will never know, but somehow they did, managing to escape and sneaking across the border by night. In 1980, less than a year later, that boy sat in one of my classes. Human cruelty can be almost beyond belief. Certainly I knew that great cruelty existed in the world. But to see for myself the human evidence of this horror inflicted on the mother and son made me shudder. But at the same time, their strength and resiliency appeared as something greater than I had ever known before. The sacrificial love of the mother and the barbaric cruelty of the police stood in stark opposition to one another. That humans are capable of either is one sign of the Christian faith's recognition of the reality of human nature. We are all flawed and capable of rationalizing even the most heinous of acts. We can also act out great love and self-sacrifice.

Barbara Moyo, another Zimbabwean student, had fled the civil war by walking miles and miles through lion country at night to reach freedom. In a Scripture Union meeting one evening soon after we had arrived, Barbara told her remarkable story of how she had escaped the violence in her home country. Speaking slowly, she explained, "I thought and prayed about it for a long time. Before I decided for sure to leave for

Botswana, I spent a day fasting and praying. While I prayed, long into the night, I received a sense of calm assurance that I would be okay. That's when I decided to go." Then she set out alone in the middle of the night, reciting the Twenty-third Psalm to herself as she fled through the bush through lion country to the border. "The Lord is my shepherd, I shall not want." She crossed the border with a sense of exhilaration and relief. She concluded, "And now I am a student at Maun Secondary School!" Not for the first time did I feel a sense of awe at the courage people could have in desperate circumstances.

A few South African students were with us hiding from their government's security forces after escaping arrest in their own country for their opposition to apartheid. Late in the school year, one of those students refused to have his picture taken with his class for the mimeographed school yearbook. He wanted to take no chance that the security forces from the apartheid regime could discover his location. Facing circumstances I could hardly imagine, these students demonstrated a bravery and resilience that aroused in me a sense of wonder and admiration. The inner strength of human beings to endure in horrific circumstances appeared far greater than I had ever imagined. Certainly I had read accounts of people enduring great suffering, but in Africa it confronted me much more directly than ever before. Because I write these words in the midst of the tragic 2020 virus pandemic, I feel compelled to note the strange, mindless reactions of some people who refuse the simple act of wearing a protective mask. When North Americans use the words *tyranny* or *oppression* in reference to such a modest act of human kindness, they demonstrate appalling ignorance of the meaning or reality of the words.

Minority Groups and Languages

The majority of the students came from one of the eight Setswana-speaking tribes, but minority tribal groups were also represented: tribes with names such as the Yeya, Kalanga, Mbukushu, and Herero peoples. A big surprise came when I discovered that a great many students entering the first year, while lacking wider world experience, could speak at least four languages. They grew up with their own tribal language, then learned the tongue of the closest neighboring tribe. Setswana came at the beginning of primary school, and finally English beginning in Standard Four. In addition, some students were fluent in Afrikaans, language of the White minority and mixed-race populations of South Africa. English and Setswana served as the two official languages of Botswana. All of the secondary school teaching, except for Setswana class, used English.

A common southern African joke:

What do you call someone who speaks three languages? Tri-lingual

What do you call someone who speaks two languages? Bi-lingual

What do you call someone who speaks one language? An American.

This proved to be an unhappy but largely accurate declaration.

I began to think that living in a different culture is like entering a conversation in the middle, not knowing the other participants nor the intricate past from which they arose. It meant not knowing their assumptions or attitudes about life, or the pains they had endured. Certainly for me, it became a kind of perpetual learning experience. My world kept growing larger.

Easing In

Students knew very little of my culture and I had just begun to learn to know theirs. Yet in spite of all these differences in worldview and language, I did not feel out of place, seeing myself as a guest of the government and of the church in Botswana, called there to fill a needed role in the educational system. As a family, we felt welcomed into the life of the school and the community. The African teachers—about half of the faculty—welcomed me and were always willing to offer advice and assistance in my new position.

Teaching courses in religious education took up the bulk of my time, given the nearly 300 students I regularly taught—and sometimes more. Marking that many student test papers at times could be agonizingly tedious. Indeed, in this case, *tedious* would have been a euphemism. Fortunately, the simple life we lived apart from any modern conveniences (especially the circumstance of having no television or telephone) made the situation seem much less rushed or harried. Despite the stacks of student papers, I felt at ease and not pressured.

CHAPLAIN

Scripture Union

Other duties faced me as well. As the school chaplain, I acted as adviser to the Scripture Union, the student Christian group. The group met several evenings each week for prayer and some joyous singing. Although I helped them plan meetings, they did most of the planning themselves, often sharing impressive testimony to their faith. In one of my first encounters with students at a chapel service, a senior student named Robert made a point of saying how important it can be to pray and care for others rather than laughing or looking down on them. He posed the example of a girl who became pregnant, a good example because so often it seemed easy for many students to look with disdain upon such a girl. As an outreach project, the SU also supported an elderly woman who had no family to care for her. Students had rebuilt her house after a storm damaged it. They continued to visit her and purchased food for her. Along with students, I helped organize weekly Sunday worship for the students. Students would suggest speakers or musical groups—choirs, brass bands—from Maun churches, two of the SU leaders usually going into the village with me to invite them.

Sunday Worship

One especially inspiring speaker for the Sunday morning worship came on the third Sunday of the term. Mr. Motsamai Mpho, the former member of Parliament, one-time candidate for president, and leader of the Botswana Independence party, one of the five political parties in the nation, spoke on the topic, "A Christian's Responsibility to Humanity." He emphasized the point that Christians are called into the whole world, to care not only for their immediate surroundings, but for others. "Christians should speak out when something is wrong: to call on the powerful nations of the world to stop building destructive weapons, to tell African leaders that peace and justice do not come from murdering their brothers." He continued, "America and the Soviet Union are called big powers, but does having more destructive weapons make a nation big? No, rather it is the nations who live in peace and who work for peace who are the big powers." Referring to the recent peace deal that ended the seven-year war in Zimbabwe, Mr. Mpho spoke of Ian Smith, the White leader who led the former Rhodesia, saying that "Ian Smith is my brother, and he is welcome in Zimbabwe now." I remembered this story from soon after we had arrived, when Chris Purves had told me that Mr. Mpho had stood up in our local UCCSA church a few months before and confessed that he hated Ian Smith, saying he knew that he could not hold onto that hate if he were a Christian. For the students, this served as a remarkable message of reconciliation and hope for the future, a powerful message of belonging to one another in Christ. Richard Kashweka, the Scripture Union president and the worship leader that morning, gave a response to the sermon, in which he admirably reinforced Mr. Mpho's message. "Yes, we know that it is necessary to forgive Ian Smith, because there is no peace without forgiveness." At the time, Bishop Desmond Tutu in South Africa had often expressed that same thought.

Some of the Sunday speakers gave less than helpful messages. More than once the entire content of a sermon consisted of the admonitions, "Study hard, obey your parents," and that would be it. But others had much more profound and moving words for the students. Rev. Kwenane, the Church of God pastor, arrived one morning and began to speak of "partaking of the divine nature." At first I felt skeptical, thinking this to be a bit too much on the mystical aspect of spiritual life. But Mr. Kwenane spoke then of God's nature being love. As he put it, "To love freely, unselfishly, from the heart and not out of obligation is to participate in the divine nature." It struck me as simple, obvious, and profound. To live in God, who is love, is to participate in that love and to be at one with God. For some days afterward, I dwelt on this thought in my early morning meditations.

Teaching Theology

In addition to my duties at the school, I met once a week with two deacons from the Maun congregation of the United Congregational Church in Southern Africa (UCCSA). When I arrived, they had finished two years of a five-year theological education program, so the Botswana Synod of the UCCSA asked me to be their teacher and guide for the three years remaining in their studies. The curriculum had been written and adapted to Tswana culture by our UCC colleague Dick Sales with guidance and input from Batswana pastors. Dick had spent years in South Africa working with pastors there before being expelled for his opposition to apartheid.

Arriving in Botswana, he found no theological seminary operating there, so Dick made productive use of his exile, developing what I came to see as a remarkable theological curriculum. Entitled the Botswana Theological Training Program, it included all of the usual aspects of a seminary education: issues of pastoral care, theology, church history, preaching, and ethics and social concern—all in the context of Tswana customs and traditional beliefs.

Consulting extensively with Botswana church leaders, Dick had put together a culture-specific program relevant to the church circumstances there. Dick and Nancy lived in the south of the country, where he continued to train tutors for the program. Because of my theological training, I could readily study the curriculum and prepare myself to teach it. This added to my reasons for feeling useful to the church in Botswana, and it gave me a stronger sense of gratitude for the opportunity I had been given. In addition, it reinforced the sense in Elaine and me that we had made the right decision in coming to southern Africa.

My two theology pupils, Mr. Dikole and Mr. Riley Molelo, served as deacons from our local UCCSA congregation. Mr. Molelo served as boarding master at the school, primarily in charge of the boys' dormitory. Mr. Dikole lived in the traditional Tswana manner, growing corn and sorghum on his land and keeping cattle at the cattle post. Typical of a majority of the population, he, his wife, and their six children lived on what they grew, regularly eating corn meal porridge and drinking milk from their cattle. With the proceeds from sale of a cow once or twice a year, they had cash for other food and necessities. Without refrigeration available, it made no sense for one family to butcher a cow themselves. Money from the sale to the butcher bought items such as tea, sugar, and a few other food items. They would then purchase occasional fresh meat from the butcher. Just as with the RE teaching, the time with these two men, I felt sure, would lead to fruitful learning for myself as well as for them.

Reveling in the teaching and the learning, coming to see their world through their eyes, I taught them and they taught me. We met every Tuesday afternoon for ninety minutes, sitting in the living room of our house. One especially enlightening session involved the explanation they gave me about traditional Tswana religion and its encounter with Christianity. The Christian message had come to Bechuanaland (the old name for Botswana) in the mid-nineteenth century through the work of the London Missionary Society. An LMS missionary, a Scot named Robert Moffat, translated the Bible into Setswana over a period of years beginning sometime before 1830. His son-in-law, David Livingstone, had traveled around the territory and converted Chief Khama the Great to Christianity. Khama, leader of the Bangwato, largest of the Setswana-speaking tribes, had been grandfather to Seretse Khama, the President of Botswana when we first arrived. Chief Khama had been given the name *Great* for his leading efforts in 1897 persuading the British government to make Bechuanaland a British protectorate separate from the Union of South Africa. This prevented the White South African minority from gaining control over the land that eventually became the free, multi-racial democracy of Botswana.

My two pupils explained to me that traditional Tswana religion called the one high God *Modimo*, which means "the one who is higher than anything else." Batswana understood this Modimo to be high, lofty, utterly transcendent, much more than we can understand. Therefore people addressed prayer to the ancestors, who, while separated from the present day, were still much closer than Modimo. As Mr. Dikole put it to me, "Traditional Tswana religion sees Modimo as so high and distant that it can be dangerous to address Modimo directly. A person is better off praying to the ancestors to go through them to reach Modimo. It's not ancestor worship; it's just that the ancestors are closer to the original creation than we are, and therefore closer to Modimo, the creator. So even if you do try to pray directly to Modimo, your prayers might take months, or even years, to get there." Thus when the Batswana heard the news of the Christian gospel, it astonished them to hear that the one high and lofty God, Modimo, had come seeking out humans in the man Jesus, sharing our own human experience, being for humanity and with humanity in a radically new way. It seemed to me that the traditional religion of the Batswana had indeed been altered, but perhaps not entirely repudiated. Given the nature of strong bonds of African community and the power of the chief, when Chief Khama had accepted Christian faith, the tribe followed.

LEARNING WITH NEIGHBORS

At School

When the school term began, Elaine and I joined a group of staff and local pastors who met each Wednesday evening for prayer and bible study. Various church and national backgrounds made for some lively and

absorbing dialogue. The Purveses, Christine and Jack, came from Mennonite and Methodist heritages. A Presbyterian couple, Mark and Susan
Shopland, were Peace Corps volunteers, Mark a science teacher and
Susan working on establishing a typing school in the village. Susan had
grown up with missionary parents in Egypt. Our friend Peter Mudiwa, a
Methodist pastor from the predominant Shona tribe in Zimbabwe who
had fled for his life from the security forces there during the civil war two
years before, served as our local UCCSA pastor. Mary Beth Gilbertson, a
young Lutheran from the American Midwest, had spent her early life in
Japan. Larry Kies, the Iowa farm boy who had arrived in Maun with us,
came from a Roman Catholic family. A Motswana pastor, Rev. Norman
Wright, led an independent church (not founded by foreign missionaries) called the Spiritual Healing Church. From Northern Ireland, the science teacher Marion Gilmour had come to Maun not long before our
family had arrived. The troubles and religious prejudice in her homeland
created a situation Marion could not abide. Finally, we had Mildred Taylor, a Methodist missionary who had spent thirty years teaching English
in Zimbabwe until her bishop ordered her to leave after two occasions of
being held at gunpoint by rebels.

Mildred had an extraordinary story. Soldiers of the Zimbabwean
National Union-Patriotic Front, or ZANU-PF, the liberation movement
headed by Robert Mugabe, had come to the mission station, beaten several people and raided the supplies there. Mildred had stood on the porch
of the medical clinic, being held with one other teacher at gunpoint,
while several soldiers went in and out to get medical supplies. She stood
there by the doorway greeting each of the men in Shona as they came up
the steps to the building. Because she understood Shona, she overheard
two of the fighters say that they were planning to shoot her and another
teacher. Then a young man came past her, paused, then turned back toward her in surprise. He called out to his compatriots, "Hey, this is Miss
Taylor! She taught me English. She once gave me a tape player." So they
decided not to shoot her or her colleague. After that incident the bishop
told Mildred to get out of the country and go to Maun Secondary School.
Upon hearing her story, I remember thinking that it really is relationships that save us. Without our connections with others, we would be
lost and without hope. The Setswana proverb makes the point this way: *A
person is a person because of others.*

Over time, the group would teach us a great deal, beginning with
that first meeting. Discussing African customs regarding death, dying,

and funerals, Pastor Mudiwa explained Shona customs from the majority tribe in Zimbabwe, saying that his people expect, even require, that everyone cry at funerals. Often, he said, a group of people traveling to a funeral would decide among themselves who would be the first to begin to cry when they arrived. He also made a striking point about crying: when a husband dies, if the wife does not cry, people think that she caused his death by some kind of witchcraft. It truly seemed a new world to us.

On another evening a few weeks later, our study group talked about giving and receiving, and what is a Christian way to deal with begging. Susan Shopland commented that in Tswana culture, it is not considered an imposition to ask someone to do a big favor for you, unlike North Americans, who are hesitant (or more often not inclined at all) to ask someone else for help. For Americans, an individualistic ethic dominates, a feeling that we must be self-reliant and not dependent on others. For Batswana, it seemed that people had little hesitation asking for help, and others quite willingly obliged. It struck me that this attitude stemmed from a sense of community belonging that had a positive quality about it. People didn't think twice about asking others to take them various places, or to sew clothes, or help in some big project. Susan commented that we Americans have a hard time saying no to requests, and when we accept them we feel burdened, but we rarely ask others to do something for us. We do know something about giving, but it is harder for us North Americans to learn what it means to receive.

Community Churches

The great number and variety of churches in the village intrigued and surprised us. At least thirty different congregations had arisen in Maun, most of them African independent churches, including such interesting groups as the Spiritual Healing Church, the Zion Christian Church, and a group simply called St. John's Church. Many independent churches took directives from the Old Testament, including the strict dietary laws. They frequently took biblical instructions quite literally. The Zion Christian Church had been so named because one of the Psalms in the Bible states, "You shall worship in Zion." The group had a most unusual ritual carried out every Saturday night. The congregation gathered in a field near the village to spend an entire night drumming, dancing, singing, and praying. A group of about a dozen men donned very large, odd-looking shoes that reminded me of over-sized beanbags. Dancing in a circle, the men frequently leapt high in the air, descending to stamp hard on the ground as a sign of stamping out the devil and his works. Sometimes we would wake Sunday morning to the distant sound of the drums still in action. The Zion Church people were well-known for the practice of showing their care for a sick church member in an extraordinary manner. The entire congregation would gather in the evening at the home of the ill person to pray, drum, and sing for him or her—all night long until sunrise!

St. John's Church, like numerous independent churches, had an African founder held in extremely high regard by all the members. The founder, a woman of quite advanced age from South Africa, held the title of "the prophetess." Once in our time there, the prophetess visited the congregation in Maun. Two of our students went with me to the church compound to request that the congregation's musical group, a small band, come to our Scripture Union meeting at the school on a Sunday evening. They did not grant permission for us to see the prophetess, so a representative spoke with us and agreed that the band could visit us. But while he spoke with us, someone else came hurrying up to us with a solemn look and a message: "We must first speak with the prophetess." Apparently, nothing could be decided without her approval. So the students and I waited about thirty minutes for consent to be given. It came at last, and the students and I walked back to the school campus. They explained to me along the way that we were not allowed to see the prophetess because the church permitted no White person in her presence. People explained that, although in her eighties, the prophetess had the appearance of a much younger woman. When we told this to Chris Purves later, Chris speculated that the woman may have had plastic surgery and thus thought an outsider might discern the truth about her appearance.

The church's band (all men) came later that evening and played and sang for us and with us at our prayer meeting. As the band departed to go back to the village, one of the men, clearly older than I, shook my hand warmly and said, "Now when I come back, I know that I have a father here." It surprised me, but I realized that he had expressed his respect for me as the school's moruti (pastor). Later on, I found that this served as a common term of respect used by the students. At evening prayers in our small chapel, a student leader would often turn to me and announce, "Now we will ask our father to pray for us."

Another surprise came to me upon discovering that despite this wide variety of Christian churches just in our own village of Maun, all of the pastors seemed to get along with each other and cooperate in community events. This cooperation extended far beyond the usual circumstances in the United States. It didn't seem to matter that Seventh Day Adventists, Church of God leaders, UCCSA pastors, the Spiritual Healing Church, Zion Christian Church, and St. John's Church had stark differences in beliefs and practices. All the pastors joined together to sit in one group at the large community meeting area called the kgotla, especially when community prayer services occurred. Time after time their willingness to come to pray and worship with our students impressed me greatly. Every one of them came at one time or another to preach at our school's Sunday morning worship, or showed willingness to visit our Scripture Union meetings either on campus or out on student retreats. Not once did any of the pastors try to convert the students to their particular church. Rev. Norman Wright of the Spiritual Healing Church and Rev. Peter Mudiwa, the UCCSA pastor, joined regularly in our staff Bible study at the school. I once asked one of the Maun pastors how they could cooperate so readily despite their differences. He answered simply, "Well, we all belong to Jesus." Coming myself from a tradition that celebrated the unity of the universal Church, I found this inspiring and hopeful. They did not allow differences to disrupt their fellowship. An ironic aspect of the history of Christian missions is that they often disrupted the unity of the tribal community, a community that showed the precise sense of responsibility and care for neighbors that supposedly should mark Christian communities.

A Church Visit

Not long after meeting us, Rev. Norman Wright, pastor of the Spiritual Healing Church, graciously invited Elaine and me to worship at his congregation one Sunday. As we walked into the church sanctuary, we were overwhelmed by powerful, joyous singing, all in four-part harmony. It appeared that people had been crammed in, jamming the building to its limit; people were everywhere, crowded onto benches, squeezed onto the floor right up to the walls on every side. A high pulpit sat at the front. Various deacons led the worship, making announcements, leading singing, calling upon random people in the crowd to pray. Pastor Wright spoke for a short time, then introduced me. People broke into great, warm smiles and clapped vigorously to welcome me. This would not be the first time that African hospitality showed its warm embrace.

Not accustomed to speaking extemporaneously, I gathered my thoughts together quickly, giving a short homily on Jesus welcoming and associating with the poor and outcast. Rev. Wright translated into Setswana for the people. More glorious singing then filled the room. After several hymns, an exuberant display of giving took place, one unlike anything I've seen before or since. At the time for the offering to be taken, two deacons went to the front of the hall and sat side by side at a small folding table. Row by row, the people came up to the table, singing and dancing in a long line, single file. As they danced and moved forward to the table, each one held a hand high in the air holding the offering money to be presented to the deacons. I watched, with a combination of wonder and admiration, as they danced up the center aisle, waving their money in one hand, and then set it on the table in front of the deacons. It took more than twenty minutes to collect the offering—quite a contrast with the solemn passing of the offering plate down each row of seated people back home in the United States. The worship that day lasted for more than three hours, not at all unusual for African churches.

8

Death of a President

THE SUFFERING OF A COMMUNITY

Mourning and Remembrance

WE HAD COME TO Botswana under the auspices of the United Congregational Church of Southern Africa, a denomination with congregations in five nations: Botswana, Namibia, South Africa, Zimbabwe, and Mozambique. The UCCSA, the largest denomination in Botswana, had in its membership most of the nation's leadership, including President Sir Seretse Khama and many of the cabinet members. The nation held Khama in high regard. The fact that he presided over the only stable multi-party, multi-racial democracy on the continent at the time made him an honored and respected leader, not only in Botswana, but in the entire region of Africa.

Thus the news on the morning of July 13, 1980, stunned the nation. In our school dining hall for morning worship, students were in tears, having just received the sad word that President Khama had died early that morning. For over a week, people from the Maun area had been meeting every day at the kgotla for public prayer services for the seriously ill president. A large open field across from the chief's house, the kgotla served as the gathering place for important meetings, political discussions, trials, and prayer meetings. Beginning the first evening that past week, hundreds of people came to the kgotla to hear the chief, several local ministers, and other local leaders speak and pray. At the time of prayer, all who attended those meetings had gone to their knees on the sandy ground and prayed aloud in a babel of voices. The meetings had always ended with the singing of hymns and a benediction. The first night, some of our students sang a popular African hymn, "The Holy Spirit Must Come Down and Africa Will Be Saved," then led everyone in the singing of the Botswana national anthem. The atmosphere seemed like a very large family gathered on behalf of a sick relative.

Twice re-elected president and greatly respected by everyone, Sir Seretse Khama had been the country's only president for the fourteen years since independence. The people regarded him as the father of the nation. That Sunday morning in the dining hall I could see in our students a deep sorrow and expression of real loss, and it moved me to be with them in their grief

Mr. Motsamai Mpho, the former Member of Parliament (and twice Khama's rival in the race for president), came to our school worship on Sunday morning with Mr. Dikole, the scheduled speaker. The two of them conducted a brief prayer service. Mr. Mpho reminded the students to think of the words of the Psalmist, "The Lord is my shepherd," especially at a time when a beloved leader has been lost. Then the service ended so everyone could attend a great gathering of the whole Maun area community in the village at eleven o'clock. Students filed slowly out of the dining hall, many still crying.

I walked with them the mile or so into the village to gather at the kgotla for community prayer. This time, more than a thousand people had gathered for mourning, prayers, and singing hymns. A few had small wooden stools, but most of them sat on the bare, sandy ground. People of all the area tribes gathered together in sorrow. I spotted Herero women with their long, full, multi-colored skirts, Kalanga men and women, Mr. Mpho's Yeya tribe members, along with many hundreds of Batawana, the majority tribe of our region. Sounds of crying and the mournful wailing of African grief rose from the crowd. Elaine and Sherry had come also, and for the first part of the meeting we sat on the ground in the midst of the crowd. All the local ministers sat at the front behind a microphone and sound system brought out for the day. Shortly after we arrived, someone brought me a chair, a gesture of respect. But no chair appeared for Elaine, seemingly indicative of the male dominance of society. But only a minute or so later, the pastor at the microphone called out to us specifically, saying, "Rev. and Mrs. Christensen, please come up and sit in front," that is, with all the other pastors behind the mike. We were guided to empty seats there. As a recent newcomer, I hadn't presumed that I should join the other ministers at the front.

The prayer service lasted more than two hours, with people continuing to stream in from outlying villages. Even though we were in midwinter, typical midday temperatures that time of year reached 75 or 80 °F. With neither clouds nor air pollution to block the sun, sitting out in the open became an ordeal. The sight and sounds of such a large gathering all joined in communal grief engulfed me, drawing me in a powerful way. The solidarity expressed in this common, shared sorrow made a deep impression on me. With over a thousand people sitting spread over a wide area, the setting offered a compelling indication of the strength of the community. Many had their own personal hymnals following along as a song leader "lined out" the words for everyone to sing. As in the week before, at one point people knelt on the ground for prayer, speaking aloud their grief simultaneously in a cacophony of sound, filling the air with different tribal languages but a unity of grief.

After the two hours, we went back to the school campus, only to return to the kgotla for more prayer and singing from 4:00 to 6:00 pm. At the end of that meeting, several of the Maun ministers came to me with an unexpected request: they asked me to preach the sermon at the prayer service of mourning to be held at the kgotla at 9:00 am the next day. I felt quite honored by this for two reasons. First, the invitation made me feel that the people did not view me as an outsider and now genuinely welcomed me into the community. Second, the next day, July 14, happened to be the national holiday called President's Day in Botswana. So I went home warmed by the hospitality shown to me and my family, but at the same time feeling a bit nervous about speaking to the huge crowd I knew would be there.

After supper, many students and some faculty gathered in the small, round chapel at the school. An assistant principal, Steve Pabalinga, spoke to the crowd. "Seretse Khama was a charismatic leader, a man who helped to fashion a democratic country with racial harmony. Unlike many other African leaders, he died without any political prisoners in jail, and has been an inspiration to many. We grieve this great loss to our nation." This seemed especially meaningful coming from him, as Steve came from the Kalanga, one of the minority tribes in the country. So often in other African countries, minority tribes had been denied rights and status, but Botswana had been more free of such discrimination than other nations.

His whole life long, President Khama had always insisted that people of all tribes and races were meant to be united, living together as equals. He had appointed both White and Black members to his cabinet, even though Whites were a small minority in the country. Additionally, in such a male-dominated society, a woman held the important cabinet position dealing with economic matters. The more I learned about the man, the greater respect I came to have for Seretse Khama.

After the chapel prayers, Steve sought out Thomas Tau, the other assistant principal. At their urging, I drove the three of us back to the kgotla for another late evening session of mourning, where some men of the village had gathered around a fire sharing and praying. In what seemed to me an especially meaningful custom, the men of a tribe gathered at night to talk about the leader who had died, sharing stories, reminiscences, and other memories of President Khama long into the evening. Expressing a sense of pride in the late president and his accomplishments, one man noted that under Khama's leadership, Botswana had become a democratic country with racial harmony in a region of the world where both democracy and harmony were rare traits.

The simple act of being together, sharing stories, not only honored the departed one but bound people together in powerful ways. To me, it affirmed the deep-rooted communal sense of life and fostered a share narrative. Thomas and Steve sat on either side of me, translating quietly for me as the men around the fire spoke of Khama's ability to bring people together to work for the common good. Listening intently, I heard the tale of how Khama had ensured that food supplies were stored in various parts of the country for times of poor harvests and the accompanying famine. As a result, no one in the country had died of starvation in the previous ten years except for six people in an especially remote village in the far northwest.

The gathering around the fire would go on for hours, but Steve, Thomas, and I left to go home late in the evening, long before the sharing finished. It had been a long day, and I had a sermon to write before 9:00 the next morning.

Preaching for the Community

In the morning, the whole school, staff and students, gathered at the kgotla with what I estimated to be more than two thousand people for the morning worship. Strong emotions washed over the crowd as they sang and prayed, and I became caught up in a sense of awe at the inspiring, all-encompassing sound and beauty of thousands of people singing in four-part harmony. I stood up to preach the sermon, nerves surprisingly calm due to the feeling of being a part of something much greater than myself. One of the pastors translated my words into Setswana. I fell into a rhythm, quickly sensing how much I could speak before needing to pause for the interpreter. Speaking of thankfulness for Khama's leadership and encouraging the people to remember always his integrity and honesty, my voice carried over the sound system to the hushed crowd. Ending with a prayer for strength, grace, and guidance for the people of the nation, I sat down and felt a rush of emotion. Even as a foreigner, I felt a sense of oneness with the crowd, people very different from me and yet the same. We breathed the same air, worried about children, hoped for a good future. The sense of unity in the midst of great sadness overwhelmed me. It remains in my memory as one of the most stirring emotional experiences of my life.

Reflecting more on the experience some months later, it kept puzzling me as to just why I had been asked to preach the sermon on that important occasion. Only recently arrived in the country, I came obviously as a foreigner with no experience in Africa. I began to notice that people with credentials of some sort (a diploma, any certificate noting expertise of some kind) commanded great respect in southern Africa. While at a local garage one day with another faculty member to have his car serviced, I talked with a young boy who assisted the mechanic. The boy pointed to the mechanic, saying to me with a great solemnity in his voice, "He has a certificate!" Then it occurred to me that perhaps I had been asked to preach for the prayer service because of being at the time the only person in the region with a master's degree in theology. But talking much later one day about the funeral with one of the seniors, I found a different answer. When I asked him what may have motivated the local pastors to ask me to preach, he immediately responded, "Your authenticity—they knew you wouldn't have a particular agenda to push!"

Prayer services continued to be held at the kgotla for several weeks at 9:00 am and 4:00 pm each day. The day after President's Day, classes resumed at the school, but the entire student body and staff left the school grounds to attend the 4:00 service. I sat again with the pastors in the second row behind the speaker's table. Once more a large crowd gathered to mourn and pray, and once more a pastor preached a sermon. Reading from the passage about Moses' death in the book of Deuteronomy, he noted that the Israelites set a period of thirty days of mourning for Moses, the same period of mourning that had been declared by the government for President Khama. The daily prayer services continued for that entire period.

The Weight of Tradition

I sat directly behind Chief Letsholathebe Moremi, the kgosi (chief) of the Batawana, one of the eight Setswana-speaking tribes who made up the vast majority of the nation's population. I had recently learned of the extraordinary amount of power and authority bestowed upon the chief in Tswana culture. He had a heavy responsibility far beyond any other individual in the tribe. The chief approved people for various government posts in the district, gave his okay to the formation of new organizations, served as a judge in all sorts of trials and disputes, and chaired the land board, which had the authority to determine the use of any parcel of land in the region. All of the land belonged to the tribe collectively, so the land board decided where a family could establish a home, where a new business could build and begin work, and how land disputes should be resolved. Furthermore, people often sought out the chief to arbitrate in marital problems and land disputes. I did not envy his job.

Earlier that year, before we had arrived in Botswana, a sad and tragic situation had come to the attention of our American colleague, Mary Beth Gilbertson. She and her roommate, Peace Corps teacher June Woods, had taken into their house a woman from the village who had been beaten terribly by her husband. They took her to see our pastor, the Rev. Peter Mudiwa, who decided that they all should visit the chief to ask his permission for the woman to leave her husband and go to Gaborone to escape further danger. Upon hearing the account of the abuse, the chief indicated great discomfort in the face of the situation, caught between the weight of tradition and the grace of compassion. After much deliberation, he decided that he would not give the woman permission to leave because it would appear that he condoned the breakup of families. The chief also stated that he would go to the husband and talk with him about his disgraceful behavior.

Because Mary Beth had intervened in the situation as an outsider, the possibility had arisen that she might have had to undergo a trial before the tribal officials at the kgotla. Fortunately for Mary Beth, the officials decided against this. But they forced the woman who had run from her husband to go back home. The chief went to talk to the husband to call him to account and order him to end the abusive behavior. Several weeks later, the woman had been found dead, having committed suicide. It seemed to me a horribly tragic result of custom and tradition triumphing over compassion. The encumbrance of tradition had obviously placed a great deal of pressure on the chief. Long-standing attitudes about male dominance and the common view of regarding a wife as property had conspired to doom the woman to a tragic end. Increased educational opportunity for women had begun to lift the status of women in the society, but old customs stubbornly remained. In the new religious education curriculum just introduced, one emphasis lay on the worth, dignity, and talents of women, and I determined to teach that lesson with my actions as well as my words.

9

Students and Teachers

STUDENTS

National Pride

WHEN WE ARRIVED IN 1980, Botswana had been a free country under majority rule for fourteen years. Proud of their new nation, students celebrated it as the only stable, multi-party, multi-racial democracy on the entire continent at the time. They knew they were free. They knew they would not be tossed in jail because of their skin color, but only if they committed an actual crime. They knew that no one would call them a *kaffir*, the derogatory term for Blacks used frequently in South Africa. Sure of the stability of their democracy, they reveled in what they viewed as the newness and the opportunity of their freedom. At the same time they stood strongly in support of the struggle against apartheid to the south.

Hearing students sing for the first time what they called the "national anthem," I didn't realize that it formed, in fact, the Setswana portion of the anthem of the South African liberation movement. Botswana's population at that time numbered slightly under a million. More than three million Setswana-speaking people lived in South Africa. Both the music and the words moved me.

> Morena boloka, sechaba sa etsho.
> O fedise dintwe le matswenyego.

Translation: "Lord, save us, save our country.
Deliver us from war and trouble."

Botswana had a national anthem of its own, but students often sang the one quoted above with powerful expression, with and for the victims of apartheid, in solidarity with them and in hope for their freedom. Each time I heard it, my spirit rose with the joy of the music. The power and the hope shone brightly in the beautiful four-part harmony sung by our 600 students.

Questions and Problems

With no television available in northern Botswana, portrayals of affluent consumerism rarely confronted our students. Numerous students, especially some of the older ones, disparaged the influence of Western culture, proclaiming it abhorrent and un-African. But when experienced Batswana teachers observed a student with a tape player or a radio, they challenged the student, "If you oppose Western influence, why are you using Western inventions? You'd better give that up. Hand it over." The student then quickly decided that perhaps some Western influence posed no problem.

We dwelt there as affluent Westerners, in the midst of a country where 90 percent of the people lived in mud huts with thatched roofs. I heard from other teachers, but never directly from a student, that some elements of anti-White feeling lay in a few of the older students. Derived from the history of colonialism and oppression in nations surrounding them, it included the belief that Whites who worked in Botswana exploited the country by taking money from the government. White colonialists in Angola, Southwest Africa, Zambia, and the former Rhodesia had regarded native Blacks as culturally and intellectually inferior, exploiting the land and labor of the people and refusing them education, so the anti-White attitudes could hardly have been unexpected. I never tried confronting these attitudes directly, believing that focusing on teaching well and demonstrating concern for the students would be the only ultimately realistic and useful response.

Reflecting on the processes and methods of education in my life, I realized that I didn't understand how the big difference between my own individual, consumer culture and the African tribal, communal culture could easily handicap my students. Recognizing how easily I could slip into the didactic, one-teacher-in-front-of-the-classroom model so common to my upbringing, I saw that this model did not honor their understanding of the community as prior to the individual, the sense of belonging to something greater than themselves. Western educational methods frequently fail to teach the importance of relationships, co-operation, and communal responsibility. Emphasis lies on individual achievement rather than on growth in relations with others. An Anglo-based school system, with its emphasis on individual achievement and competition for grades, seemed to deny a fundamental aspect of their culture. Although the RE curriculum put great emphasis on the nature of community, I stood in front of a classroom every day with neat straight rows of students all facing me. For a long time I did not recognize the paradox inherent in the process. Only when I began to ask students more closely about their own lives, and question them about issues and how they handled them, did it become quite evident to me that I had more to learn than they did.

It became my habit to listen carefully to student concerns and ask them questions about their culture and customs, hoping to pick up on what worried them, what they found hopeful, what dreams they had for the future. I once asked a class what Zimbabweans had been hoping for during the liberation struggle against the White minority government in the previously-named Rhodesia. They gave a firm, immediate response: "They wanted their country back!" The push for liberation from colonialism loomed large everywhere in southern Africa.

In time, students began to open up more to me. In a class after lunch period one day, the students seemed obviously restless and upset. When I asked what bothered them, several spoke up at once to say that they had no lunch; the corn meal porridge served at lunch had been filled with insects. They couldn't eat it. They were hungry and annoyed. Just the day before, we had been talking about the Gospel stories of Jesus in class, looking at the account of Jesus' temptations during the forty days in the wilderness. Taking the opportunity to remind them of their lesson, I said, "Well, you know what Jesus said to the tempter in the wilderness when tempted to turn stones into bread." And they all broke into laughter remembering the line, "Man shall not live by bread alone."

They in turn questioned me about life in America. At times this made for odd conversations. One day discussing funeral customs in Botswana, we talked about the strong sense of community in the people's practice of coming to sleep at the bereaved family's compound overnight.

They questioned me about funeral customs in America. Explaining common practices, I told them of the job of the mortician, who took care of the body and prepared it for burial in a special building solely for that purpose. The thought of a person whose full-time occupation involved preparing bodies for burial seemed one of the craziest ideas they had ever heard. They were accustomed to family members nailing together a simple wooden coffin for a deceased person. When they asked me if houses in America were different from African dwellings, I tried to tell them something of the variety and prices of houses in America, but they simply refused to believe me. It sounded outlandish and incredible to them that building a house might cost $50,000 or more.

Still another means of understanding the culture came to me when I discovered that a person's name often indicated something of the circumstances of their birth. Grateful for the birth of her daughter, one of the school's secretaries named the child Mpho, which means "gift (of God)." I had students named Boikanyo (faithful, or trustworthy), Batlhalefhi (the cleverest ones), Matswenyego (troubles). With a slightly joking tone of voice, I once asked a boy named Matswenyego how he had received his name. I immediately regretted my tone when he answered, "At the time I was born, my father was in jail." When a boy named Kelapile stopped at the bursar's office one day to present his school fees to Elaine, she smiled and asked, "Does that name fit you?" He smiled and sighed a bit, saying "Yes." His name meant, "I am tired," most likely referring to his mother's state of mind at the time of his birth.

School Fees

Students had to pay school fees of P180 per year to attend secondary school. I had no idea what a difficulty this could be until witnessing a couple of incidents in our second year. A Form Two student named Petros failed to show up for the second term starting the first week in May. I saw him in the village on the Saturday after the term began, and he hastily explained his late arrival. The area around his home village of Shakawe, far to the north near the border with Namibia, had been suffering from serious drought. He had tried to sell two cows to get money for the school fees, trying everyone he could find, but he could get only a pittance of P40 for some meat from each cow. The usual price for a single such animal would have normally been P150. In an expression of despair and disappointment, he told me that he simply gave the meat he could not sell to his brothers. The drought had been much worse in his area than in other parts of the country. People around Shakawe had failed to grow any crops that year because of the drought, cattle had been dying, and the government had begun to send food to the region as part of the drought relief program. People quite simply had no cash. Petros told me that a kilogram (2.2 pounds) of meat sold for ten thebe (about twelve cents), because people were not willing to pay more. So he had come to school with less than the amount he needed for his fees. Not knowing how to help him initially, I inquired and found that the school could give him some scholarship help. I felt relieved for him, but the whole situation made me anxious, worried that more students might face similar circumstances. I feared their parents might easily decide not to send them back to school.

That same year, the high value many people placed on education came to me more forcefully than ever. A week after the opening of third term, Tjingovera, a fine student in one of my Form Two classes, came to me with a plea. "Mr. Chris, I have a problem. During the term break I didn't receive any mail because I remained at the cattle post. When I came back to school, I found a letter telling me that I must pay my school fees by September twenty-seventh or I'll be sent home. My parents have no money and most of my other relatives do not think a formal education important enough to spend the money. I have only one uncle who encourages me and has helped with my school fees in the past. But he has gone to Namibia and I can't get in touch with him." I could not imagine being a young boy highly motivated to get an education, but the family thinking it a waste of money and refusing their support. He asked my permission to return home to sell his last two head of cattle in order to pay his school fees for the year. He had to do it himself, because the family back home refused to do it for him. Because he lived in Tsau, fifty miles north in the Okavango, finding transportation would be a problem.

I spoke to the principal, who gave his permission for Tjingovera to go home. He traveled to his village to sell the only two cows he owned. In Botswana, as in many other African cultures, cattle are the traditional means of life. They represent food, drink, wealth, status, plus the equivalent of an IRA and social security. Selling his last two head of cattle meant real sacrifice. He returned to school Friday evening six days later, walking up the path from the river by our house. As soon as he came into the house, he mentioned that he had nothing to eat all day. I took him in right away and gave him some bread and hard-boiled eggs—which he wolfed down immediately.

It had taken him from Monday morning to 11:00 pm Tuesday night to travel from Maun to Tsau, two days of walking and hitchhiking to get home and then two days back. With the P100 he received, he paid the bulk of his school fees for the year. He explained, "I also had an ox that I have given to a friend, who will sell it to the Botswana Meat Commission. I will get that money in a few weeks to pay the rest of the fees." When I expressed concern that he had sold the only cattle he owned, Tjingovera responded, "I'm not going to worry because my uncle has told me in the past that he will give me some of his cattle next year to pay those fees." When cattle provided such a basic commodity for people's lives, seeing this measure of determination aroused in me a keen sense of admiration.

Mandela's Influence

Being located immediately north of the apartheid regime in South Africa made our students intensely aware of and keenly in touch with the situation of oppression and injustice in that neighboring land. Many students could recite from memory the final statement of the long speech Nelson Mandela gave at his 1964 trial in Rivonia, South Africa, where he had been sentenced to what eventually became twenty-seven years in prison. They would recite it always with a sense of reverence, indicating the profound respect they felt for a hero of the struggle for liberation from the evils of apartheid. The first time I heard someone quote it, in a class discussion on the meaning of freedom, I could sense in the student's voice the powerful influence that Mandela exercised over so many, both in his own country and in others:

> During my lifetime I have dedicated myself to this struggle of the African people. I have fought against White domination, and I have fought against Black domination. I have cherished the ideal of a democratic and free society in which all persons live together in harmony and with equal opportunities. It is an ideal which I hope to live for and to achieve. But if needs be, it is an ideal for which I am prepared to die.[1]

Hearing that for the first time, it suddenly occurred to me that real freedom does not mean being able to do anything you want, as many

1. "I Am Prepared to Die," para. 141.

modern people like to believe; rather real freedom has to do with what you are willing to give up. I later came to witness this personally—and powerfully—with anti-apartheid activists on my visits to South Africa.

In the Classroom

Those first months in Botswana often gave me surprising insights and revelations about the attitudes and perceptions of the people. I once asked students in a class, "How do you think Jesus speaks to us today?" One boy immediately raised his hand. "In dreams," he answered. Not the first answer I expected, but I then mentally slapped myself on the side of the head, remembering the numerous examples in the Bible when God speaks to someone in a dream. African tradition puts great stock in the power and meaning of dreams, so his answer should not have surprised me. Slowly I learned to see more of their worldview.

Respect for elders played an important role in Tswana culture. When young persons entered a family compound, approaching adults seated around a fire, the youth always walked up to the elders and immediately crouched down in order to be on the same level as the adults. They considered standing above an older person to be disrespectful. In the classroom with me, whenever a student came up to the front to hand in a paper, each one would make a little bow and offer it to me with the right hand, the left hand placed on the right forearm. Offering the paper casually with only the right hand would have been highly disrespectful. I always felt honored at this gesture, humbled to be held in such regard.

Racism

Students came to our door, often on Saturdays, expressing interest in our life in America. We invited them in, sitting down together in the living area of the house. We had photo albums on the table that quickly drew their attention, along with a picture book of photos of the USA. They asked question after question about life in the United States: what kinds of houses do people live in, what is school like? And then a question that truly startled us: "If Black people go to the US, do they put them in jail?" It became immediately and painfully obvious to me that the depth of the tragedy of racism in the United States registered as a grave moral stain evident to the rest of the world. I thought that if these young people from the far north of a remote district of Botswana held that impression of the racism in the United States, then it seemed more than likely that impression must be widespread in Africa and other parts of the world. The tragic persistence of racism in the United States obviously made the United States look like hypocrites when claiming to promote and support human rights in the rest of the world.

I hardly knew how best to answer their question. Caught completely by surprise, I struggled to answer it in a way that would be honest in acknowledging the pervasiveness of racism in the United States, yet correcting their somewhat distorted version of the reality. After responding to their question, saying, "That's not true, usually," I described some of the circumstances of racial discrimination in housing, schools, and jobs, saying that the nation continued to fall disgracefully short of its stated ideals. I told them a bit of the history of some of the struggles of the civil rights movement trying to gain the right to vote for those denied it. But hearing their startling question opened my eyes to the perceptions of many people outside the United States. The effects of the evils of slavery and the stubborn legacy of racism continued—and continues—its long-standing grip on American society, remaining glaringly obvious to the wider world.

On a religious education paper during exam week in August, a Form One student wrote an answer to a question that referenced an example of racism in Botswana. In reference to the Basarwa people (commonly called "bushmen") often being treated as inferior, one boy wrote the following answer to the question, "Write an example of something a Christian student or students could do to help build the kingdom of God." His answer: "Sharing with others what you know about God's love; e.g., when I get home during this holiday I am going to tell my friends who treat Bushmen badly that God accepts anyone in every nation who fears God and does what is right. And He does not judge people by their age, color, language, or intelligence. So I will tell them not to judge Bushmen by their color and language. This means that it is my own idea which I am going to do to help to build the kingdom of God." For the end of my first term of teaching, such sentiment touched me and made me feel fortunate that we had come to Botswana.

Exams

The exam period showed me what a difficult time it could be for the students. They had exams every morning and afternoon all week long, writing their exams in a kind of frenzied intensity and obvious anxiety. Seeing their demeanor, I realized more than ever the stress they were under. It also seemed obvious how much they cherished an education. Seeing how much time it took to grade all the exams, I also learned to have more respect for the teachers. For several days afterward from early morning until late at night, I marked the examination papers of 236 students from Forms One and Two, then recorded the marks in the record book. I found it almost maddening reading the same phrases over and over.

FACULTY

Abel and Philip

Throughout 1980, opportunities arose to get better acquainted with my faculty colleagues. In those initial months in Maun, I discovered the artistic talents of a Motswana English teacher, Abel Manatsha, a soft-spoken, earnest young man. After seeing some of his drawings at a staff meeting, I thought he would be intrigued by some slides I had brought with me to Botswana. On a 1971 trip to Norway, I had visited Oslo's Frogner Park, a large area of strikingly original stone sculptures. Each one illustrates in a different manner an aspect of the range of human circumstances and human emotions. At our invitation, Abel's eyes lit up with obvious interest and he came to our house one evening, talking about his art. "I want to draw the world," he declared. We viewed the slides. Just as I had been when I first saw the sculptures, Abel sat in stunned amazement at the powerful, evocative images. A man and a woman sat with foreheads touching and arms around each other, with serious, almost angry looks on the faces. A huge, slender obelisk contained nothing but human figures of all ages—even babies—climbing over one another in apparent attempts to reach the top, the whole work seemingly cut from one giant rock. A woman, half-bent over, sheltered a group of five or six small children with her whole body, her arms holding them tightly. A man reached down with both arms to pull up another man who had stumbled. The emotions aroused from the many scenes of human struggle, intimacy, and love left Abel speechless for a time. We both sat in silence. Abel finally spoke. "Amazing, amazing," he said. "They are so powerful! I've never seen anything like it before." Pleased that he found the sculptures so riveting, I said, "I had the same thought when I first saw them! I'm very glad I could show them to you." Replying with a smile, Abel said, "Yes, thank you, thank you! This gives me many ideas."

Late in October that year, students in the photography club asked Abel to design and draw something for the cover of a mimeographed yearbook for the school, celebrating Maun Secondary School's tenth anniversary. He produced a charcoal portrayal of a road into an African village, leading off into the distance toward a large full moon lying in the night sky close to the horizon. Students photographed the picture, then ran off copies of it for the yearbook cover. As a title for the yearbook, they chose a statement of the benefits of education: "Tsela kopo e isa Boipelong," explaining it in the following way: "The word TSELAKOPO means *the difficult road*. A road can be difficult for many reasons. It can be either twisty or steep, for instance: School life is difficult, just like the steep twisty road. There is a Latin saying that states that the roots of education are bitter but its fruits are sweet; the other word is BOIPELONG, which means *to happiness*. It explains what the difficult road through MSS leads to." Students, proud of their achievements, often referred to the road they traveled as long and hard. Abel's art gave insightful expression to their feelings about their education.

Philip Monnaatsie, a Motswana who chaired the English department, became an especially helpful colleague who gave me wise advice on numerous occasions. A dignified, well-respected man always open to my questions, he explained to me matters such as how grading should be recorded and the reasons for some of the rules of the school. When I raised objection to him privately about the beatings sometimes used by teachers to punish students, he told me, "I realize that this is not a very good practice. But you must understand, parents expect their children to be disciplined in this way. If we failed to do this, the parents would complain that the school did not carry out its proper responsibilities." I still objected, because it seemed to me that other forms of punishment could certainly be used, a common one often given being the use of scythes to slash and cut tall grasses around the school grounds. But I understood the bind the school found itself in. Abandoning practices of long standing is never easy.

Mary Beth and June

Our American colleague Mary Beth Gilbertson, another missionary teacher sent by our mission sponsor, the United Church Board for World Ministries, had been in Maun for a year before we arrived. A soft-spoken, kind, conscientious Norwegian-American in her mid-twenties, she threw herself into her work with energy and creativity. Students always found her approachable and willing to offer suggestions and advice for their writing. Always willing to help with student retreats, she proved herself many times as a valued colleague and friend.

Mary Beth shared a faculty house like ours with June Woods, a Peace Corps volunteer from Colorado. Both taught English, each with at least 200 pupils each term. A petite woman in her fifties recently widowed and retired from a school district in Colorado Springs, June took on her new task with energy and a good sense of humor joined with what Elaine termed a "permanent twinkle in her eye." She needed both energy and humor, as she and Mary Beth were burdened with huge numbers of English essays to grade most evenings each week. I thought I had a big load, but the two of them had even heavier ones, spending most of their time outside of class with impressively high stacks of student essays piled on their dining room table, on chairs, and on the floor around a big sofa. Coming into their house one day, I found June crouched on the floor picking up one of four big piles of essays lying on the floor. Mary Beth sat in a big chair with other stacks on the floor in front of her. Their red pencils moved swiftly and tirelessly as they corrected grammatical and factual errors, sometimes ones quite surprising. In one essay assignment about famous inventions, several students startled June by claiming that steam engines ran airplanes.

June's son Scott, a college student back home in Colorado, had picked up his mother's good-humored nature. As an old saying has it, the apple doesn't fall very far from the tree. One day June received a letter from Scott informing her that he planned to drop out of college and get married—obviously unwelcome news to June. A week later, she received another letter saying, "Just kidding! What I'm really doing is changing my major." He thought that if he prepared her with the shocking (fake) news, she would more readily accept the real news. June responded with a big sigh of relief, a shake of the head, and a smile. Scott's ploy had worked.

10

Doubling the Size of Our World

THREE-WEEK ORIENTATION

Classes

MY FIRST TERM OF teaching came to a close at the end of July. All the grading had to be completed immediately because on August 4, Sherry, Elaine, and I were flying to Gaborone for a Setswana language course offered at the Peace Corps' Botswana Orientation Center. The flight to the capital in a small plane took just two hours, a welcome improvement over the all-night train ride and the eight-hour drive when we first traveled to Maun.

In the capital, a teacher from Gaborone Secondary School met us at the airport. He took us to his home for afternoon tea, then drove us to St. Joseph's College, a secondary school in Kgale, just south of Gaborone, where the religious education workshop had been held back in April. The Irish nuns at St. Joseph's, Sister Carmel, and Sister Therese showed us generous hospitality, preparing an apartment for us where we would stay each night for the next three weeks, and kindly serving us a simple but delicious supper of bread and soup. One of the nuns drove into Gaborone daily for some shopping, so that became our ride to the Orientation Center each day.

From the first day of the language course, we found a good-natured enthusiasm among the teachers and the other students. People attending the course came from a variety of agencies and organizations. We met folks from the Mennonite Central Committee, International Voluntary Service, and the World University Service of Canada. We made friends with the Reimer family, Mennonites from Lancaster, Pennsylvania. It delighted Sherry that the age of one of their children matched her own, and the two quickly formed a friendship.

Our small group's teacher, a young woman named Malefo, led us in an enjoyable time of learning simple conversational skills as well as valuable insights into the culture. The most common greeting in Setswana (after one says "Dumela") is actually a question: "A O tsogile jang?" (Did you rise well?). Malefo made a point of telling us that *tsogile* is the same verb used in Christian faith for "resurrection." Farewell is expressed by "Tsamaya sentle" (lit. "Go away well"). We learned to say the ever important "Ke itumetse" (Thank you). One especially interesting fact about Setswana caught my attention: the language has no separate pronouns for male and female. The single word "O" means "he," "she," or "it." Still another revealing point about Tswana culture arose when we discovered that Setswana has no word for "revolution." The Batswana strongly prefer talking through differences rather than fighting to resolve them. I heard a report of a Zimbabwean supporter of his country's independence who spoke at a rally in Botswana, ending his speech with the slogan, "Let the revolution continue!" For the Setswana-speaking hearers, the Motswana interpreter translated the words as, "Let fellowship increase!" Learning a new language and culture doubles the size of one's world.

Malefo showed great patience with us, carefully repeated many common phrases for us in her gracious manner. We would never be experts in the language, but we learned enough to be able to carry on simple conversations. It gratified us that we would be able to speak at least a little more with people in Maun.

The program at the orientation center featured more than language training. One afternoon we viewed an extraordinary film portraying a group of ten Basarwa (or Bushmen) tracking and killing a giraffe in the Central Kalahari. By 1980, Basarwa people had mostly given up their nomadic way of life, so the old black-and-white film portrayed an event hardly ever occurring any more. Moving stealthily in a half-circle, the hunters crept up close to the giraffe, firing their poison arrows, then trailed the animal as it attempted escape. Hunters had to be patient and persistent, as the poison took its time bringing down the animal. No hunter chanced getting very close to the giraffe because the big animal could suddenly strike out with a powerful kick that could easily kill a man.

When the animal's death came, the hunters made full use of their prize, cutting off the skin to dry and taking portions of meat back to their camp to share with their whole band. Nomadic desert dwellers traditionally took advantage of every resource they could find, sharing everything with one another, a sharing which demonstrated the tight-knit nature of their community life. Survival itself came only with dependence upon one another. Self-reliance would have seemed a foolish, even dangerous, trait to uphold. The film gave us another example of the African insistence on the priority of the community.

In the Big City

Being in the capital city of Gaborone after three months in the village of Maun seemed like a real vacation to us. We could get ice cream, go to the only movie theater in town, and ride in some busy traffic, none of which ever happened in Maun. We found it strange to walk into a market and find a wide variety of canned goods, cheeses, and cereals, rare sights in the little general stores in Maun. In our village, only one kind of cheese would usually be available, and frequently we would open a box of cereal bought in a little shop, only to find it full of bugs. Many cereal boxes quickly found their way to the trash. In the capital, we kept discovering and enjoying numerous items that had been unavailable to us for the previous three months, such as ice cream bars, potato chips, and what seemed a real treat: cold, pasteurized milk. Only shelf-stable milk could be found for sale in Maun.

A rather unnerving occurrence happened on our lunch break on the fourth day of our course. Standing in line in a take-out restaurant in the Gaborone Mall, Elaine abruptly thought that her purse felt lighter. Looking into it, she saw that her wallet had vanished. As it had over 200 Pula (about $230) in it, she felt panic-stricken. For a brief moment all three of us thought that we had little to no chance of ever recovering the money. To our great fortune, two young boys about ten years old excitedly told us that they saw the thief go out of the restaurant and head up the mall. So I asked them to come with me and point out the thief. Thinking more quickly than I, the boys split up—one went with me in the direction of the thief, while the other boy ran in a different direction to locate a policeman. The first boy and I ran in the direction he had pointed out, and upon rounding a corner of a building we saw a policeman holding onto a shabbily dressed young man in a long gray coat. Running up to them, the boy with me said, "He's the one," pointing to the lower front of the man's shirt. The policeman reached and pulled out Elaine's wallet. I verified it as hers. Surprisingly, all in the space of about five minutes, we received the wallet back with all our money. The fast police work amazed us, but we certainly were even more grateful for the quick and kind help of the two boys. If they had not spoken to us right away, we never would have found the thief. The two boys seemed happier than we were at the outcome. Obviously the restaurant could be called a "takeout" place in more ways than one.

The next morning, Elaine and I attended the court hearing for the thief. The courtroom, a large room furnished sparingly with the judge's bench, a witness stand, small tables for the prosecutor and the defendant, along with a couple of rows of spectators' seating, had only a small number of people present. The police had taken the Pula bills out of Elaine's wallet as evidence, leaving the US dollar bills alone, likely assuming they were worthless in Botswana. To our surprise, the defendant acted as his own defense attorney, which we discovered later not to be uncommon. At the time, Botswana had too few trained lawyers to provide defense attorneys for every accused person.

The defendant called Elaine to the witness stand to testify. He stood at his spot, a rather cocky look on his face, and asked her one question: "Did you see me take the money?" He knew she had to answer no, which she did. But that question constituted his entire defense, as he had been caught with the wallet and money almost immediately after the theft. After a few more comments from the police, the brief trial ended with our money returned to us and the thief sentenced to time in jail. Because he had several previous offenses, the judge gave him no leniency.

Each evening after our language class, we went back to St. Joseph's, said evening prayers with the sisters, then enjoyed a cup of tea with them. We felt such warm hospitality from them, adding to our sense of being at home in our new African setting.

A New Car

The language and orientation course lasted three weeks. On the second weekend we were greatly pleased to discover that we could buy a car. Visiting Dave and Joy King, British missionaries working at Moeding

College with Derek Lindfield, we drove into their yard and saw a Chevrolet Nomad—somewhat like a jeep—with a "For Sale" sign in the window. We had seen a vehicle much like it in Maun not long before, thinking it seemed ideal for the three of us. As with so many of the missionaries we met, the Kings were people of generous and open hearts, inviting us in immediately for tea and conversation. After talking it over together, Dave offered to drive the Nomad to Gaborone on Monday afternoon and pick us up from the language class. Upon arriving with the car the next day, he had me drive it back to St. Joseph's, where Joy showed up in their Volkswagen. After agreeing on a price, Dave explained the location of the jack and a few more details and left the car with us. We had hardly expected such quick action.

Now I can imagine the reader thinking that they were unloading a clunker on us, but not at all. The Nomad had a front seat wide enough for three, a good engine, and cushions on both sides in the back where Sherry could sit or lie when on a long trip. The vehicle traveled well in sand (a necessity for Botswana!) and featured good gas mileage. We bought two gasoline cans holding about six gallons each, then went to a garage and had a metal rack fashioned and welded to the front of the car, setting the two cans into the rack. The fourteen-hour drive between Gaborone and Maun had long stretches of hundreds of miles where no gas stations existed, so we deemed the extra storage a necessity.

Final Week

In the third week we all had a choice of either going to a village to stay for the week and practice our language skills, or staying at the orientation center for continuing classes. Because Sherry had made friends with the Reimer family, all of whom were going to live in the village, she decided to go along with them. It surprised and impressed Elaine and me that our shy young one showed such willingness to go to an unfamiliar place. But almost immediately the thought struck me, "Ah, she's going with a friend—and without us for once!" Elaine and I stayed at the center for the formal classes that week.

On a free Tuesday afternoon during the third week, we decided to return to Moeding to visit Joy and Dave one more time. They introduced us to Albert Lock, a retired British missionary from the old London Missionary Society. A distinguished-looking man with white hair and mustache, Lock (a White man) had served for a time as the Speaker of the Botswana Parliament many years before. It signaled to me both the high regard Botswana had for missionaries and the commitment President Khama had held to a non-racialist society.

TRAVEL BACK HOME

On Friday, the final day of our language class, we welcomed Sherry back from the village and began to prepare for our trip back to Maun. By chance, we ran into Mark and Susan Shopland in Gaborone late Friday morning, where they had been visiting the Peace Corps office for medical checkups. Since they were headed back north, we were glad to offer them a lift. We arranged for them to stay overnight with us at St. Joseph's so we could all leave together early the next morning. They planned to leave us at the crossroads at the village of Palapye, where they would hitch a ride to Serowe, site of Seretse Khama's grave and the headquarters of the Bangwato tribe.

The trip home featured some surprises for us. A few hours north of Gaborone, we crossed the Tropic of Capricorn, where a person can stand up straight in the sunshine about noon each December 22 and cast no shadow at all. Each year at that day and time, the sun is directly above. Soon after that spot, dozens of antelope called tsessebe began appearing alongside the road. With brown fur similar to the common North American deer, and a pair of horns each shaped like a crescent moon curved inward at the top, tsessebe usually ranged over wide plains and in the Okavango, so Susan said that it surprised her to see them in that area of the country. Standing in the middle of the road, one animal became startled upon spotting us, quickly jumping off to the left. Attempting to jump the barbed wire fence meant to keep cattle off the road, the underside of the animal became snared on the barbed wire. Struggling frantically back and forth trying to shake himself loose, the antelope's stomach became cut and bleeding, but he finally freed himself and dashed off into the wooded area. Only a few hundred yards farther along, another surprise: five wildebeest stood along the road, creatures also not often spotted in that area. Powerful-looking creatures resembling buffalo, they had broad shoulders and thick horns.

After dropping off the Shoplands at the crossroads to Serowe, we hurried on to Francistown, hoping to reach it by noon. In southern

Africa, all the gas stations (and other businesses) closed each Saturday at noon, not reopening until noon on Sunday. We missed the deadline by thirty minutes. After staying overnight in a hotel, we waited until noon for the fuel, then set off on the long journey to Maun.

The eight-hour journey between Francistown and Maun had little to offer in the way of sightseeing. The flat desert landscape stretched out endlessly, trees and bushes scattered along the way with little to attract our attention. The first 120 miles featured paved road and smooth driving, but then came the difficult part we remembered so well from our first trip to Maun. The rough dirt road extended for over 200 miles and vexed inexperienced drivers like me, occasionally making me unsure where the road ran. Joking, I remarked, "I guess we just point the car in the right direction and drive!"

Just after sunset, we came around a small grove of trees. Suddenly, right in the middle of the road in front of us stood the largest giraffe I had ever seen. It towered so far above us that because Sherry sat in the back, she had to lean down lower to look up and out the front windshield to see the animal's head. An extraordinary sight, the giraffe loomed as tall or taller than any of the trees near the roadside. Having so recently seen the film showing Basarwa people in the central Kalahari hunting a giraffe, we immediately recalled mention of the giraffe's enormously powerful kick. At that moment, not having our windshield kicked in became a far more important goal than getting home quickly.

We stopped the car and sat still.

Unsure who felt more threatened, we or the giraffe, we sat unmoving for a minute or two. At first facing away from us, the giraffe turned its head and looked lazily at us, then turned back. He slowly walked a few steps away from us straight ahead on the road toward Maun, seemingly unbothered by our presence. Attempting to pass him on either side seemed risky at best. Elaine spoke first, with a kind of nervous laugh, saying, "I hope at that pace he's not on his way to Maun!"

But then something else caught our eyes. On the road about fifty yards farther ahead, large numbers of animals crossed the road in a steady stream from right to left. Because darkness had almost fallen, we had difficulty determining what they were. They looked like horses, so we decided they must be zebra. The giraffe moved a couple of slow steps in their direction every few minutes, and we followed, slowly and tentatively. Coming closer, we watched in awe as hundreds and hundreds of the black-and-white striped zebra poured across the road for more than ten minutes, a mass migration for water in that driest part of the dry season. Then it hit us—the giraffe acted as crossing guard for the zebra crossing. Pun intended!

Luckily for us, the giraffe soon decided to walk a few steps off the road to the left, in the direction of the migrating zebra. Thinking we could slip by him while he faced away from us, we took our opportunity and drove by slowly, passing within fifteen yards of the animal. He stood next to a telephone pole, the only object in sight taller than the giraffe, an awe-inspiring presence. The flow of zebra seemed to be coming to an end, but we still had to be careful driving through the zebra crossing. When we reached that spot, two scared zebra charged across the road right in front of us, barely missing the front end of the car. We passed through the crossing spot and then sped off to be on our way.

Arriving home after the eight-hour journey, we found a pile of mail stacked up for us. In the midst of numerous cards and letters lay a package from my mother, one we quickly opened. Among other goodies, the box contained a bag of chocolate chips, packed carefully and, remarkably, not melted together. Since no shop in Maun ever carried such an item, it served as a rare and welcome treat for us. We were still learning how the simplest items and unexpected experiences could bring joy and pleasure to our lives.

11

Scripture Union and a First Retreat

FINAL TERM OF THE YEAR

THE DAY BEFORE THE new term began, I opened the hood of the Nomad to check the engine. When a group of teachers gathered around to peer into our newly purchased car, Philip Monnaatsie walked up and said to me, "Moruti, are you baptizing your new vehicle?" We had become more and more at home and at ease with our surroundings and our school colleagues, but challenges still lay ahead.

A Cultural Lesson

On the school campus, I regularly attended Scripture Union evening prayer meetings in the small round chapel on campus, sometimes learning surprising lessons about living in another culture. One evening, I sat while students followed their usual practice of taking turns praying, reciting memory verses of Scripture, and leading singing. In the midst of all this, one boy came up to the lectern with a cut-out newspaper photo in his hand. With a solemn demeanor, he held up the picture saying, "A great man has died, Leonid Brezhnev." The Communist Premier of the Soviet Union—not quite the figure I expected to be revered in a Christian worship setting. At first it puzzled me, and I briefly thought of objecting, but I stopped myself upon realizing that these students had a very different view of communists and the Soviet Union. The Soviets had provided a good deal of aid to Botswana in an attempt to gain influence in Africa. Not only that, but the small Communist Party of South Africa strongly supported and participated in the leadership of the African National Congress in South Africa in their struggle against the apartheid regime. So the students were understandably sympathetic. They viewed communists as allies in the struggle against racism. I had learned a lesson about how different the world can look from the perspective of another cultural setting. I saw again how dwelling in another culture doubles the size of one's world.

Overnight Retreat

The last weekend in September, Mark Shopland and I took about twenty-five students for a Friday overnight retreat, going a few miles away to a beautiful spot along the Shashe River. Because students knew the river to be crocodile-free, most of them almost immediately went in for a swim, while the several boys designated as cooks started dinner. This being my first such experience, I watched the dinner preparations in some surprise and admiration at both their methods and their efficiency. Starting a fire with one small log of mophane wood, useful because it burns for a long time, they prepared to cook. Dinner featured soft porridge, called bogobe, made with corn meal, sugar, and water, cooked in a big round black kettle that reminded me of the first scene in Shakespeare's *Macbeth*. Taking water from the river, they boiled it in the pot, threw handfuls of meal in and let the mixture boil for about twenty minutes. Then they mixed in the sugar, using considerably more than the cooks would ever use back at the school dining hall. When on their own, students seized the opportunity to make bogobe to their own tastes. Other than the pots, they had no other cooking equipment. I couldn't help thinking how people in the United States would see the whole process as terribly unsanitary because the boys used a big branch broken from a tree to stir the porridge. Having bogobe for the first time, I found that I really liked it—no doubt due to all that extra sugar.

Another first for me came when I wandered down by the river and spotted a lilac-breasted roller, the national bird of Botswana. Unlike anything I had ever seen, the roller flew over me, showing off its brilliant sky-blue wings with dark blue edging, the lilac breast, tan crown on the head, a gorgeous sight.

After supper, we had a campfire, sharing some ideas about what it means to trust and to have faith. Faith, we came to agree, is trusting that God never abandons us. The Seventh Day Adventist minister, Rev. Dimbungo, arrived after a short time to speak to the students, encouraging them to persist in loving our neighbor even when it seems most difficult. After he left, the whole group of us stayed up until midnight, singing, sharing stories, and dancing in a circle around the fire. I loved watching them laughing and teasing one another, all of them feeling a carefree delight at being together. Students relished these times of fellowship, free from the pressure of school work. I felt privileged to be part of it.

Mark and I put our sleeping bags down near the river and went to sleep on what seemed a perfect evening—completely clear, with a full moon shining so brightly that it cast vivid shadows all around us, no wind at all, the air just slightly cool. The students, still enjoying themselves, stayed up much later, singing around the fire.

We all awoke by 6:00 the next morning. The cooks served breakfast of soft porridge—the regular fare of the Batswana people for breakfast and supper every day—and then everyone gathered together to sit on a grassy spot in the morning air. Some students lay on their stomachs, elbows propping up heads. Others sat cross-legged on the grass, upper bodies hunched forward eager for the morning discussion. We began with a Bible study on being called by God, trying to emphasize that God calls us in many situations to act with love and compassion for others, to overcome divisions between people. One of the boys asked, "If I hear my friends speaking badly of a person because he's from another tribe, does that mean that I have a responsibility to say to them that they should not have prejudice against the person?" I replied, "Yes, I would say that's like a call from God to overcome barriers between people. The New Testament letter to the Ephesians says that Christ has broken down the dividing wall of hostility between people." Others raised the issue of prejudice against the Herero people in Botswana. I responded by telling them of the sign of reconciliation I had seen in the UCCSA church in Maun, where Herero and Batswana worshiped together.

In the second half of the morning, Peter Mudiwa, the UCCSA pastor and part-time RE teacher, came to give a talk on a subject very popular with students: courtship and marriage. Always enthusiastic and engaging, Peter spoke of the importance of communicating, emphasizing the

importance of a couple being sure that they talk with one another seriously, listening to one another carefully, coming to know and understand
each other well. The students gave Peter their full attention, responding
with a big round of applause in gratitude for his presentation.

At the time for lunch, the cooks used two big pots, one for porridge
and the other for meat. In order to make a hard porridge, they cooked
the corn meal longer than in the morning. Into the other pot they threw
large chunks of meat in with a little curry powder and salt. Curiously,
they also had raw carrots, but they didn't throw them in to cook with the
meat. When I asked them if they put the carrots in the pot to cook, the
boys gave me a rather odd look of astonishment. They didn't say it out
loud, but, I could see them thinking, "What a silly idea!" They never did
such a thing. They always ate the carrots raw.

We ended our retreat with a favorite student activity: a question time,
when students raised questions about faith, morals, or the Bible. It brought
out a wide variety of issues, some of them surprising to me. "Is joking a sin?
Is God a man or a woman? How do you keep from falling in love?" Both
Mark and I had the most trouble trying to answer that last one.

Ending the afternoon with a swim, we all packed up and went back
to school, quite satisfied with the fellowship and learning we had all experienced. It felt energizing to be with the group of students in an atmosphere outside the bounds of school and study.

12

Life in Maun

SHOPPING ENCOUNTERS

Village Obstacles

"Watch out for the goat!" Elaine exclaimed as we drove the school van through the village one Saturday morning. I honked the horn. The goat slowly stood up in the middle of the sandy road and wandered off. Along with driving on the lefthand side of the road, other roadway challenges faced us whenever we went to the village. The occasional cow or donkey walked casually onto the path in front of the car. Goats, especially, liked to lie in the sand right in the middle of the road. A variety of trails in the sand meandered throughout Maun, winding in no discernible pattern around houses and other buildings in such a way as to leave new drivers uncertain how to find anything. Also, pockets of deep sand often loomed in front of the van, making it easy to get stuck. Whenever a deep spot of sand appeared just ahead, I drove faster to get through it.

One of Elaine's tasks as treasurer involved mail pickup and delivery in the village. Before we obtained our own car, she usually went alone or with Sherry in the school van, but sometimes I drove the van so that we could combine a weekly food shopping trip with the mail pickup. We always looked forward to mail from home, but we also discovered occasional surprises from strangers. One day a package arrived for us filled with macadamia nuts. A United Church of Christ congregation in Hawaii sent them to missionaries all over the world, calling their endeavor "Nuts to Missionaries." We appreciated the gesture and their sense of humor.

Though a large village, Maun had no such thing as a supermarket, and no store had refrigeration. Shopping meant visiting six or seven little stores and a bakery or two in order to find everything we needed. We walked around the cramped, crowded narrow aisles of the shops with our small shopping basket, searching for whatever we could find. Even then, we often returned home without some desired items. We never could find chocolate chips or marshmallows. The bakery would often be out of bread. In the summer rainy season (December into February) flooded areas frequently blocked the road to Francistown, preventing trucks carrying foodstuffs from getting through. We went through one entire summer with no margarine available in the shops. Often cheddar cheese would be the only cheese available, so homemade pizza with cheddar cheese appeared regularly on our supper menu. Or sometimes we had a hard time finding oats. A staple for us usually available in cardboard packages, oats couldn't be bought that way because they, like other cereals, were often filled with bugs and had to be tossed out. If we wanted oats, we had to buy a brand called Tiger Oats in tightly sealed metal cans. At times, someone who had been shopping would arrive back to the school and announce to everyone they saw, "Riley's store has Tiger oats!" And several people would rush off to get them. Another kind of treat came once while shopping alone, when I happily found a rare treasure: canned apple filling. Taking it home right away, I made my first-ever apple pie, surprising both Elaine and myself. Easily tempted by the rare treat, the three of us finished it by dinner time that night.

In those first few months when we used the school van, each time we stopped at a store, we encountered another teacher from the school, who either wanted a lift back to school or asked us to take packages back so they wouldn't have to walk around town with them. So few people had cars that everyone expected anyone with a car to give rides to others. On one Saturday morning, we came back to the school with three more people than when we set out shopping.

Unexpected Requests

On two shopping trips Elaine and Sherry took together, they encountered a bizarre and unusual request. On both occasions, grown men approached Elaine, surprising her—and making Sherry quite uncomfortable—by stating quite matter-of-factly, "I would like to ask to marry your daughter. Do you give your permission?" Each man appeared to be obviously considerably older than Sherry. But it seemed not an uncommon occurrence in the culture. Neither one spoke to Sherry at all, but only to Elaine, who felt somewhat like being in a bargaining session for a commodity. Sherry clung closely to her mother while Elaine explained carefully and kindly to each of the suitors that we did not view marriage as acceptable or possible until a young person had reached at least eighteen. The fact that Sherry had received two marriage proposals before she turned thirteen failed to impress her, which she made quite clear after these incidents. She said later that she felt very odd and ill at ease. The first time it happened, later that same day she exclaimed more than once, "That was weird!"

Life at Home

Not long into our new life, Elaine noted pointedly that the three of us were not sharing cooking duties in an equitable manner. Sherry and I, embarrassed at our neglect, realized that we obviously were leaving too much for Elaine. So together we all made a schedule for cooking and dish-washing. Each of us cooked two nights a week, and one night we went into the village to eat at a restaurant. Some of Sherry's cooking favorites were tuna-cheese toasties and creamed hamburger. On each of my two evenings, I baked two loaves of fresh oatmeal bread, which we always enjoyed hot out of the oven and slathered with butter or jelly. Elaine improvised numerous creative dishes, including the aforementioned homemade pizza with cheddar cheese (since no mozzarella could be found anywhere), vegetable soup with fresh broccoli from the school garden, vegetables in a cheese sauce made into a casserole, or beef baked with onions. She also made bread-and-butter pickles from a Betty Crocker recipe and watermelon pickles from a recipe given to her by the principal's wife. On Sundays after the morning worship with the students, we often had tea with fresh-baked muffins.

Sitting at the supper table, Elaine and I would sometimes look at one another in wordless wonder and amazement that we had entered into this unusual and blessed life, each of us at a point of wrenching change in our

lives, open to new possibilities. The call to Botswana had created a new
life for us that we had never imagined possible.

NIGHTS AND DAYS

Night Time Beauty

Living in the midst of a flat desert hundreds of miles from any urban
area, the pure, clean air aroused in us still another sense of wonder. The
nights, always absolutely clear and dry, presented a palate of light the
like of which we had never seen. With no pollution or humidity to mask
them, thousands of stars shone bright and plentiful, as though a huge fire
in the distant reaches of the universe had thrown off thousands of sparks
that remained shining in place. The first time we viewed that glorious
panorama, we were awestruck at the view of the more than 2,000 stars
visible to us. Different stars shone in the night, quite unlike the northern
hemisphere. We could see the Southern Cross, a constellation not visible
in North America. Orion the Hunter had been turned upside down so
that it looked as though he had a necktie instead of a belt. Occasionally, on nights with a full moon, several of the American staff would go
outside, sit down cross-legged on the tennis court with a deck of playing
cards, and play a game of hearts. The brightness of the moon shed so
much light that we could see everything clearly. Sometimes I looked up
at the stars and marveled that many of them no longer existed; the light
we observed had started out millions of years ago from stars that had
long since burned themselves out. On those nights, the vastness of the
universe and our tiny place in it overwhelmed me.

Peanut

Soon after our arrival in Maun, we inherited a black cat from a Peace
Corps woman about to depart for the United States. Long-haired, with a
single white spot under his chin, the cat received his name from a popular grocery item called Black Cat Peanut Butter. Thus Peanut became the
newest member of our household. Elaine and Sherry loved cats, having
lived with several outdoor cats around their house in Pennsylvania. Before leaving for Botswana, Sherry asked her mother if she could have
pets in Africa. "Honestly, I don't really know," Elaine had told her. The

cat came as a pleasant surprise, providing a bit of help to Sherry's mood in those first difficult months when so much seemed so strange and new.

In the big house where we lived for the first month in Maun, the dining room sideboard became a favorite place for Peanut. He hid there, waiting for someone to go by, then leaped out and startled the passerby. A couple of times, he jumped out and grabbed hold of my leg. I think he wanted my attention. Never owning dogs or cats earlier in my life, it took me a while to warm up to him. After moving to the smaller house, Peanut still sensed this initial reluctance on my part, so one afternoon he made a valiant attempt to win me over. As I sat alone in the dining area, Peanut entered the house through the kitchen screen door, walked to where I sat and put a bird down on the floor in front of me. "Here I am, a mighty hunter, be proud of me!" For a split second, this impressed me. But then the bird opened its wings and began to fly around the room. It took some persistence and more than a few minutes to catch it and let it out the door to freedom. Peanut never tried that again, but I did indeed warm up to him. Numerous times when I sat grading student papers on the screened-in porch, Peanut stretched out on the table beside my stack of exams, never disturbing the papers.

Catching birds did not turn out to be our cat's only talent. Peanut also served as a weather forecaster. During the rainy season, if we couldn't find him, we knew it to be a sure sign that a storm loomed close. He had become an integral part of our household.

Elaine kept a garden, a difficult task in the extreme heat so often afflicting us. Because the ground remained bone-dry much of the year, the soil required constant watering to grow any flowers. But Elaine persevered, planting geraniums and repeatedly watering the garden soil. The wet ground became a refuge from the heat for Peanut, offering him a comfortable place to lie. Several times I came home from a hot afternoon class to find Peanut lying in a semi-circle on the cool earth around the geraniums.

Our house became something of a center of activity. In our first year, we hosted a July 4 celebration for sixteen Peace Corps workers, featuring magnesium flares courtesy of Mark Shopland's science lab. Elaine began to give haircuts to several of the school staff, then a couple of other expatriate workers in Maun who heard of her skill sought her out. Our sense of hospitality had expanded. Carol Schaad once remarked to another friend of ours, "When I want someone to talk sense to me, I go to the Langendijks and talk to Goke. When I want comfort, I go to the Christensens."

Morning Prayer

After some months in Maun, I developed the habit of rising early each morning to pray for an hour before Elaine and Sherry woke up. In the stillness and silence of the darkness before sunrise, I sat in the comfortable chair by the big plate glass window in our living room, looking out as the morning light slowly brought into focus our lemon tree that produced lemons the size of softballs. The hotter times had me on the screened-in porch looking out over the gentle slope leading down to the river running alongside the school grounds. Peanut stretched out on the table next to me. I relished the quiet, so peaceful because at that early hour the village chickens, goats, and dogs had not yet begun their morning symphony of screeching, bleating, and barking that greeted each new day.

In the years prior to my life in Botswana, my experience with silence showed me that I had a great deal to learn about listening. The experience had come on several eight-day retreats in silence at a Jesuit retreat center in southeast Pennsylvania. Rambling thoughts and images had always filled my attempts at contemplation in silence. Mystics speak of emptying your mind of images, resting one's mind and heart on God alone. I always found that nearly impossible. It's unlikely that I'm unique in that. It always took me at least the first two days of the eight to calm down from the hectic pace of my everyday life and center my concentration on honest prayer. It actually is not a question of stifling all the thoughts and images that arise when one is trying to listen to God with one's whole self. It seems better to say that the word of God is present in the midst of all those images.

Beginning with ten minutes of stretching and one or two other brief exercises, I then sat in silence for the remainder of the hour and watched the first rays of the sun light upon the tops of the bushes and trees. I prayed for the students in my classes that day, for Elaine and Sherry, for myself, then ended the hour by reading two of the Psalms. By then, the animals' morning symphony had begun. Elaine and Sherry had wakened and dressed, and the three of us ate our breakfast together. A short time before the school's 7:00 am morning assembly commenced, Elaine sat with me for five to ten minutes to pray together from a collection of morning and evening prayers, a time we treasured every morning.

SCHOOL DAYS

Daily Schedule

Just before 7:00 am I took the path through the hedge dividing our yard from the driveway, and walked past the administration building to take my place on the morning assembly ground. Facing an elevated concrete speaker's platform, 600 students stood in straight lines in the open air, arranged by class for the opening of the day. About half of the number boarded at the school, and half lived in the surrounding area. Students had uniforms—white blouse and dark blue jumper for the girls, gray pants and shirts for the boys. Winter term saw a navy blue sweater added. Teachers stood at the front facing the students. On the platform with steps leading up either side of it, the principal stood up to make announcements, followed by a rousing, hand-clapping song, the 600 students raising their voices in a stunning and glorious four-part harmony. Staff members took turns, each for a week at a time, telling a story or giving a short word of advice. The assembly ended with a short prayer and the students were off to their classrooms. My forte: telling stories from folklore, history, and various cultural and religious traditions, stories which taught a lesson. One morning I told a story of US President Abraham Lincoln, who at a White House reception during the Civil War made a complimentary remark about a Confederate general—obviously an officer in the enemy Southern army. Surprised by this, a woman in the group said, "Mr. President, that man is your enemy! It's your job to destroy the enemy." To which Lincoln replied, "Madam, if I have made my enemy into a friend, have I not destroyed my enemy?"

The faculty modeled a miniature United Nations. We had US Peace Corps volunteers, along with teachers on two-year government contracts from the Netherlands, Northern Ireland, Germany, Denmark, England, and India. Also, wanderers came from other African nations as far away as Sierra Leone in west Africa, and exiles from the terrible seven-year civil war in Zimbabwe that had recently exhausted itself and mercifully come to an end. Part of the Zimbabwe contingent included several American Methodist missionaries who had been in Africa for many years. Another American couple had fled from turmoil in Angola. All these expatriates comprised about half of the faculty. The other half were native Batswana assigned to Maun by the government, some of them working there reluctantly because they considered this village in the far north an out-of-the-way, undesirable posting, far from any urban attractions.

The first of eight class periods began at ten past 7:00. Because buildings had no heat, in the second (winter) of the three twelve-week terms of the school year, classes began an hour later to deal with the colder mornings. Even so, many students wore gloves in class the first part of the morning. Except for science and agriculture classes, students remained in the same classrooms all day, while the teachers moved from one room to another. A mid-morning break of ten minutes and a longer break halfway through the day served as rest times. At the longer break students could visit the clinic if they had health issues. Classes ended at 1:40, then lunch. The unbearable afternoon heat in the first and third terms necessitated ending at that time. After the regular classes ended, the school required students to attend an additional one-hour study period, an especially burdensome time as the heat put numerous students to sleep at their desks. After supper, the boarding students had another mandatory study period Monday through Thursday from 7 to 8:30 in the evening.

Much to my initial surprise, only one faculty member oversaw all sixteen classrooms during the afternoon study hour. A student prefect, or monitor, sat at the front of each classroom. The single faculty member made the rounds of the classrooms once or twice during the period, only occasionally encountering any discipline problems. Little wonder, I soon realized, considering the heat!

Facing Differences

The first few times I stood in front of a class—always forty students, five rows, eight students to a row—I felt overcome by the vast difference between my own life experience and theirs. It seemed that a great deal of time would be needed to educate myself. I didn't know how they would view me or even accept me. But I soon found that students held teachers with strong educational credentials in high regard. I recalled Christine Purves telling me of the student who, upon hearing that I had a master's degree in theology, responded by saying "Ah, now I will pay close attention in RE [religious education] class!"

After a while I began to feel that I had some familiarity with their lives. But while I knew something about their lives, much remained far outside my middle-class North American experience. Students eagerly explained the traditional life in Botswana, the custom of a typical family having three homes: the family compound in the home village, a cattle post where they kept the family's cattle, and a place simply called "the lands," a third area where the crops grew. These usually included corn, sorghum, and occasional vegetables. They told me of the normal custom of boys being sent to the cattle post away from their village, drinking fresh milk from the cows and eating bogobe, the corn meal porridge that served as the staple of the national diet. A herd boy faced danger at the cattle post, needing to keep a fire going at night to scare off the lions who often attacked cattle. Girls often stayed in the village, gathering firewood for cooking and taking care of younger children. In a male-dominated society, older people often thought that girls did not need to attend school, but thankfully, that seemed to be changing with many girls attending secondary school.

So much lay outside my own experience. I had never lived without easy access to good medical care, or some basic foodstuffs. Nor did I need to worry about the threat of drought. But in Botswana, if the rains did not come, the grass did not grow, and the cattle died. Cattle were the main source of wealth in that entire region of the continent, so people kept cattle like many other people in the world held bank accounts. Batswana teachers often used part of their monthly salary to purchase more cattle. When a period of drought occurred, the threat of famine loomed large. Students told me of the government policy of storing food in several areas of the country as a cautionary measure in case of drought. They reminded me of the six people who had died of starvation some years before in a remote village far to the northwest. But because of the government's policy, those had been the only deaths resulting from hunger in a long time.

Visiting the tax office in Maun for the first time, Elaine discovered how integral cattle were to the society when she faced questioning required to register for taxes. "How many cattle do you have?" the official asked. Elaine answered, "None." The man looked astonished. "None? Not even back home in America?" He could not imagine such a situation. He shook his head in amazement, baffled as to how someone could survive without something so basic to normal life.

One day at the end of a school year, I sat silently in a Form Three classroom proctoring an English exam. Looking out on the students busily writing, I began to remind myself how easy it can be to believe in the superiority of one's own culture and values. When Jesus spoke of the poor in spirit, he meant for us to recognize the poverty of all that is in us and to be aware of the richness and grace we do not possess. While true that many people in the country did not have the education I had, that really made for a dangerous temptation to regard my opinions and experiences as more worthy than theirs. But my opinions and perceptions came from my own limited experience, with no guarantee that my insight and understanding were anything to boast about. The culture and values of Botswana contained riches that I had not yet fully appreciated.

Numerous times I witnessed the tendency of people to ask for help with all sorts of tasks. They asked without hesitation in circumstances where a North American would not dream of asking unless the request came from a very close friend or relative, one whom he or she would expect to repay. A ready willingness to help seemed to me to stem from a greater sense of community and belonging than we have in the United States. In that African setting, where people put great emphasis on sharing and giving time to one another, it struck me that we in the United States often kept ourselves and our families insulated from the pain and passion of others. I thought of the contrast between this African sense of community and the individualism held up in the United States which causes us to overemphasize self-reliance as a virtue. That means, in turn, that we North Americans often fail to see that we belong to one another in a profound way not always evident in our culture.

The thought came to me that the church in the United States lacked the deep realization that when one suffers, all suffer, when one is not free, no one is free. The North American church has too often understood salvation as being solely rescue from punishment, when in fact it is more complete than that. Salvation is the restoration of community. The New Testament expresses this quite clearly. In the Gospel of Luke, Zaccheus finds salvation when he makes things right with his neighbors; the one leper whom Jesus heals finds salvation in going to the priest as the law commanded and then being restored to fellowship with the community. It is in the community that people are forgiven, where peace and reconciliation take place. We belong to one another in Christ. I began to realize, as never before, that salvation is not primarily individual, but communal.

The students sitting in front of me had a more acute sense of both their own freedom and their own sense of belonging, living as they did in such close proximity to South African apartheid's oppression and yet embraced by a communal sense of belonging to a tribe and to their recently independent nation. Their eagerness for learning appeared to me a sign of their hopefulness for a better future. It gave me a satisfying feeling to think that I could play a part in that future.

African Hospitality

Living in southern Africa, we found one of the most appealing aspects of life to be the gracious hospitality shown by so many of the people we met. Deeply ingrained in the culture and also shared by all the missionaries we encountered, it influenced our own lives. Whenever I went to visit a family in the village, either by myself or with Elaine, the hosts would immediately bring out some kind of chair or other items for us to sit on and offer us tea or an orange fruit drink. If possible, they would make sure that we were seated in the shade. They made every effort to have us feel comfortable. The endearing quality of it always put us at ease.

In turn, we learned to be open and welcoming to visitors both expected and unexpected. At times, young travelers from a variety of nations stopped at our door asking for an overnight stay. We would invite them in, give them some tea, and listen to their travel stories. One young Australian woman had set off on a journey from Capetown on the southern tip of the continent, intending to travel all the way north to Cairo. US Peace Corps workers would get word of Americans living at the secondary school and arrive at our house asking for lodging for a night. Travelers threw their sleeping bags on the living room floor or on our screened-in porch and spent the night. The next morning, we would feed them breakfast and see them off.

The students themselves demonstrated a care and respect for me for me in some unique and sometimes unexpected ways. In a Form Two class one day, I stood next to the teacher's desk explaining one of the lessons. Several students began waving their hands as though they wanted me to call on them, but as I hadn't finished the point being made, I put them off, saying, "Just a moment, let me finish my thought here." Unable to contain himself, one boy came marching up to stand in front of me, speaking quickly but quietly. "Mr. Chris, your zipper is down." Simultaneously grateful and embarrassed, I thanked him, turned and remedied the situation.

Once a year we held a big overnight retreat for the Scripture Union. Usually about a hundred students would participate, all of us walking several miles upriver from the school to camp out overnight. On one retreat experience with them, I watched in the evening as the students began to spread out all along the sloping bank of the river to settle down to sleep for the night. Three student leaders walked over to me. Pointing to a spot by a tree a bit farther away from the river, they explained to me that I should sleep there. As I started to ask why, they noticed the puzzled look on my face and gave me an entirely unforeseen explanation. "Oh, Mr. Chris," one said, pointing again to the tree, "You should sleep over there. That way, all of us students will be between you and the crocodiles."

Suddenly I saw what genuine hospitality meant. They wanted me to know that they cared for me and wanted me safe from danger. Readily accepting their proposal, I did wonder how they protected themselves. But I decided that they must have known what they were doing. And they did, building a fire which held the crocs at bay. The night passed with no casualties.

13

Believing is Seeing

MAGIC SPELLS

Facing a New Worldview

AT THE AGE OF eight, I became fascinated with magic tricks. My next-door neighbor Bobby had an uncle who ran a magic shop, a place of many wonders for the two of us. Learning a variety of simple tricks and illusions, Bobby and I fooled and entertained other kids on our street. My personal favorite involved filling a glass Coke bottle with water, holding it uncapped upside down—with no water falling out. (Sorry, but magicians don't reveal their secrets!) But we knew that rational explanations always existed for the "magic" we performed.

However, in southern Africa, the presence of magic charms and spells presented a world seemingly beyond my capability to comprehend. Belief in magic pervaded every-day life. Our students frequently received slick, glossy catalogues in the mail from South Africa with odd-sounding names like *Kansas City Warehouse* advertising various magic charms and potions. "Use this potion and make the object of your desire fall in love with you." "Wear this charm and find the valuable item you have lost." Belief in magic infused much of the cultural setting. At our school, one of the Zimbabwean teachers claimed quite seriously that a man he had known back home had an invisible spell on him that lasted ten years.

While utterly mystifying to me, he clearly accepted it as nothing strange or unusual.

But this worldview, so contrary to my own Western mind, had a dark side, as I soon discovered. One morning only a few months after our arrival, the day students walking in from the village came to school buzzing with a kind of fearful excitement. They brought a startling bit of news. A dead body had been found about 200 meters down river from the school. They called it a ritual murder—someone killed for the purpose of using body parts in magic spells. One student quickly assured me of my own personal safety: "Don't worry, Mr. Chris! White people's body parts don't work in magic spells." This gave me no comfort, feeling quite alarmed as I did thinking about the danger to the students. To live in a world with a real possibility of ritual murder seemed like some sort of scary alternate reality. Students also told me of the strange belief held by many that if you killed a rich person, you would become rich yourself. Even though this didn't threaten me personally, I felt it no less disturbing. The students viewed the threat to be so real that when some from the village walked to the school campus for an evening program, they traveled in groups, often carrying clubs for protection.

With the ritual murder, it suddenly seemed that my world had shifted. I felt that I had been hurtled abruptly back in time to a world where spirits, magic spells, and a different fear than I had ever known surrounded and inhabited the society. A few months later, as a Westerner from a disenchanted secular society, it proved easy for me to conclude that the illness of a student resulted from tension and the extreme pressure of important exams. That explanation seemed preferable to that of a magic spell. But the connection between mind and body is such that the strong cultural belief in magic aroused a very real fear in people. I learned about strong beliefs subjecting a person to powerful forces. Early that year our local pastor, Rev. Peter Mudiwa, had preached a sermon on fear and faith, remarking that fear is overcome only by faith and trust in a power greater than the spells and charms.

Early in the first term of 1981, one of the girls at the school developed a sore spot on her foot, and she began to express what to me seemed another strange idea: she became convinced that she had a needle in her foot which would travel through her body to her heart and kill her. Students described this to me as a fairly common notion. The girl began to believe herself bewitched. She heard voices telling her not to study or go to class. What I thought of as normal pastoral counseling—listening to her fears and attempting to help her work through them—proved entirely ineffective. The only solution seemed to be to send her to her home village, where she could consult a traditional doctor. Only then would she be convinced that she would receive the help she needed. With a mixture of fear and sadness, I agreed. The fear stemmed from the possibility that her family would decide that it would not be worth sending a girl back to school. But she went home and came back two weeks later. With a beaming smile, she told me excitedly, "I went to the ngaka [traditional doctor] and he got the needle out!" Whatever happened, seeing her again brought me great relief. I began to see that the traditional doctors (ineptly called "witch doctors" in English) are not charlatans, as Westerners often assume, but are actually quite knowledgeable about various kinds of cures.

Uahangana's Illness

Another striking instance of the belief in magic spells arose at the beginning of one school year when two Herero students came to our house on a Saturday afternoon. Uahangana stood outside our kitchen door with a plea: "I have a problem, and I need to ask for your help." His friend Ngaikunue stood by him. "Come in, come in, please," I said as I pushed the screen door open. We all sat down in the living room. I knew that Uahangana had been ill with stomach pains and intestinal troubles for about ten days, so I already had concern for him. He suffered from constipation and had endured a great deal of misery. The school nurse had no answers for him. Nothing the nurse tried had helped. So Uahangana had written to his mother about it and had just received a reply by mail. "She tells me that she consulted a witch doctor about me, and he told her that I have been bewitched by one of my uncles. That's why I'm sick. She told me that I should come home right away so that the witch doctor can kill a sheep and break the spell over me." Startled by such a claim, I hesitated a bit, struggling to decide how to respond.

Because Uahangana served as one of the leaders of the Scripture Union, I did not feel entirely certain that he believed this. I asked him what he thought, and he shook his head wearily, responding, "Yes, this happens in our tribe. And if someone bewitches you, unless you go and have the sheep killed, you will never get well and you will die." "So it's important for you to go home," I replied. "Yes, it's very important to do it." He needed my permission as his class teacher, which I readily provided.

I then instructed him to go to the principal, who also needed to give his permission for Uahangana to go home for a few days. Fortunately in this situation, the American principal wisely took the situation seriously and granted the request.

I certainly did not understand it at all from my Western scientific rationalist background. Although skeptical, I had learned by that point not to take talk of magic spells lightly. If Uahangana believed it, he would not have received any relief until the traditional doctor performed a ritual on his behalf. Uahangana had no means of transportation for his trip to his home village, a tiny place out in the bush fifty miles to the north of us. He had no choice but to walk. Gathering a few provisions for the journey, he then set off to the north on foot. As I discovered later, the trek took him almost two full days.

The next Friday, early in the evening before sundown, Uahangana appeared at our kitchen door, a big smile on his face. "I am well!" "Please come in and tell me all about it," I said as I opened the door, eager to hear his story. He sat down, stretching out his legs, looking far more relaxed than he had six days before. A remarkable and intriguing tale unfolded. When he arrived in his home village after the two-day walk, he greeted his family. His mother took him immediately to see the traditional doctor, who called the entire extended family together. About thirty people gathered, sitting in a circle on the ground. The ngaka went around the circle asking each person if he or she had "bad feeling" toward Uahangana. When he came to the uncle, the one whom the ngaka had blamed for Uahangana's illness, the uncle did not say yes or no, but seemed to hem and haw a bit. Finally he admitted that he did have "bad feelings" toward Uahangana. But the uncle agreed that he no longer desired that to be true, expressing sorrow that he had caused harm. As I listened, I thought to myself, "Obviously, family pressure must have been a factor in his confession!"

Once that expression of apology had been made, the ngaka directed two of the men of the family to bring a sheep from the family flock. They slaughtered the sheep right there in front of everyone, a sign and instrument of peace being made in the family. The ngaka permitted no one to leave until the sheep had been roasted, everyone shared in the eating of it, and the bones and other inedibles burned so that no trace of it remained (and presumably, no trace of the anger and bad feeling either). "When the sheep had all burned," Uahangana said, "I started to feel better and began to get well."

Correctly assuming that I likely held a skeptical view of what he had described, Uahangana quickly explained to me, "Mr. Chris, the ceremony with the sheep is not magic! It doesn't mean that I'm completely cured. I could get sick again. It just means that peace has been made in the family. This is the way we do things in our tribe. I will still go to the hospital to have myself checked." Then I realized that he had it right; what he described ought not be labeled *magic* in my Western sense, but rather the ritual with the sheep overcame division and disclosed the African emphasis on magic as dealing with repairing disharmony in the community. African tradition recognizes that where disharmony in personal relationships exists, the whole community suffers. The actions of the ngaka had an effect on the harmony and disharmony of the community.

The thought immediately came to my mind, "What a great way to solve family problems!" Then I felt moved by the beauty of the ritual, where people are reconciled at the blood and death of a lamb. I thought of the obvious parallel to Christian tradition: "Lamb of God, who takes away the sins of the world." It also began to dawn on me that the traditional doctors were actually even better psychologists than I had imagined, and certainly not charlatans. But as a Westerner, I did find it hard to wrap my mind around the notion that such possibilities existed in the world. But I certainly began to realize how seriously one must take the connection between the mind and the body. Believing that someone could cast a spell on you can place you under its power.

The Case of the Missing Science Notebook

Oddly enough, when students spoke English, they frequently used the term "witch doctor," as Uahangana had. Spells could be used to create both harmony and disharmony. One morning in my first period class, as I took attendance, one of the girls came up to my desk with a determined, angry look. "Someone has stolen my science notebook." I started to respond, but she interrupted me. "I'm going to the witch doctor on Saturday and have him put a spell on the thief and kill him!" Startled at her vehement stance, I thought that before letting her resort to such drastic measures, we should try another avenue. "Listen everyone, I want you all to look around the classroom and just outside to see if you can find the notebook." Mercifully, later that day one of the other students discovered the notebook inside another desk. Upon hearing the news, I felt as though I may have saved someone's life.

Reflections

Larry Kies, our American colleague and friend, once had an upper level student helping him with his understanding of the Setswana language. At one session, the two of them began to talk about the common belief in charms and spells. Larry asked the student, somewhat in jest, "So, could someone cast a spell on me?" The student smiled, replying, "No. You don't believe it." This seemed a particularly astute observation by one who obviously understood the reality of cultural context and the mind-body connection. To put it another way, the old saying, "Seeing is believing," can be reversed: believing is seeing. Believing that someone else has the ability to do you magical harm can make you quite fearful. Nowadays I often wonder how Botswana students read the Harry Potter books. Somehow I doubt that they see the stories simply as entertaining fantasy fiction.

A parallel came to mind in the Gospel stories when Jesus encounters unbelief in his hometown of Nazareth. Mark 6:1–6 reports that "he could do no deeds of power there because of their unbelief." Failure to trust or have faith creates a barrier to healing, a resistance to a gift. Believing is seeing the world in a new way. This applies to religious faith as well as to a fearful belief that someone has power to cast a magic spell. We cannot "see" without belief.

Did I believe in magic spells? That may not be the right question. Confronted with the obvious reality of Uahangana's experience, I found it difficult to disbelieve it, even though it did not square with my own view of the world. On the other hand, I realized that a simpler, more rational explanation might be possible for his healing: it may be that his two-day fifty mile walk to his home village shook his bowels loose and put his painful constipation to an end. That seemed more reasonable to my Western mind. But I also needed to accept the possibility that there are phenomena in the world I simply cannot explain, that my mind may not be big enough to include such mysteries—which made the idea of the mind-body connection all the more complex and fascinating to me. Maybe this required a little more humility on my part. It continually causes me to ask the question: what else might I be refusing to accept, what else might I be refusing to see? Or, how often do I look, but not see? Perhaps we Westerners are more closely connected than we realize and fail to see those connections. So after hearing of Uahangana's experience, one question for me becomes, do we have effective ways of dealing with broken relationships? Could we have better ways? This is a challenge for families, the church, and for society as a whole.

The world, I thought, is a strange and mysterious place. And it is stranger and more mysterious than we know. At the least, the whole experience with Uahangana helped me to recognize once more how powerful a true sense of community can be and how influential is the culture embedded in each of us. My African education continued.

THE TRAGEDY OF DIPHENG

Trauma for the Community

In students' lives, a combination of eagerness and anxiety loomed as a constant presence. Eagerness to learn came from the fact that without a Junior Certificate awarded upon successful completion of the Form Three examinations, chances of a good job would be nonexistent. Students also knew that they were extremely fortunate to have the opportunity for education. The high anxiety stemmed from both the threat of magic spells and the great pressure of the J. C. exams at the end of the third year. At times, the anxiety proved to be more than they could bear.

On a Friday afternoon in November at the end of exam week, I had gone into the village for an errand. Returning about 5:00 pm, I met Mary Beth near the walk way to our house. She greeted me with a distressed look of sadness and a question,

"Have you heard the news?"

"What news?" I said.

"Dipheng committed suicide at his home just a little while ago."

I felt stunned, disoriented, unable to imagine such wrenching tragedy for his family and for all of us at the school. Mary Beth taught English and served as Dipheng's homeroom teacher. Dipheng sat in one of my religious education sections. The week prior to exams he had been tense and anxious. Wednesday that week, he had been badly upset, suffering from such high anxiety that his heart raced and his chest hurt. School staff took him to the hospital to be examined, and he had been sent home. The principal allowed Dipheng to take the first couple of exams, but his results were poor. Friday morning the hospital had discharged him so he could take another exam. After only five minutes in the exam room, he left, telling Mary Beth that he could not concentrate. The principal and another staff member took Dipheng a second time to the hospital. They took a blood sample and sent him home. The principal informed his parents that Dipheng could have a place in school the following year to retake his Form Three. The parents accepted this offer gratefully, but Dipheng remained sullen and silent. After 1:00 pm, Dipheng's father went to work for the day, while his mother went out to visit their pastor, Rev. Peter Mudiwa. She also stopped at the hospital for Dipheng's blood test results.

About 4:00 pm while alone at home, Dipheng took his father's gun and shot himself. His mother found him when she returned. The shock overwhelmed the whole family, as well as the school. I walked in a daze, suddenly much more keenly aware of the enormity of the pressure students faced. The other students, also quite shaken and crying, wandered around campus with stunned expressions as though they had lost a beloved family member.

To North Americans, November means frost, football, harvest, and turkey. For school students in Botswana, however, November meant hot weather—temperatures reached 110 °F by noon each day—and the tension of final examinations. Form Three students endured a time of particularly high stress. The Junior Certificate (JC) examinations were national qualifying tests in math, English, Setswana, science, history, geography, agriculture, and religious education. These held their full attention with good reason. Without passing the tests, they could not advance to the next level of education. Failing them meant they received no more formal education. No JC certificate meant far fewer job possibilities.

As a further distraction and cause of severe anxiety, that pervasive fear of harmful magic charms and spells gripped many students. They knew that someone in their extended family could hire a traditional doctor to cast a spell which could supposedly cause a student to perform poorly on the exams. Frequently a student's aunt or uncle whose own child had not been admitted to secondary school would, out of jealousy and spite, have such a spell cast on their niece or nephew. Keenly aware of this, students' tension and anxiety levels could easily skyrocket before and during the exams.

As a result, numerous students became convinced that Dipheng had been bewitched by a magic spell. Unsurprisingly, I had never faced this problem of pastoral care in the United States. As the school chaplain, only a few months in the country, I felt less than confident in my ability to respond in any effective way. Without sharing their worldview, one that included magic, I wondered how I could discuss it with them. It all seemed so wrong. To kill oneself over an exam? But the combination of physical distress and the heavy burden of the significance of the exams for his future had proved too crushing.

In the few weeks before exams, Dipheng had been acting up frequently in class, speaking out and laughing often. Then the last day of class before exam week, he had answered questions and looked motivated—a real turnaround in attitude. Students became so anxiety-ridden and high-strung at exam time, I had not recognized how serious this could be. Suffering a pang of uneasy guilt for not paying more attention to the problem, I thought that I should have been more observant, perhaps encouraging Dipheng to speak with the psychiatric nurse at the hospital. A shrewd and perceptive Motswana, the nurse would have certainly understood the tribal culture better than I.

After supper that evening, assistant principal Steve Pabalinga and another teacher drove with me into the village. We arrived at Dipheng's family compound, several small round thatched-roof huts ringed by a waist-high mud wall. Covering much of the large open space in the compound were bedrolls, cots, mattresses, and blankets spread out in the open air. Someone explained to me the custom that when news of a death came, friends and members of the extended family came bringing bedding, and slept there, sometimes for as long as a week, in solidarity with a grieving family's suffering. I realized once again the strong sense of community and the deep extended family ties that existed.

We walked slowly into the hut where Dipheng's body lay. One small window on the lefthand side let in the dim light of the twilight hour. A blanket hung dividing the hut in half. A single candle burned in the room, and a kind of musky smell permeated the small space. Dipheng lay on the floor behind the blanket, six women of the family sitting with him. All appeared to be in shock, overwhelmed, and speechless. Tswana custom had the deceased laid out on the floor of the hut, the lighted candle at his feet. We sat down on the earthen floor with them in the meager light of the candle, greeting the family. We made an attempt to express our sorrow for the family. Steve spoke first and then translated as I spoke. We then sat in a solemn silence broken only by occasional muffled sobbing. After a few minutes, someone from the family asked me to pray. I spoke a simple prayer for mercy and strength to endure. We all sat in silence for about thirty minutes more and then said our goodbyes for the evening. I knew that nothing I could say could take away their pain or fill the empty space so unexpectedly thrust into their lives. Silence seemed the only fitting response to such deep sadness.

Back on the school campus, Mary Beth and I decided to look for some students to listen to their grief and hurt. We found a group in the small chapel on campus, sat with them and prayed and sang together. Afterward, Steve Pabalinga spotted me and took me to a meeting with our local pastor Rev. Peter Mudiwa, the school's principal, and a few others to plan the funeral for the next day. When I returned home, Elaine, always keenly aware of others' feelings, put a gentle hand on my arm and said, "You should go check on Mary Beth and see how she's doing." I walked down the lane and entered the house. When I walked into her living room, I found her with eighteen of her students, Dipheng's classmates, who sat or lay in the room, living portraits of stunned disbelief and despair. Some sat leaning forward, arms on their knees, chins held up by balled fists. Others sank backwards, half lying in their chairs. They seemed dazed and exhausted, like people lost in a trackless desert with no idea which way to go. They had gathered there because they trusted Mary Beth and knew of her obvious compassion. She had been listening to their pain and sense of loss. I sat down, silent for a time, not wanting to cut off their expressions of grief. Some students, convinced that Dipheng had been bewitched, thought that he had a spell cast on him that caused him to take his life. Listening to their expressions of shock and sorrow, I attempted to respond to their grief by observing that sometimes we endure only by depending on God and each other. I wanted to help them to find ways to remember their friend, so tried to give them some tentative suggestions for doing that. I told them that nothing could take away from them the experiences they had shared with Dipheng, that they could honor him by holding those memories in their hearts. Finally, about 11:00 pm, I took the short walk down the lane home.

Community and Identity

In Tswana culture, as in much African experience, relationships hold prime place in a person's life and identity. The tribal community is the primary source of identity. I once asked a class section of mine, "What's more important in your culture, the tribe or the individual? What has priority, the community or the individual person?" Their unanimous answer: "The community." They gave the answer with an underlying tone of surprise, as though I had asked a nonsense question: "The community." I would never get such an answer in a North American classroom. A Tswana proverb says, *A human being is a human being because of others.* Africans have a conviction that the human experience is one that is shared, that life is life-in-community. This sense of life-in-community could be seen clearly in important transitions of life: birth, marriage, a death. Families held a big party when a new baby received its name. Wedding celebrations lasted for days, with feasting, joyous singing, and dancing. All this and the funeral customs revealed the strong feeling of interdependence.

The Basarwa people (commonly called Bushmen), who once freely roamed the central Kalahari Desert south of us, lived in small bands as their ancestors had for thousands of years. Men of the tribe would rarely hunt alone. But if one did, he took along with his own arrows an arrow from another hunter's quiver. Not only did this mean that the hunt would be symbolically shared, but he would be borrowing a portion of his neighbor's skill and courage for the hunt. And he always told the others where he planned to go. Any food he killed or found he shared with the community, an essential act for survival in the harsh desert environment.

The community extends even beyond death. Among the Herero people in the Maun area, a common fear existed that they would not be remembered as part of their original community if they were not buried back home in Namibia with their ancestors. Africans know that they belong to one another.

Kenneth Kaunda, former president of Zambia, once observed that the cultural contribution of the Eastern world is mysticism, the contribution of the West is technology, and that of Africa is human relationships. Extended relationships of family connections hold people together in powerful ways. I could see this in the funeral preparations for Dipheng and in the funeral itself. And I began to understand more fully than ever that, as when learning a new language, to be immersed in another culture doubles the size of one's world.

Preaching and Mourning

Waking the next morning, I knew that I had a daunting task before me. As the school chaplain, it fell to me to give the funeral sermon before a large crowd of almost a thousand people that would include all of our students, Dipheng's extended family, and many people of the church and wider community. The funeral of a suicide is agonizing and difficult any time, but this one made me struggle a long time throughout the morning to find words of meaning and strength for all those who would gather at the family compound that afternoon. I chose the simple message from Romans 14:8, "Whether we live or die, we are the Lord's."

Elaine and several other school staff left with me for the family compound about 2:00 pm. Arriving at the scene, we expected the funeral to begin in thirty minutes. But the family had decided that seemed too early, so we waited. Men and women in Tswana culture had different roles. The men went to sit in the shade of a large tree, while the women sat in and around the hut where Dipheng lay in a newly made coffin of simple wooden planks. Long-standing custom dictated that women gave loud and visible expression to the grief felt by all. To prevent the body from deteriorating too quickly in the extreme heat, quantities of sand, mud, and water surrounded the coffin. At that time of year, the temperature reached over 100 °F.

All the other attendees sat outside, scattered on the ground around the compound, while the men finished their tea and lunch. After a half hour, on a signal undetected by me, everyone stood, lined up, and filed into the hut past the coffin one last time. In spite of the sand and mud surrounding the coffin, the body had begun to deteriorate. Dipheng's lips appeared quite swollen. Viewing him in that condition put a dull ache in my heart. The crowd then gathered outside, while inside the hut several men closed and nailed the coffin.

The funeral unfolded right there in the open area of the family compound. Since Dipheng had not been baptized, by custom the funeral could not take place in the church building itself. The large crowd that had gathered to be with the family filled the compound. Most sat on the ground, some on the low walls surrounding the compound, and a few on benches, all joined together in the burdensome heat and even more burdensome grief.

The worship included hymns, prayers, and a long list of speakers. Terribly uncomfortable sitting in the hot sun, I sat in my suit and tie in the afternoon heat with a white handkerchief spread over my head for a bit of protection. I thought of the tragic unexpectedness of it all, how there would now be an empty space in the family, always there in their midst. Family members spoke about the boy, the school principal and several teachers gave their greetings and condolences, and a student leader expressed his sorrow and sympathy. Fortunately for me, they were (mostly) mercifully brief.

My time to speak came last. I knew that I could not take away their pain or fill the empty space. But I stood up to deliver the homily. In front of me were students with fears of being bewitched themselves, family members suffering agony compounded by a sense of helplessness and resignation at this terrible loss of a beloved son, others mournfully sharing the sorrow in solidarity with the family—all ensnared by the magnitude of the grief. Another teacher translated my words into Setswana as I gave the following sermon:

> It is a very sad and difficult time for us all today. It is a sadness that is deep inside us. It cannot be taken away by simple answers or by speaking a few words, no matter how comforting they are. We do not really understand what happened. We do not understand the distress that Dipheng felt, and we feel hurt, confusion, and pain.
>
> But in the midst of the sadness, there is a message for us that gives us some light and hope. One verse in the New Testament book of Romans is especially meaningful to me. In chapter fourteen, Paul says, 'Whether we live or die, we belong to the Lord. For Christ died and rose to life in order to be Lord of the living and the dead.' No matter what happens to us—if we are in pain, if we are distressed, even if we die, we belong to the Lord. We are not left alone. That is good news for us. In the gospel of John, the night before Jesus knew he would die on the cross, he said to his disciples, 'In my Father's house are many rooms. I go to prepare a place for you.'
>
> The message for us is: we have a home. In my Father's house are many rooms. There is room for Dipheng and there is room for each of us. We have a home, we are not left alone. We belong to a Father who loves us with a love greater than we realize, a love so strong that it goes beyond death. In life and in death, we know that we belong to someone. There is no trouble and no sorrow that can stop that from being true. We have a home. We belong to the Lord, and maybe that is the final comfort for us at a time like this.

For Dipheng, all sorrow is ended, and death itself is past, and he has found the peace that the world cannot give. He is at home with God, whose love and forgiveness is greater than we imagine. Whether we live or die, we belong to the Lord. Remember that. And remember something else. Dipheng's life was a gift to us, and nothing can take away from us the experiences we shared with him. The years of his life were a gift from God to his family, his friends. We can never lose that. We will always have the memory as part of our lives. We will always have that memory to make us see what a great gift life is for all of us. It will make us realize how valuable each day is. It will make us treasure each experience we have with our families and friends, and we will be able to give thanks to God for all these gifts that we receive.

Whether we live or die, we belong to the Lord. That is the one final hope for all our lives. He is a Lord whose love is stronger than death, and he gives us the hope that one day in his presence we will all meet again and there will be no more crying, no more sorrow, no more pain because we will have a home with God. And we will be able to say, Thanks be to God who gives us the victory over death through our Lord Jesus Christ.

As I finished, grief-stricken family members began again the mournful wailing that expressed so much anguish and depth of suffering. The coffin then having been loaded onto a school truck, the crowd followed, walking behind for a distance of more than half a mile through the scrub brush to the cemetery. Rev. Mudiwa conducted the graveside ritual. The people sang several hymns in lovely, mournful four-part harmony. The coffin went into the ground, and several men shoveled the dirt to fill the grave. By ancient custom (and no doubt for health reasons), they also threw into the grave a large bag containing all the sand and mud that had surrounded the coffin. Because of Dipheng's family's close relationship to Chief Letsholatebhe Moremi, chief of the Batawana, the chief's wife stood at the graveside as numerous people came up to the grave with flowers and written messages to be placed on the grave. One man read aloud the message on each bouquet, which Mrs. Moremi then placed on the grave. The graveside ritual went on for about an hour. Later that evening, Elaine said that the biggest impressions on her that day were the sounds: nails being driven into the coffin, the wailing of the grief-stricken family, dirt thumping on the lid of the wooden coffin as they filled the grave. A sense of finality.

Returning to the family compound, we saw three large metal dishes set out in the open area. As we entered the compound, people dropped money for the family into the dishes. Everyone sat down then and listened solemnly as several elders of Dipheng's family expressed their deep appreciation for all that had been done by the secondary school staff and other neighbors and friends. I noticed again all the bedding lying on the ground around the compound, the strong signs of the powerful sense of community alive among extended family and friends who would sleep there overnight for the week ahead.

As we returned home about 7:00 pm that evening, tired, hot, and drained from the long day, we thought how different the mourning vigil and funeral had been from our American experience: no funeral home, no expensive casket, no embalming of the body to mask the reality of death, no hesitation about loud expressions of grief, so many people sharing and connecting with that grief. People in the U.S. resist discussing death, frequently finding it difficult to write living wills or directives about their own dying. Many people die in hospitals rather than at home so that death is frequently out of sight. When several students asked me in the days afterward to tell them about American funeral customs, they expressed the same astonishment other students had expressed to me previously to hear that a separate building and specialists exist to prepare a person's body for a funeral. Initially they refused to believe me. It all sounded crazy to them. The more I thought about it, the simplicity and openness of this African funeral seemed to me somehow a fuller and more honest expression of grief.

The following week, at my regular session with the two local deacons studying theology with me, they told me that many people had greatly appreciated my funeral sermon for Dipheng. "People have been talking about it all week," Mr. Molelo said. Knowing that my words had some meaning for the people, a strong sense of gratitude rushed through me.

14

Wisdom Is Like a Baobab Tree: A Single Person's Hand Cannot Embrace It

—West African proverb

COLLECTIVE WISDOM

Tribal Discernment

DURING THAT FIRST YEAR we lived in Botswana, the rapid spread of foot-and-mouth disease ravaged cattle herds in the country, a fearsome threat to a culture so dependent on cattle. The government instituted numerous policies to combat the disease, including restricting movement of cattle from one place to another, and compelling vehicles to drive through water troughs set up on roadsides between villages. Our first trip to Maun in April involved two stops where we all stepped out of the van and were told to walk through a small trough of shallow water with a white disinfectant to wash any trace of the disease from our shoes. Then we drove the van through the trough to clean off the tires.

One Saturday morning in September, I sat at a meeting with over a thousand people from the area, called together by the chief of the Batawana, the dominant tribe of our northwest region of Ngamiland. As the home of the chief, Maun hosted the meeting at the kgotla, the large, open-air meeting ground in the village where the tribe conducted criminal court proceedings, elections took place, and other public meetings occurred. A few people brought small carved wooden stools for sitting, but most sat on the bare ground as I did. They held a discussion of the government's plans to protect the cattle. Even though I still had minimal knowledge of Setswana, I thought it likely that tone of voice, manner of speaking, and facial expression could all show me the mood of the people.

As the saying about the baobab tree indicated, African tradition generally regarded wisdom as residing with the tribe as a whole. The collective wisdom of the community could not be ignored. The kgotla meeting demonstrated this belief in striking ways. The chief presided. Remarkably, at least to my eyes in the unfamiliar setting, the chief gave everyone who wished to speak the opportunity, no matter how long it took. It made for a powerful example of real grassroots democracy. Sitting in this crowd of over a thousand people, I realized, such a meeting could obviously take a very long time. Africans generally seek to reach a consensus on issues, so they were willing to go long hours to achieve that consensus. This amazed and impressed me. The chief denied no one the chance to speak. Time did not seem to matter. But, as people explained to me later, a Setswana proverb asserts, "The chief is chief because of the people." That is, a chief's authority rested on the regard of the people. If the chief had not allowed the opportunity for all who wished to speak, he would not have been doing his job and would have lost the respect of the people—and thus lost his authority.

Person after person rose to speak, a few with obvious anger and frustration, others more calmly and thoughtfully. With my limited knowledge of Setswana, I couldn't understand very much, but I could easily see how deeply concerned and distressed many people were. Ordinary village life depended upon cattle, and numerous people complained about what they saw as the government's inadequate response to the danger. On and on the discussion went, with no signs of letting up. Late in the morning I had to leave for home and lunch with my family. That evening another teacher told me that the kgotla meeting had lasted until after 5:00 pm. So for more than eight hours the crowd had listened to one another. No one's contribution could be left out. That day I learned great admiration for the power and importance of African community, for the impressive exercise of democracy, and for the stamina of the chief. The communal decision-making clearly illustrated the strength of community ties. The Setswana proverb says, "A person is a person because of others." I could see that in tribal society, it would be impossible to be a human being apart from the collective knowledge, wisdom, and assistance of the entire community.

Classroom Experiment

One afternoon in a Form Three class, I decided to test this notion of collective wisdom by posing an ethical dilemma to the students. In the midst of discussion on a section of the RE curriculum on "Respect for Life," I posed a scenario that created quite lively interchange. Explaining my opposition to my own nation's practice of building and maintaining nuclear weapons, I told them that upon returning home the next year, I would face a moral dilemma of whether or not to pay taxes which help pay for these weapons. I asked them for some advice about what to do upon returning home.

Intrigued by this issue, many students sat forward in their seats, thoughtful expressions on their faces. Eager responses poured forth from the group, giving me a variety of answers and suggestions. "You must pray for change," one student suggested. An especially earnest boy pounded his desk with his fist, saying heatedly, "Start a new political party to work for the change you want." Another offered, "Get all the Christians together to work to influence the government." Still another idea came from a boy in the back of the room. "You could choose to go to live in another country." Most of the class didn't think much of that idea, many shaking their heads and several speaking out to say, "No, no, that's no good!"

I thanked them for their ideas, then asked a further question: "Do you think it would be right for me to refuse to pay my taxes and perhaps go to jail to oppose these weapons?" A bright, thoughtful student named Bernard Bulawayo responded right away by saying, "No, I don't think so. Don't refuse to pay taxes. Many people will not understand why you go to jail. Besides, you won't be able to work for change as easily if you're locked up." A particularly perceptive comment, I thought. "Good point," I said. Then I presented another possibility. "Perhaps I could live very simply, earning only a limited amount of income, and thus not paying any taxes because my income would not reach the level at which a person owed taxes." The class considered this a possibility, though they were dubious about the practicality of it. Most indicated that working for change in some way would be best.

The whole discussion made me see once again the importance in their lives of working for the well-being of their own nation, and the strong predisposition of concern they all felt for what they often termed the "building of our country." The communal culture of the tribes in

Botswana strongly encouraged the participation of all in political decisions. Their nation had become free and independent a little more than ten years before, and they clearly thought themselves capable and ready to contribute to the wider community. I admired their recognition of the power and desirability of freedom as well as their determination to use it.

SIGNIFICANCE OF COMMUNITY

Responsibility

Over time, the meaning and significance of communal life in African culture became clearer and clearer to me. Most African tribes have a communal approach to life. A person is an individual only to the extent that he or she is a member of a tribe, a community, or a family. A person has an obligation to live harmoniously with others in the community, and to make a contribution to work done in the town or village. When a person breaks the harmony of the community, he or she is not simply damaging present-day relationships, but also offending the ancestors and offending God. With harmony broken, everything is out of balance, because everything is connected. Failing one's responsibilities ruptures the harmony of this whole connectedness. It struck me that for my students to accept individualism as an ideal would have been just as difficult as for me to accept the sovereignty of a tribe in my life. In a communal society, youth who have the opportunity to go to school are considered responsible for using their education to uplift others, to teach others what they have learned in school.

    A popular African story, related to me by another teacher, illustrates this sense of communal responsibility. It goes something like this:

> Suppose that there is a village suffering from great famine. There is no food; only one loaf of bread is left for the whole village. The starving people can divide the bread and each get a crumb, or they can cut the loaf in half and give it to two of the strongest young men who, with the additional strength they get from eating the bread, can walk the miles to the nearest place to get food to bring back to the waiting village.
>
> So you, the few of you among the many who cannot go to secondary school, have been sent to this store of knowledge and you must gather all this food and take it back to your families and communities who have made such great sacrifices to send

you to school. The energy is not for yourselves alone but so that
you can help others, and teach others.

This story showed me how students bore a heavy responsibility, not
simply for their own personal development, but for the development and
progress of their family, community, or tribe. A family's future might depend on one young person's ability to read or do sums. I began to see why
students became so anxious at exam time and wrote so copiously and
furiously on exam papers.

Friendship

One unit of the religious education curriculum held up friendship as a
key element of any community. Noting that appreciation of the value of
friendship is prominent both in African tradition and in the Old Testament, the lessons used the stories of David and Jonathan in 1 Samuel, as
well as Ruth and Naomi, to show the similarities with African friendship.
Jonathan defended David; David took care of Jonathan's crippled son.
Ruth showed care and faithfulness to her mother-in-law even though not
required to do so, accompanying her back to her homeland in Israel. In
African tradition, people always viewed friendship as a close relationship
between two people, but also community oriented: trust, loyalty, generosity, and concern for the other's kin were expected.

As we ended the unit on friendship, we talked about the openness
Jesus showed to all sorts of people: tax collectors, Roman soldiers, societal outcasts, and others. Students observed that seeking out relationships
with those who are different from you can require real struggle, but it
began to dawn on them that such friendships can be a source of creativity
and new insights. Nearing the end of the class period, a thoughtful boy
named Bakgadi asked a rather revealing question, "We've talked about
this good way of being a friend to someone, but I want to know this: is
it possible to be a friend like this to someone who doesn't take Religious
Education?" A touching query—it indicated that he saw what a desirable
way of living we had been discussing, but he doubted that anyone who
hadn't learned this could act in the same way. I responded, "Bakgadi, it
seems to me that if you try to live as a friend to someone, accepting the
other completely and showing what a friend can be, then the other person will see what a good way it is to live." I pointed to an African proverb
noted in the student book: "The best way to have a friend is to be one,"

observing that this sentiment is expressed in many cultures. Bakgadi slowly shook his head yes in in a sort of tentative agreement.

One morning in a Form Two class, one of our Herero students described a striking demonstration of friendship, a story of discouragement and the help of a friend to overcome it.

Ngaikunue explained that he had failed his Standard Seven examinations, mostly because of math. Consequently, he had not been accepted into secondary school. Quite discouraged, he felt like quitting school altogether. But his friend Uahangana, a year behind him in Standard Six, encouraged him, saying, "You should repeat Standard Seven. We will be in the same class, and I will help you." So he explained that he did repeat Standard Seven, Uahangana helped him with math all through the year, and they both did well on their Standard Seven exams. "And now," Ngaikunue said with a feeling of real satisfaction, "we are both here at Maun Secondary School." The sense of kinship and loyalty between friends could not have been stronger. That kind of loyalty and support is a great gift, illustrating vividly what true friendship can mean.

Identity

The tribal community gave people a strong sense of identity and belonging. I could see this over and over in the pride and loyalty of students for their tribe and their place of origin. Even students whose parents or grandparents had long before been refugees from Namibia or Zimbabwe expressed this. The Herero people were native to Namibia, on the western border of Botswana. In 1904, the German colonialists in Namibia began slaughtering the Herero. Before the Germans began the killing, the Herero population numbered around seventy thousand. When the Europeans tired of the slaughter, sixteen thousand remained alive—the first, and least remembered, genocide of the twentieth century. Many Herero fled to the only place possible: inland, away from the sea, away from the ports, away from the European invaders who had so cruelly disrupted their land. The refuges walked east, into Bechuanaland (the old name for Botswana), settling there, the women with colorful full-length dresses copied from the German missionaries who worked in Namibia.

Talking with several Herero students one day, I learned the story of this massacre. Many students had ancestors who had fled inland to Botswana to escape. A Herero boy named Mbeuta told me the story of his grandfather, one of the refugees. He had just received word that the grandfather had died at age ninety. Mbeuta explained to me that in 1904 his grandfather, at age twelve, had walked over a hundred miles inland to escape the horror. Both of Mbeuta's parents had been born in Botswana. Since South Africa had taken over Namibia later in the century and imposed apartheid, Namibian rebels under the name of SWAPO (Southwest Africa People's Organization) had been conducting a guerilla war fighting for the country's freedom from South Africa's grip. As a result, neither our Herero students nor their parents had ever set foot in Namibia. So it surprised and moved me when Mbeuta said with a sense of resolve in his voice, "When Namibia is free, we will go home."

Imagine that. "We will go home." He had never lived there or even seen the place in his life. But there lay in him and other Herero a sense of pride of place and heritage that could not be abandoned or forgotten. Difficult for me to grasp, this strong emotion had been embedded in the minds of people who had gone through such a history. This proved to be one of numerous occasions in southern Africa when I could sense the powerful determination of people to control their own destiny, to rid themselves of oppressive forces that stripped people's dignity away. Not sharing this experience, the meaning and significance of tribal identity and the strength of community became much clearer to me that day.

A few days prior to the beginning of the 1982 school year, a Black man originally from Namibia came with his English wife to visit our school. The husband, a student at Oxford, explained to us that his doctoral project involved researching the Herero people. He would be in Maun for a week attempting to interview some Herero people. I eagerly told him that I taught a number of Herero students. "I will be glad to put you in touch with several of them, and I am quite sure that they would be more than happy to speak with you." Delighted with this unexpected good news, he quickly accepted my offer.

I sought out Uahangana and Mbeuta, two of the students I thought would already be there for the beginning of the school year. They were delighted and pleased to be asked, so we arranged for the researcher and his wife to have a conversation with five Herero students the next day. The next afternoon, they all had a long, fruitful conversation. Afterward, the Namibian researcher and his wife came to thank me, both of them expressing their strong admiration for the students. They had obtained a great deal of valuable information, and added, "We were most impressed with the fact that every one of the boys indicated that they expected to return someday to an independent Namibia, their ancestral home." Those boys, like almost all Herero in Botswana, had been born and raised in Botswana and had never seen Namibia, so this showed the researcher a remarkable determination on their part. The Oxford man then added, "They all feel that they are preparing themselves for a future in which they will contribute to their country when it gains its freedom from South Africa." At that moment I felt greatly honored to know and have the opportunity to teach students with such strength of character and purpose. They seemed utterly unwilling to accept any future scenario other than a Namibia free from the grip of the South Africans. Their hope for freedom remained undaunted.

Mbeuta did make it home, just as he had vowed, joining the SWAPO fighters in 1985 and finally celebrating Namibian independence in 1990. Eventually, Mbeuta served his country as the Namibian government's Minister of Information and Communication Technology.

Solving a Family Problem

A day later, still more insight into the strength of the communal nature of African society came to me in an encounter with a former student who sought me out to help him deal with family troubles weighing heavily on him. I had a surprise visit from Molapo Moruti, a recent graduate of our school. In his last year, he had been in the important position of head boy for the school, assigning and supervising the student prefects for each class section. Appearing at our door that evening, Molapo said that he needed to ask my "help for a difficult problem." He needed a lift for him and some members of his family to a small village away from Maun "to settle a family problem." About noon the next day, I drove out to meet Molapo and three men from his family. Two of the men were dressed in coats and ties. They gave me directions and we started out on the road toward Francistown. After about twelve kilometers, one of the men pointed off to the right into the bush. I couldn't see any sign of a road, but I turned where he pointed, trusting he must know the way. Worried that the car had been overheating, I drove ahead, discovering to my great relief that our destination lay only a couple of hundred yards off the main road. We came suddenly upon a family compound off by itself. Giving an inward sigh of relief, I parked outside the low wall of the compound. A young boy ushered the five of us in.

People in Botswana always treated visitors politely and respectfully. Whenever visitors arrived, family members pulled out some kind of seating, usually from the nearest hut, and the hosts tried to ensure that their visitors sat in a shady spot. At first, we sat down on the ground in some inadequate shade cast by a rather skimpy tree. But very quickly, a small boy about eight years old brought out a large metal bucket for me to sit on. After setting it down and realizing that the bucket had been sitting in the blazing sun, he ran back into a hut, grabbed a piece of burlap, and spread it carefully over the bucket, sparing me from sitting directly on the hot metal. We sat quietly for a while, waiting for the representatives of the family to join us. Soon three Herero men and three women from the household gathered around sitting on the ground. The oldest man from Molapo's family began to speak in Setswana. After he finished, several members of the Herero family made responses. There appeared to be no acrimony, no harsh words. After the Herero responses, everything seemed to be settled.

Then the eldest man from Molapo's family looked at me and explained in English what had just happened. "Molapo's brother is the father of a child of a daughter of the Herero family. We came here to settle the matter. We admit that the young man is the father, and we promise that our family will give some help to the young woman and her baby. And so now the matter is settled. We are all agreed." I took the most important point in the discussion to be that Molapo's family admitted their son's responsibility for making the girl pregnant. Without any open acrimony, the whole event lasted less than twenty minutes. I served as an honored witness to the proceedings. Molapo and his male relatives said their farewells and then departed with me, Molapo thanking me effusively for providing transportation.

The willingness to sit down and talk through a disagreement or problem again made a deep impression on me. I knew from the history of Botswana that its people had an ingrained preference for talk rather than anger and violence. One famous incident in the mid-twentieth century saw Seretse Khama, the future chief and first president of the nation, argue with his uncle Tsekedi over Seretse's role in the tribe. When the two could not come to an agreement, Tsekedi took his immediate family and moved some distance away rather than continue to disagree openly with Seretse. He returned quite a few months later and the two finally reconciled. This had been the history of the Batswana for centuries. They kept moving further inland from the coasts of southern Africa because they preferred to settle differences without open conflict. Relationships held prime place in society. To deny or abandon relationships with others would cause the breakdown of society.

15

Christmas Travel Adventures

CELEBRATIONS AND TROUBLES

Achievement and Goodbye

OUR FIRST SCHOOL YEAR came to an end in November 1980, marked by several happy celebrations. The Form Five classes completed their Cambridge exams, rejoicing at the end of the ordeal of the difficult exam week. We also attended the official opening of the Nthoo Typing School, founded by Susan Shopland. For her Peace Corps project, she had been working to establish the school to provide more work opportunities for people of the area. All of us who were still on campus attended the November 29 opening ceremonies. Lady Ruth Khama, widow of the late president, made the long trip north to serve as the main speaker and declare the school open. She made a point of saying how important such projects were for the growth of the nation, complimenting all involved in the new school. Batswana had a flair for special events; along with Lady Khama, this one featured other local speakers, singing groups, and traditional dances by groups of children. Barefooted dancers pounded the hot sand with their feet, spraying sand into the air around them. The whole affair went on for three hours. As part of the large crowd gathered, we felt quite pleased for Susan and for the community, celebrating the results of her two years of effort.

Sadly, for the three of us in our household, the Shoplands were preparing to leave Botswana, having come to the end of their two-year Peace Corps term. We had known them just eight months, but had become close to them, appreciating their spirit and talent. Both of them had shared insights with us on life in Botswana in comparison with the United States, helping us to see more clearly the contrast between individualism and community in the two societies. Susan's friendship with Sherry had been one big factor in helping Sherry become more at ease in Maun. The honesty the Shoplands displayed in our weekly Bible study, raising hard questions that made us reconsider how much we were willing to give up for the sake of others, deepened our understanding of faith and the meaning of true friendship. They helped us to discover the truth of the Setswana proverb, "A person is a person because of others."

In an effort to give them a gala send-off, all the expatriate faculty—the only people left on campus at that point—organized an elaborate progressive dinner. We had hors d'oeuvres at the principal's house; salad with Carol and Marion; meat, rice, and rolls at the home of June and Mary Beth; cake and fruit salad at our house; and wound up with coffee and tea with our Dutch neighbors, the Langendijks. We all talked and laughed so much that the party went on until after 11:00 that night. Mark and Susan said their farewells the next day.

Danger

Just a few days later came a distinctly unwelcome surprise—an outbreak of typhoid in the area. In our isolated part of the country, our local hospital did not possess enough vaccine to inoculate everyone. They hurriedly sent someone to fly to Gaborone to obtain extra medicine. The hospital reported four cases of typhoid in the span of three days, one case being another of the Peace Corps volunteers in Maun. Due to the great concern over fear of an epidemic, we had to boil all of our water just to be safe, because they had no way to identify the source. Sadly, one village woman died, but it happened because she waited too long before going to the hospital. Alarmed at the thought of how easily typhoid spread, we tried to be as careful as possible. The possibility also arose that the local authorities might not allow people to leave the area. Boiling water to use for cooking, drinking, and brushing teeth turned out to be only a small nuisance, but the scare certainly did make us much more aware of how we took clean water and sanitation for granted back in the United States.

TRAVEL AND LEISURE

A Happy Visit with the Jones Family

After a week and no further signs of typhoid, Elaine, Sherry, and I made the trip to Gaborone for Christmas. Because I had gotten our car stuck in the mud on a trip to an RE conference in Francistown earlier in November—and had to be pulled out by a government truck—we decided not to go by car. The unpredictable rainy season stretched from November to February, so we began our journey with a ten-hour bus ride to Francistown.

Arriving there weary after a rough ride over poor roads made worse by the rains, we stayed overnight with our friends Tony and Betsy Jones, taking the happy opportunity to visit with them and their two little girls in the morning. Tony told us of "a bit of a quandary," as he put it, they had faced the day before. Having written a letter to the South African government objecting to the detention without trial of a prominent activist, they were all set to mail it. Then it occurred to them that when the letter went into the police files in Pretoria, the two of them would be effectively barred from ever obtaining a visa to enter and travel in South Africa. They pondered this—briefly—and then mailed the letter.

Gaborone Surprises and Hospitality

That evening we took the train south overnight to Gaborone, having arranged to stay a couple of nights with the Purveses before heading to the Reimer household, the Mennonite family we had met at the language course back in August. Jack and Chris Purves had moved to the capital to work on a two-year project for the Ministry of Education. Much to our surprise, we found Mark and Susan there also, on their way home via the long route. They planned a trip through Zimbabwe, then on to east Africa, hoping to climb Mount Kilamanjaro, spend a month in Egypt, and finally go to London before returning home to the United States. It became a delight to be together with them one last time. One evening the Purveses took us all out to the Gaborone dam, site of the city's water supply, to watch the sunset. Sitting on top of the dam, we could see all around us beautiful colors in the clouds and on the water. The sky, several shades of blue and turquoise, acted as backdrop to clouds reflecting unusual colors somewhere between yellow and copper. We sat there with a deep sense of satisfaction at the lovely evening and the joy of friendship. After dinner the next evening, the Shoplands headed off for their trip on the night train.

The Reimer family had generously offered us the use of their house in the capital for a week. The parents and all three children greeted us warmly, while Sherry brightened up seeing the friend she had made at the language class again, even if briefly. Their whole family planned to attend a conference in Lesotho for that time, so we appreciated their graciousness in providing us a free place to stay. Since Lesotho is a country entirely surrounded by South Africa, the trip had to go through a portion of South Africa, for which they needed a travel visa. But the South Africans, having expelled all Mennonite missionaries sometime before for speaking out against apartheid, had refused to grant the visa. But just before we arrived in Gaborone, the apartheid government relented, granting the family a twelve-hour travel visa. The fact that the drive from Gaborone to Lesotho took eight hours made us see South Africa's reluctance to let them in at all. If they were to break down while in South Africa and overstay the visa, the police likely could have arrested them and forced them back to the Botswana border.

With warm welcoming hugs, all the Reimers ushered us into their house on Sunday evening. They made tea, showed us where to find things in the house, and pointed out to us that they had recently received a new videotape from home: the recently released *Muppet Movie*. Talking with them for a short while before they finished preparing for their trip, we discovered that they lived in Lancaster County, Pennsylvania, familiar ground to us. The Reimers departed Monday morning for Lesotho, leaving us to enjoy a relaxing week. We celebrated Elaine's birthday with a dinner out and did a little Christmas shopping at the Gaborone mall. As a bonus, we consumed as much ice cream as possible—a favorite treat impossible to find in unrefrigerated Maun.

TRAVEL TROUBLES AND BLESSINGS

Mix-ups and Discomfort

A few days before Christmas we headed back to Maun. Gathering up our belongings, we made our way to the train station, only to find dense crowds on the platform almost crushing the conductor who assigned the travel compartments. After managing, with great difficulty, to get the conductor's attention and obtain our seating assignment, we found ourselves pushed along by the crowd of Christmas travelers. People crowded onto the train all around us. We three found our assigned compartment and went in to sit down, relieved to be out of the crowd. But after only a few minutes, a Black family of three entered the compartment, saying that we were in the wrong one, as they had been assigned to the same one. They questioned why we were there. I checked the compartment number again, and found it correct. Railroad officials had obviously double-booked our compartment. Understandably, the other three refused to leave. I felt really uncomfortable and at a loss as to what to do.

After a short debate about it, we all decided to wait for the conductor to come by collecting the tickets and ask him to fix the mix-up. We waited and waited, but he never came. So I went looking for him, only to find him in the next car, angry and frustrated. He had given up when dozens of people had pushed their way onto the train without assigned seating. When I asked him, he refused to do anything about the confusion, even refusing to give us bedding for the night. Not that we could have used it, because with six in the compartment it would have been impossible to pull down the sleeping berths from the side wall. We had nowhere else to go because the overcrowded train had been overwhelmed. As a result, the six of us sat, physically uncomfortable and quite ill at ease, crowded in a three-person compartment for the eleven-hour all night journey. No one got much sleep, and the other three people, understandably resentful, hardly spoke a word to us.

Hospitality and Family Stories

Arriving in Francistown early the next morning, we made our way to the home of our friends Tony and Betsy, who welcomed us, fed us some breakfast, and commiserated with us at the news of the night's discomfort. When we related the tale of the overcrowded train, a combination of surprise and sympathy came to Tony's face. He blurted out, "And you couldn't get any help from the conductor?" Betsy, quickly realizing how we were feeling, said, "When you've had what you want to eat, go right in and use our beds and just sleep for however long you wish." We more than happily took her up on her offer.

Later that day, refreshed and eager to visit with our hosts, we sat and talked throughout a leisurely afternoon and evening. Our hosts told us the tale of meeting one another while teaching at a school in Uganda some years before. Having grown up in a wealthy family in Boston, Betsy reacted against the affluence and accompanying materialism there by entering the Peace Corps for service in Africa. As she said this, I remembered feeling a similar sense of being out of place in American culture, part of my reason for the urge to get away from the United States to get a different perspective on life after the divorce. While teaching in Uganda, Betsy met Tony, a science teacher from England, discovering that he shared her great discomfort with the consumerist, materialist lifestyles in their home countries. When they married, they made the decision to remain working in Africa and raise their two little girls in the simpler life they found there. Speaking with a firm sense of conviction, she told us, "Africa gets in your blood, and you don't want to leave." As an ironic reminder of what the couple wished to avoid, Betsy had recently received a birthday gift from her parents. Having requested a simple wrist watch, Betsy opened the gift package to discover a diamond-studded watch.

The Final Leg Home

Saturday morning they drove us to the public bus which would take us to Maun. We had to get there more than two hours before the 1:00 pm scheduled departure in order to get seats. After sitting for about a half hour, we were surprised by Carol Schaad climbing onto the bus and waving heartily. Just arrived from Bulawayo, Zimbabwe, she had encountered the Shoplands there and seen them off on their train ride to Harare, Zimbabwe's capital. Botswana being a country with a small population, running into people we knew happened frequently, creating a sense of familiarity and interconnectedness. Leaving Francistown at 1:00 pm, we arrived home at 11:00 at night, discovering to our delight the large pile of Christmas cards and other mail awaiting us. We were pleased to be home.

CHRISTMAS DELIGHTS

And the Word Was Made Flesh and Dwelt Among Us

After arriving home from our stressful travel experience, we had a relaxing few days before Christmas. A joyful holiday began Christmas morning with the unexpected opportunity to attend a service of the Eucharist conducted in English by an Anglican priest in the UCCSA church in the village. As often occurred in Africa, the worship had been arranged on very short notice, a complete surprise to us. We had no idea of the identity of the priest or where he came from, but as soon as we heard of it, we drove into town and joined a few others at the church building. A simple time of worship, it seemed especially beautiful to us, with the words of thanksgiving and grace so meaningful, putting us in solidarity with the worldwide community of the church. Living in southern Africa now made us much more conscious of this than ever before.

Unexpected Beauty

A few of us who remained on the school campus decided to share the evening meal together. We gathered at our house for a Christmas supper to which everyone contributed, making an altogether joyous day. The next morning a group that included Larry, Carol, Mary Beth, and the three of us traveled to Lake Ngami, a huge shallow lake west of Maun. We arrived there to find hundreds and hundreds of storks, pelicans, ducks, and flamingoes resting on the lake. What we viewed made up only a fraction of the bird life in southern Africa, a variety so striking that I thought that the riot of bright colors must be nature's way of offsetting the dull scrub brush and sandy soil of the Kalahari: brilliant blue-winged lilac-breasted rollers, red and blue carmine bee-eaters, black-headed crimson shrike, the flamingoes we saw on the lake. As the early morning sun lay as a backdrop on the horizon, an incredible drama unfolded: all of the flamingoes rose from the lake, hundreds of them flying up against the sunrise. A magnificent sight, they had white bodies, with a streak of bright pink and a black border on their wings. At the time, I thought it must be the most overwhelmingly beautiful spectacle I had ever seen. We all stood awestruck at an extraordinary beauty we had never seen before, a most fitting climax to our Christmas holiday.

16

Transitions, Troubles, and Death in a New Year

A NEW YEAR BEGINS

Successes and Anguish

THE WEEK BEFORE THE new school year began for 1981, we received the results of the 1980 national Junior Certificate examinations. We were all elated that 90 percent of our students had passed—not the best record in the nation, but close. St. Joseph's Secondary School at Kgale in the south had scored a 93-percent pass rate. Students who scored in the highest percentiles individually received a first-class pass, a very difficult feat to achieve. The 1979 class in Maun had achieved just one first-class pass. But in the 1980 class, four of our students had achieved first-class passes, two of them from the Form Three section I had taught for religious education. By government rule, anyone who earned a first- or second-class pass could be admitted to Form Four, the upper level of secondary school. Our school had only sixty spots for Form Four, which meant that a few of the students with second-class passes had to be assigned to another school.

Independent in 1966, Botswana determined from the start that education would be a major priority for the nation. In a stroke of good fortune, diamonds had been discovered in the northern Kalahari in 1968, giving the government a steady source of revenue. By the 1980s, in what

I admired as an impressive act of wisdom and foresight, the government dedicated one-third of the entire national budget to education, building schools, training teachers, and hiring teachers from other countries in Africa and around the world. Even with this effort, not nearly enough schools existed to accommodate all those who completed the seven years of primary school; only half of those who successfully completed Standard Seven could be admitted to secondary school. With so few people having a chance to complete secondary school, let alone attend it in the first place, I saw vividly how frustration and discouragement could strike families.

The school year began the third week in January. For several weeks prior to that, parents besieged the office of the school principal, insisting that he admit their children to the first year of secondary school. Parents lined up, filling the corridor outside his office. Some came to his house at night, each one pleading for their child to be given the chance for an education. He had the painful experience of telling them that the government had already told him whom he must admit on the basis of test scores. No more room could be made. A week before classes began, one of the school's cooks walked into the principal's office and announced that she wouldn't move until he gave the okay for her daughter to be admitted. But he had to turn down her demand.

Imagine having to plead for your child to be allowed to attend school, and then be told that it's impossible because there is no room in any of the schools in the entire nation—and that therefore your child has no chance for anything more than a seventh grade education! Even if Botswana had built many more schools, they would have been woefully short of teachers to staff them. When we arrived in Maun, only twelve of the twenty-eight teachers were Botswana natives. The others were all expatriates, many of them on two-year contracts. It meant a constant turnover of staff from year to year, making continuity difficult.

A Faculty Dispute Resolved

The school year began on a Tuesday. Early Monday morning at the first staff meeting for the year, a real uproar arose regarding the class schedule for the term. Whoever had prepared it had made a real hash of it, resulting in multiple conflicts, including numerous examples of two teachers assigned to teach in the same classroom at the same time. In addition, many class sections lacked the proper number of weekly class periods for some subjects. Anger and disgust filled the room, many teachers loudly complaining to the principal that they faced an impossible situation. Everyone in the meeting realized that we had less than twenty-four hours to redo the entire schedule for all sixteen class sections—a seemingly impossible task.

I could easily see what a real mess we faced, a major headache for all of us. I could not see how the tangled web of conflicts could be fixed. But we had no choice. Someone had to take on the task of straightening it all out. To the enormous relief of all in the room, the Zimbabwean math teacher Kelly Nare volunteered. A highly capable and talented teacher well-regarded by others, Kelly had many gifts, among them successfully coaching both the school's soccer team and the chess club. In May 1980, only a month after we had arrived in Botswana, he had celebrated a reunion with his brother whom he had neither seen nor heard from in seven years. The brother had been one of the freedom fighters in the bush country all that time, and when the civil war ended and Zimbabwe began majority rule, the family finally heard from him.

Confident that Kelly knew his business, but seeing that he obviously needed some assistance, I offered to help. We had less than twenty-four hours to fill in the entire class schedule for sixteen classrooms, eight periods a day for each individual weekday. Picture the dilemma this way: someone had thrown sixteen decks of playing cards, fifty-two cards to a deck, each deck with different markings, high in the air, then had to attempt to put all the cards together, each in the right deck and in the right order. Except that the complications were even greater—not only did we have to make sure that two teachers did not occupy a classroom at the same time, we also had to plan so that each class section had the proper number of class periods for each of the eight subjects in the curriculum. Furthermore, each subject did not have the same number of class periods per week. English, for example, had seven periods per week, while religious education had two. Hercules and Sisyphus had easier tasks than this one.

After the shouting and angry debate died down, the turbulent meeting ended about 11:00 am. Kelly and I went to one of the science classrooms. We spread out large pieces of paper on several of the big work tables, and began to work on a completely new schedule. Aside from forty-five minutes for lunch, we worked straight through until 1:15 am Tuesday morning. Jack Langendijk, our Dutch neighbor, stayed with us much of the time, laboriously making copies of individual class section schedules. If it had been only a few years later, we could have done the task in a fraction of the time with a computer. Unfortunately, we were forced to plug classes into the time slots in pencil on the big sheets, ensuring that each subject had the proper number of class sessions for the week. We wore down an enormous quantity of erasers, as we had to write everything in pencil and make countless corrections. It proved to be a byzantine, messy, and extremely frustrating business. We would finish, thinking we had everything straightened out, only to discover that one Form Two class had too few geography periods in the week. So then we would begin shifting classes around to fix the problem—and uncovering more conflicts. It exasperated us at times, but we kept on pushing. Kelly displayed a tireless determination to get the whole schedule correct and ready for the next day. His patience and persistence seemed unending.

During our long slog through this academic swamp, we were pleasantly interrupted by several people bringing us refreshments or meals at various times. Late in the afternoon, Mary Beth brought us some cake and cold drinks, then a bit later Marion came in with some fresh mangoes and watermelon. Elaine brought us sandwiches and drinks for supper, and later in the evening Goke Langendijk served us tea. All of it sustained us through the burden of the day and night. But we finally figured it all out. After checking and rechecking every detail, we grabbed a few hours of sleep, and woke early in the morning to begin the school year. I have always been enormously thankful that I never had to do anything quite like it again.

Good News

In a striking bit of good news for us Americans on campus, on the day after the school year began, we heard the BBC radio news announcement of the forty-four American hostages being released from captivity by the Iranian government in Teheran. They had been held for over a year, and a failed rescue mission attempted by Jimmy Carter had contributed to his loss of the presidency to Ronald Reagan. The good news of their release cheered us, but the election of Ronald Reagan alarmed us. We had good reason for this because Reagan soon affirmed his strong support for the unjust apartheid regime oppressing our neighbors in South Africa. He reasoned that the South African government strongly opposed communism. But the apartheid government used that opposition as an excuse to hold 80 percent of the population under strict control, dictating where people could and could not live and denying basic human rights. Reagan may have opposed communism, but, we thought bitterly, he seemed to have no concern for freedom and justice in South Africa.

Entering the beginning of a new school year, after that day and night of the timetable calamity, Elaine, Sherry, and I faced a variety of new learning experiences. One day on a break in class during the first week, I went to her office to see Elaine, who sat with a bemused look on her face. Several parents had come in to pay their child's school fees for the year, one of them bringing not cash, but a live cow for the payment. Not being quite sure what to do, an impish smile came to her face as she said to me, "How do I deposit a cow in the bank?"

That year, Sherry began Standard Seven classes at the English Medium School in the village (English being the medium of instruction), relieved, it seemed, to have a bit more structure in her days. Elaine and I also felt relieved, because assuming Sherry did well on her Standard Seven exams at the end of the year, she could be admitted to Form One at Maun Secondary School for the 1982 school year.

Bible Knowledge

New matters faced me also. I had been assigned to teach the Cambridge Bible Knowledge class to Form Five. That year the topics included the Gospel of Mark, the book of Acts, and the Sermon on the Mount from Matthew. Students would take the examination from Cambridge University in England in November. Numerous British Commonwealth nations made use of Cambridge examinations in most of the subjects for seniors in the secondary schools, the exams being similar to what the British termed "O" levels. To my surprise, the British university even marked all the exams. We would mail them off to Britain in carefully wrapped, tamper-proof packages and receive the results in January. But I faced a serious problem—I had no specific curriculum material available, and therefore had to rely on copies of old Cambridge exams to get an idea of how and what to teach. It did not take long for me to realize that I needed to put a lot of work into lesson planning, much more than necessary for the more structured RE curriculum for the younger students.

That year I had fifty-three students in two sections, all good students whom I enjoyed teaching. More mature and easily engaged than the younger groups, they provided not only more satisfaction in the classroom but also at times a dose of good humor. One day one of the sections came from an English class where they had read the book and then viewed the movie *To Kill a Mockingbird*. They came into class animated, talking about the film. Nchunga Nchunga asked me, "Can we get a film about the book of Acts?" I said, "I'm sorry to say I don't think one exists." Then, out of honest curiosity, I asked them if they had any trouble understanding some of the accents of the American South they heard in the film. One boy spoke up rather sarcastically, as though I had insulted them, saying, "No, we're Form Fives!" I replied, "Oh yes, certainly. I realize that. It's just that I am not from that part of the United States, so I remember having a little trouble understanding some of those accents when I first saw the film." With a kind of sly, good-natured smile on his face, Nchunga responded with a little shrug and the remark, "You're not a Form Five."

Sports Season Begins

For ten days at the end of January and beginning of February, the initial weeks of the first term of the school year, we had day after day of rainstorms, some short and hard, some long and soaking. In class, we could hear the rain pounding on the metal roof of the classroom building. It amazed me how much the grass grew, springing up quickly and growing thick and high. It seemed so remarkable considering that in our first five months in Botswana, we had seen not a single drop of rain. The rain gave life to the Kalahari and to the water channels of the Okavango Delta. Thick grass provided food for the cattle, in addition to furnishing nourishment for the sorghum and corn crops which served as staples for the people. The rainy season usually stretched from December to February, but we never knew exactly when the final rainstorm would be. When the rain stopped, the land almost immediately dried up in the hot sun, the ground becoming hard, sandy, and dry. This brought the beginning of sports season.

Botswana secondary schools played football (soccer), softball, tennis, and netball. Softball had been introduced by US Peace Corps folks just a few years before we arrived. At the time we lived in Botswana, boys' and girls' teams played softball, volleyball, and tennis. Only boys played football, the most popular sport in the world (except in the United

States!). Netball, a game somewhat similar to basketball (but limited to clever passing to move the ball—no dribbling because of the rough, sandy ground), engaged only girls.

Before the school teams had played any matches, some of the boys, not including any of the football team members, challenged the teachers to a football game. We played on a Friday afternoon when students had no school work to do for the next day. The African teachers organized our team, designating who would play which positions. They also followed the common African custom of giving every team member a nickname. Supposedly, the nicknames usually indicated a particular trait or skill of the player. Jokingly, and for some unfathomable reason, Zakes Mahlanza, one of the geography teachers, gave me the name "Mastermind." He designated me goalkeeper, kind of a joke in itself as I had never played an organized game of soccer in my life. I had a minimum knowledge of goalkeeping, knowing at the least to come out from the goal to cut off the angles for the opposing player advancing with the ball. On only a couple of plays did I touch the ball and kick it away from my end. All the students had played the game since they were small boys, so they were not only better, but faster than the older teachers. Playing on a field of stones, dirt, and sand, not grass, when the game started, I felt destined for failure. Because of the condition of the playing field, diving for a ball would have been a disaster, so I couldn't do it. That, plus the reality of the teachers' less than sterling defensive capabilities meant a long day. By the end of the first half I had an enormous blister on the ball of my left foot, so I could not run any more. Someone else took my place.

The teachers lost the game, five to one. But everyone enjoyed the afternoon, especially all the students cheering on their friends. The teachers gathered together afterward at the middle of the field to commiserate with one another, although with quite a bit of good-natured joking and complimenting one another. When the following year, the teachers lost four to one (with me again as goalie), I teased the students, "if I were here four more years, we could beat you!"

Refrigerated Delights

In a surprising and most welcome development, near the end of February a new food store opened in Maun. For the first time in anyone's memory, the owners had arranged for a refrigerated truck to come from down south. To our delight, it brought a variety of fruits and vegetables, cheese, and best of all, ice cream. On our first visit to the store, Elaine found two real treasures: heavy cream and Philadelphia cream cheese. Arriving home with the goodies, Elaine and Sherry immediately used the cream cheese to produce a delicious cheesecake. Good news about food always traveled fast, so the cheesecake disappeared by early that evening because seven people came to our house to sample it. The next day, Elaine and Sherry attempted to make whipped cream with the heavy cream. This did not turn out to be a success. In order to make whipped cream, both the bowl and the beaters needed to be chilled, something impossible in the heat. So the attempt failed. They wound up, not with whipped cream, but with butter.

A Special Celebration

A happy event came in early March as Elaine and I celebrated our first wedding anniversary. We both experienced a sense of wonder that we had found so much happiness together, talking openly and sharing our lives honestly and joyfully. We had found that praying together each morning and evening strengthened our life together. Elaine found a short piece of writing as a gift for me, a beautiful statement about having two loaves of bread and selling one to buy hyacinths, because flowers are so important. She said to me, "I'm glad you know the value of hyacinths."

Earlier I asked Mary Beth to teach me how to make a paper crane in the Japanese origami style of paper folding. I made two of them out of green Christmas wrapping paper and gave them to Elaine. In the simpler world where we were living, it occurred to me that we had been conditioned in our home culture to think that something expensive is a more appropriate gift for a loved one, but that seemed really foolish. We had been in Africa for about a year, coming to love the life there, the pace of it, the climate, the work, and the people—and we knew we had made the right choice.

DEATH OF CHIEF LETSHOLOTHEBE MOREMI

Shocking News

Living in the midst of the Tswana culture often brought surprises, frequently due to the striking differences between the nature of community life there and back home. Almost every week we learned new and often fascinating lessons about tribal life which caused us to ponder what it meant to live in a more communally focused culture. As we learned the customs, our respect for the close relations of the community increased more and more.

In the middle of March, a shock hit the whole village and surrounding area. Letsholathebe Moremi, Kgosi (Chief) of the Batawana, died suddenly and entirely unexpectedly. Just forty-one years old, he suffered a stroke while in the capital Gaborone on business. One of the eight major Setswana-speaking tribes in the nation, the Batawana predominated in our area. The chief played an outsized role in the life of the community, bearing an enormous responsibility for many aspects of tribal life. The tribe expected the chief to be the settler of many minor and major disputes, the judge for some criminal trials, a personal adviser for individuals, and a politician in charge of various appointments. For example, he chaired the land board, the group which assigned land grants to businesses and individuals. The tribe owned the land collectively, and therefore people had to get the permission of the tribe's land board to build a new business. On top of all that, the chief also served in the House of Chiefs, an important branch of the nation's government. He seemingly had vast powers, but they remained in place only if he commanded the respect of the people. As a Setswana proverb expressed it, "The chief is chief because of the people." In my eyes, it seemed an overwhelming and almost impossible job. It obviously had taken its grim toll on Chief Letsholathebe.

Gathering of the Community

The day we learned the news, everyone from the school went into the village for prayers beginning at 6:00 pm at the kgotla. People gathered from all across the region. A discussion broke out almost immediately after the prayer service began, raised by several people who were intent upon insisting that only Batawana should be allowed to go to bring back the chief's body from Gaborone. "It should not be anyone else," someone declared firmly. With widespread agreement expressed, several persons were appointed for the task and left the next morning.

The 6:00 pm prayers continued each evening, with large crowds praying, at times aloud and simultaneously. On the third night, I watched the grave being dug and brick vault being built in the hole. The gravesite, to my surprise, sat at one end of the kgotla area in the kraal (the fenced in corral for cattle). The gravediggers had torn up part of the kraal fence to dig the grave. I realized that I shouldn't have been surprised, as the burial site signified the central importance of cattle in the life of the tribe. A student explained to me that chiefs were always buried in the kraal in unmarked graves. A man sitting near us remarked that the chief had talked about forming a burial society soon before he died, and the people took that as a sign that he hadn't long to live.

Funeral Agony

The funeral took place on March 7, the kgotla overflowing with mourners. Several ministers from Maun led the service, occasionally calling on elders in the crowd to stand up and pray on behalf of the whole gathering. Many people knelt on the ground praying. According to custom, women loudly expressed their grief with wailing and crying. Large numbers of women became hysterical and fainted, falling to the ground with those nearest trying to console them. Stretchers kept shuttling back and forth between the crowd and the edge of the kgotla area, carrying fainting women to a more open space where others could attend them. The people normally expressed grief in this way, unlike back home in the United States where it's not unusual to find people who disapprove of such loud and open mourning. I could easily see how this outpouring of grief could be healthier than trying to hold it inside. Watching one after another falling to the ground, I became intensely aware of the powerful emotions and the strong connections among the people. We sat there for at least two hours, swept up in the grief of the gathered community, feeling the strength of the tribal connection.

Every death and every funeral in Botswana left me more aware of the glaring differences between African and North American customs. When the extended family built the coffin, gathered together to sleep at the family compound, dug the grave, and buried the body, the clear sense of strength of the community in Africa demonstrated itself. The loud, unrestrained wailing seemed to me to be a setting free of emotion, giving full expression to grief and pain. People neither covered up their grief nor obscured the reality of death.

Election of the Regent

About a month later, the tribe held an election to choose a regent, the one who would temporarily act as chief until the chief's son came of age. Two candidates stood for election: the chief's widow, and the chief's younger brother. In spite of the fact that the younger brother had a less than stellar reputation, he won the election overwhelmingly. That surprised me, but someone explained to me the simple reason: the chief's widow came from the Kalanga tribe. Almost no member of the Batawana wished to have a regent from another tribe. When they counted the vote, the numbers were approximately two thousand for the brother and eighteen for the widow—an especially striking indication of the tight-knit nature of tribal life.

When the tribe installed the new regent, the vice president of Botswana attended, giving a speech with advice for the regent. "You will be liked by some, and disliked by others. You will have to learn to deal with that." As advice to the whole tribe, the VP said, in effect, "You wanted this fellow as chief, so now if he fouls up, don't come crying to the government!" Other speeches followed, and then the whole crowd raised their fists in the air, shouting, "Pula, Batawana!"

Weeks later I heard a surprising and curious report from one of my theology students. After the installation ceremony, the new regent refused to go to the celebratory luncheon with the vice president. Apparently, he feared that his food might be poisoned, and his advisers counseled him not to go. Undercurrents of jealousy and bitterness could easily take hold of people, even though outwardly they remained hidden. Suddenly understanding that I had been viewing the society with the proverbial rose-colored glasses, I realized that I had wrongly believed it to be a more peaceful and idyllic community.

17

If You Never Raise Your Eyes, You Think That You Are the Highest Point

—African Proverb

WITNESS TO THE FAITH

Students Speak Out

Time and again, students at our school impressed me with demonstrations of integrity and public witness to their faith, including their openness to those who came from different backgrounds. In early February 1981, the vice president of Botswana visited Maun, speaking at the kgotla to address a controversy regarding the Herero people, the minority tribe originally from Namibia. He explained that Herero people were being encouraged by the South Africans (who had illegally occupied Namibia for years) to go home to Namibia. The liberation movement for Namibia, the Southwest Africa People's Organization, had been waging guerilla warfare against the occupation for a long time, so it seemed odd to me that South Africa would want more people likely supporting SWAPO residing in Namibia. The vice president addressed Herero directly, saying, "You should know that the war in Namibia is going to get worse, and thus more people will die. Also, if anyone does wish to leave Botswana, they will not be allowed to take any cattle with them." I imagined this must have caused great distress among Herero people, because many Herero were rich in cattle and would hardly be willing to dispose of them, even by selling them.

Two hours of debate and discussion ensued, with questions, complaints, and other comments flying back and forth. At one point, Kandjeusa Kahiya, a 1980 graduate of our school, stood to speak. The chief recognized him, and Kandjeusa declared quite bluntly, "I wish to observe that if people here treated the Herero better, they wouldn't want to leave. The people here in Ngamiland need to accept them more as part of the community." Then one of our top senior students from the school, Richard Kashweka, rose to follow up on Kandjeusa's remark. "I have seen a Motswana boy acting scared of a Herero woman," he noted, and then asked a question. "Why would he be scared unless someone had told him that these people were bad?"

Their fearlessness in confronting the whole community with accusations of prejudice impressed me. I couldn't help but admire them for their boldness in speaking out so strongly.

Later that day another teacher explained to me some of the underlying—and complicating—aspects of the earlier community discussion. Apparently some Batswana viewed the Herero as cattle thieves. Herero did not brand their cattle, and when Herero stole cattle, they would not take unbranded ones because they belonged to other Herero. Or at least that's what Batswana claimed. I remembered seeing Herero people as part of the congregation at the UCCSA church in Maun, which appeared to be a sign of the power of reconciliation of Christian faith.

SCRIPTURE UNION

A Lesson in Patience

Patience may be a virtue, as the old saying has it, but it didn't take long for me to learn that patience has a different quality to it in Africa. In the United States, if we are kept waiting ten or fifteen minutes beyond the designated time for an event or a meeting, we begin to get annoyed. But in Botswana, I saw people calmly and willingly wait for hours for someone to return to an office, or sit at ease for an entire morning waiting for a bus. At times, people on a journey waited days before finding some means of transportation to their destination. Some of our students from the swamp areas of the Okavango Delta took as long as a week to travel to school at the beginning of a term, even though they lived barely fifty miles from Maun. Traveling part of the way by canoe, they often had to wait three or four days for a ride on a government truck going in the right direction. Then they walked to the school from wherever the truck let them off.

Everyone accepted all this as normal. People simply expected that buses would break down, cars would get stuck in deep sand, or that meetings would be delayed until all participants arrived. It took an outing with the students for me to learn from them an important lesson about patience.

On a Friday afternoon in late September 1981, a large group prepared for an overnight Scripture Union retreat. Over one hundred students gathered excitedly at the school gate, eager to get away from the dormitories, do their own cooking, and spend the evening and the next day talking and singing. Even though I felt weary from a long day of classes, I looked forward to the chance to be together with students in a casual setting for an extended period of time. I organized the students into groups for the ninety-minute walk, and we set off on the main road out of Maun under a hot sun with a temperature hovering near 100 °F (but zero humidity). Chatter and laughter filled the air. Gaining energy from the students' enthusiasm, I walked with the group as we trekked seven kilometers along the road and then off into the bush to arrive at our campsite on the banks of the Shashe River.

Along the way, the students continued my education in African culture and practices. They pointed out the usefulness of various trees we passed. The mophane tree provided the best firewood, they explained, because being a very hard wood, a small branch would burn a long time. One branch of mophane wood, about eighteen inches long and eight inches thick, burned with a steady flame long enough to cook a large iron pot full of corn meal porridge. At the time, many village dwellers were forced to travel increasingly longer distances to find usable firewood, making any mophane wood a valuable find. As we walked, some students began to break small, thin branches from another smaller tree, showing me how to use such a branch to clean their teeth. Not for the first time did I witness the surprising resourcefulness of people possessing few modern conveniences.

The campsite area, a beautiful spot, featured a variety of large trees and big open areas for gathering and for sleeping. A staff member with one school vehicle had driven ahead, bringing two large black iron cooking pots to make cornmeal porridge, a staple of the diet everywhere in the country. Part of the plan had been for Elaine and Mary Beth to drive a school truck a bit later on bringing all the food and blankets for the group. Then I would take the truck into town to pick up the Seventh Day Adventist pastor, Rev. Dimbungu, the speaker for the evening. But after waiting for some time and seeing no sign of the truck, I thought I'd better take two students and the other vehicle into town to fetch him.

Thus began twenty-four hours of a combination of comedy of errors and missed meeting times. As our first task, we were to pick up Richard Kashweka, the SU president, at a tent meeting being held by the Seventh Day Adventist Church on the north side of Maun. Two students drove into town with me, and we drove around the meeting area searching, but no Richard. Leaving one of the students at the truck, I took Nchunga Nchunga, a senior student, and the two of us walked around through the crowd for almost an hour, with me becoming increasingly frustrated. We found Rev. Dimbungu, who told us that Richard had gone out to the camp with Mary Beth, and that he himself would be out there a little later. Feeling annoyed at these mix-ups, I took the two students and headed back to the campsite. Just a short distance from the campsite, the car bogged down in a stretch of deep sand, and we struggled mightily to free it. We finally wrestled it free and wearily made it to the camp, discovering that Rev. Dimbungu had arrived right before us. He spoke to the group about the reconciliation brought to us through Christ. After he left, students began to scatter their blankets around the open area for the night. But many continued singing and sharing experiences and testimonies around the fire late into the night.

The next morning, everyone woke up early. Eager student cooks threw large quantities of cornmeal into the cooking pots, added some milk, and began to stir the pots with branches broken from a nearby tree. Being away from the school dining hall, they could cook as they pleased, so they also threw big quantities of sugar in the pot for a much sweeter porridge. The dining hall cooks would have never used so much sugar. We ate the soft, sweet porridge, some bread, and finished breakfast with cups of tea, each of which also had multiple spoonsful of sugar added.

Still tired and feeling frustrated from the previous evening, I prepared to go into town once more to pick up the local Church of God pastor, Rev. Kwenane. I found this to be a curious aspect of life in Africa. Pastors from a variety of churches showed an openness and willingness to share their time with us. As I had noticed at Seretse Khama's funeral earlier, it impressed me that the grace of reconciliation seemed more important than identification with a specific Protestant denomination. All the pastors I met seemed less narrow-minded, much more open and ecumenically minded than many of their counterparts back in the United States.

I decided again to take two students with me because of the Friday night debacle in the sand. The trip into town should have taken about twenty minutes. But the truck became stuck in deep sand not once, but twice on our way. Each time we bogged down, it took the three of us over a half hour to dig out of the sand. When we did finally pick up our speaker in town and drive back to the campsite, we proceeded to get badly stuck in sand yet a third time about a half mile from the campsite. With a headache from lack of sleep and the seemingly unending string of mix-ups and delays, I felt that my level of frustration had about reached its limit. Murphy's Law—if anything can go wrong, it will—must have a corollary, I thought: Murphy's Law is always right!

The pastor and I exited the car, left the two boys with the car and walked the rest of the way, joining the students in time for mid-morning tea. Several other students went to assist the two boys in pushing the truck out of the ever-troublesome sand. We had been gone, not for twenty minutes, but for over two hours. In the meantime, Elaine, Carol, and Mary Beth had gone ahead with a Bible study and discussion, so even though I had been enduring a frustrating morning, the actual program carried on. Rev. Kwenane spoke on the theme "Loving your Neighbor," emphasizing the grace of God overcoming barriers between people who were of different tribes.

For lunch we had a delicious beef stew served with hard porridge (that is, stiffer porridge made with less liquid). After clean-up, some students began to cut some stiff reeds from near the river, carrying them a short way upstream. They stuck the reeds into the bottom of the riverbed, sticking straight up out above the water surface in a line across the width of the river, each reed set no more than a foot away from the next one. Then many of the students went swimming, posting one student on the bank beside the reeds. Slow to recognize what the purpose might be, I finally caught on. I realized, in a rather odd combination of admiration and alarm, that if the reeds moved suddenly, the spotter keeping watch would yell to everyone to scramble out of the river. Moving reeds indicated crocodiles heading downriver toward the swimmers! It certainly gave a whole new meaning to the term *lifeguard*.

Tired from the heat, frustration, and lack of sleep, I had few positive feelings about the whole experience. But later on, it occurred to me that I felt disturbed and frustrated only because our plans had not worked the way I thought they should. That stemmed, at least in part, from the cultural trait in the United States, expecting most things to work in proper order and be on time. But Africans had a different sense of time. People were much more at ease waiting for scheduled events to happen. It didn't bother others that we had changes in our schedule—only me. The retreat had gone well, and younger students kept asking me the following week if we would hold another one that term. The experience gave me a welcome lesson about what it meant to have a more patient and less anxious lifestyle.

Visiting Speakers

Unwelcome Leadership

Scripture Union, widespread in Africa, had chapters in all the secondary schools. Each nation had its own country-wide organization with national officers who advised and helped local groups. Occasionally SU officers traveled to visit schools, participating in their chapel services or speaking at overnight retreats for a local group. Sadly for our students, the quality and effectiveness of these officers varied widely, from the use of distorted and manipulative words and actions to the presentation of highly effective and clear teachings of the grace of God.

As often happened, two young men from the national offices on a tour around the country showed up in Maun with no advance notice the last weekend in May 1981. At our evening chapel prayer service, one of them gave a message manipulating the listeners with guilt trips—as though scaring people into being a Christian had the possibility of leading anyone to a genuine and meaningful faith. The next morning in our Sunday worship with all the boarding students, the second man gave a rousing appeal to students to become Christians, which ended with the statement, "The way to pass your examinations is to become a Christian, and Jesus will write your exams for you!"

"Stunned" would be a good word to use for how I felt at that moment. I could hardly imagine a more irresponsible, preposterous statement. The students obviously thought the same. I could hear a number of them grumbling because they knew what he had said to be outrageous. It made me angry to hear such nonsense. Afterward I spoke with the two visitors, attempting to make clear how entirely inappropriate and unhelpful the final statement in worship had been. The speaker retorted, "But

Jesus promised to be with us!" I replied, "But the Lord doesn't expect anyone to be irresponsible. He doesn't expect students to neglect doing the work they need to do to learn and grow. That's part of what it means to be a human being, to play your part as a contributing member of the community." They looked at me dubiously, as though thinking that I obviously did not have a very strong faith. After a bit more grumbling, and appearing somewhat annoyed, they quietly left the campus.

Later in the afternoon, I spoke with a group of our school's SU leaders, who confirmed that, for the most part, the students thought that the morning speaker had been spouting nonsense. After I told them of the conversation with the two visitors after worship, they all nodded their heads vigorously in affirmation of my words to the two. Returning home, I felt fortunate to be a part of the fellowship we had at our school.

Outstanding Leadership

In stark contrast to those distinctly unhelpful visitors, our 1982 overnight retreat featured Timothy Tavaziva, the Scripture Union secretary for Botswana, an excellent leader who livened things up with his guitar-playing and straight talk about the faith and matters of morality. The retreat the year before, for me, had been the experience of one frustration after another—missing connections with people, vehicles getting stuck in the sand—but this one went much more smoothly. About 120 students and I walked out for four miles along the Thamalakane River, camping at a beautiful spot with some lovely shade trees. The whole group arrived weary and thirsty, but fortunately many students carried plastic water bottles with them. Just before we arrived at the campsite, I asked a group of girls for a sip of water from one of their bottles. After I drank and handed the bottle back, one girl smiled and quoted Jesus' words from the twenty-fifth chapter of Matthew to the rest of the group: "I was thirsty and you gave me a drink." That Scripture had just recently been one of the lessons in the RE curriculum. I chuckled and responded, "I'm glad you remember your RE lessons!"

During the entire retreat, the students all did their work well, cooperating cheerfully with the cooking and cleaning. We did no swimming that time, because they knew that the Thamalakane contained bilharzia, a nasty parasite which caused serious stomach pains. Energetic and thoughtful, our guest speaker Timothy made a big impression on the students with his guitar-playing and his effective speaking style. I thought it all especially helpful because he did not give students simple answers and did not attempt to pressure or manipulate them into a decision about becoming a Christian. On Saturday afternoon, toward the end of the retreat, he did ask for people to come forward if they wished to make a commitment, but he did it in such a way that made it very clear that no one should do so unless they were serious. He wisely said, "Don't come forward because you like my guitar playing, or because you like my way of speaking, but come forward if you are seriously thinking that you want to follow Christ. You can joke with me and fool me if you come up here and you're not serious, but you can't joke with God." Sixteen students came forward, Timothy prayed for them, and we arranged with Timothy right away that those students would meet in the school chapel the next morning prior to Sunday worship to talk with me, Timothy, and his associate, Belpert. That night, a large number of students stayed up quite late singing around the camp fire, caught up in a joyful sense of togetherness.

The next morning, back at the campus, Timothy and Belpert both spoke to the students who had made a commitment, emphasizing to them the importance of continuing in the faith. In an interesting twist, they used the slogan from Zimbabwe's liberation movement, "A luta continua" (the struggle continues) to emphasize the importance of growing in one's faith and service to others after one becomes a Christian. "It's always a struggle," Timothy observed. "You need to remember the importance of the practices of Bible study, prayer, worship, giving, and service to others. And it's important to support one another in these spiritual practices. The more we support one another, the stronger we will be." His message had a big impact on the students. For a considerable time afterward, I thought that the entire retreat had been an experience many students would long remember and point back to as an important point in their lives.

18

Games, Stories, and Celebrations

ENTERTAINMENT

Games and Debates

IN 1980, TELEVISION DID not exist in most of Botswana. Indeed, television had not been introduced into South Africa, the most highly industrialized nation on the continent, until 1975. In those days, before computers became a widespread bane and blessing, students made their own entertainment, soccer games and debates being two of the more popular activities. They also watched an occasional movie via old-fashioned projector on a Friday or Saturday evening, or organized a scavenger hunt with the various sections of the dormitories competing against one another.

I remember one scavenger hunt in early 1982 featuring an especially creative list of items to seek out. Students had come up with such an eclectic mix of items that each dorm section had to send groups of three or four students at a time to range over the whole school campus searching. They asked me and two other teachers to help tally the points for each team. Numerous times, students were in and out of our house excitedly seeking one or more items on the list. They would appear at our door asking, "Do you have any ____?" Elaine and I then invited them in, saying we would look. The lengthy list included five empty matchboxes, a rock as big as you could carry, stamps from five different countries, 200 milliliters of water, five insects (alive!), and much more. At the end of the hunt, one boy came back with a large, heavy rock in a wheelbarrow, cleverly observing, "The rules don't say *how* you're to carry it!" The other judges and I had to admit that he had a point. His group won the prize for the most complete collection.

A most enjoyable task for me came several times when students invited me to be a judge for a formal debate. Mary Beth advised the debate club for our school, arranging debates among our own students as well as scheduling debates with other schools. A debate usually took place on a Friday or Saturday evening, always drawing a big crowd. The school dining hall filled with students. Only the boarders were required to attend, but the audience always included many day students who walked in from the village.

Occasionally an unusual topic would be the subject. I remember one featured the proposition, "Resolved, that Botswana should adopt a barter economy using cattle to replace paper and coin currency." Actually, it seemed unusual only to me; obviously, cattle played a central role in the culture and the economy. Interestingly, the students arguing the affirmative position that night seemed to make the better argument.

The other secondary school in Maun, a private school that survived as a rather makeshift operation with few facilities and lack of materials, sent its debate team to our campus one October evening. It reminded me—again—of the difficult growing pains of a nation only sixteen years removed from colonial rule, and I felt sad to see students trying to get an education under such severe handicaps. One of the boys from the private school, a short, thin fellow who looked younger than the others, wore a sad-looking ensemble: unlaced tennis shoes that were too big for him, plain gray pants, a black-and-white checked sport coat much too large for him, and a green t-shirt with a neckline sagging halfway down his chest. It seemed that he had tried especially hard to look his best for the event, and his efforts met with decidedly mixed success. He turned out to be the best debater for their team.

Administrative Disarray

Because the weekend entertainment events gave the students a needed (and much appreciated) diversion from their studies, a real uproar developed one Friday evening due to some bumbling by the school's administration. At morning assembly early that day, the principal announced that students would be required to go to evening study in the classrooms that night if no film arrived in the mail. Evening study had not normally been scheduled on a Friday or Saturday night. None of the teachers had been notified that no plan existed for the evening, or we could have come up with some ideas. No film arrived, but no message came out to the students. When the loud whistle blew signaling time for study, students felt uncertain about what to do. Most did not show up for study. Because I had no responsibility for that evening, I sat at home, not realizing that the administrative staff had gone out searching to round up straying students. The boarding master and matron, principal, and a couple of other staff people had scant success. When confronted, most students refused to return and went running off into the fields in the darkness. A lack of clarity plus lack of planning resulted in a serious breakdown of discipline.

The next day, instead of gathering together some student leaders that morning in an attempt to resolve the situation, the administrators made another self-defeating move when they announced that evening study would again be required. In what should have been no surprise, exactly the same scenario unfolded Saturday night. When the whistle blew, students scattered in all directions. Having badly handled the situation, the authorities proceeded to make matters even worse by announcing a two-week suspension of thirty-seven of the most obviously rebellious students. It all seemed senseless to me. I couldn't understand the decision-making, thinking that if we had had the chance (and advanced notice!), some of the teachers could have planned a game night of some kind. A primary result of all this came in the students' loss of respect for the authority of the principal, clearly not a healthy situation. Fortunately for everyone, that principal retired just a few months later.

Shakespeare in the Dining Hall

In marked contrast to the chaos of that one weekend, we did have occasions when special guests brought excitement and passion with them to entertain the students. The British Council, a cultural affairs group working in Botswana and other Commonwealth nations around the world, occasionally sent small troupes of actors out to secondary schools to perform. We happily welcomed one such group who showed up unannounced in Maun one Saturday. Word spread quickly among the students, and that evening the dining hall filled with a big crowd. Comprised of only two actors, a man and a woman, the troupe offered renditions of Shakespeare to a large crowd of students that evening in our cavernous dining hall. With wit, enthusiasm, and creativity, the two actors created scenes from the bard's plays. Presenting excerpts from *Julius Caesar* and *A Midsummer Night's Dream*, they made the words come alive for the audience, who watched enthralled. The actors made it even more fun when they included the crowd as participants in the action. Dashing here and there around the hall, the actors called on groups of students to shout out a line of dialogue or let out a cheer or a groan to portray a scene. It thrilled everyone. Students jumped up to shout out their assigned parts, clearly enjoying themselves immensely. It served as a delightful example of creative drama. With no props, no scenery, only two actors acting and coaxing the student body into action, Shakespeare came alive. The students loved it. And so did I. "British actors and Shakespeare—what could be better?" I thought, sitting there marveling at their talent and the great creativity that arises when people have few resources to draw on.

This creativity and inventiveness showed up in the common life of the village. Children often took bits of wire, twisting and tying them together to fashion toy race cars with empty round shoe polish containers for wheels. An old tennis ball could be used for an impromptu soccer match. Other games could be played with stones moved back and forth among a series of shallow holes dug in the ground—the ancient game of mancala. Time after time, I experienced a keen sense of admiration at the creativity, resiliency, and effort of children who had few material assets. Their sense of imagination seemed endless.

Storytelling

Occasionally, several teachers gathered in the evening around a fire in the field near the tennis court, swapping stories and enjoying the night air. Zakes (Zaccheus) Mahlanza usually joined the group. He had bestowed upon me the soccer nickname "Mastermind" when the teachers played the students. Always one with a smile, a joke, or a story, Zakes especially loved telling African folk tales. The one I loved the most featured the Rabbit and the Elephant. The hare, or rabbit, often stands out in African folklore as a small, seemingly weak animal who cleverly outwits bigger and stronger beasts. In southern Africa, the rabbit is named Mmutla. The tale Zakes told went as follows:

One fine day Mmutla hopped along through a field of grass, merrily making his way without paying much attention to where he went. He hopped at one point, crashing right into the side of the head of a very large elephant. Elephant picked Mmutla up with his trunk and scolded him. "Mmutla, what is the matter with you? Why don't you watch where you're going?" Mmutla tried to soften him up with flattery. "You are looking fine and strong today. But I want to challenge you to a test of strength, because I am stronger than you are!" Elephant roared so hard with laughter that tears came to his eyes. "Oh Mmutla, you are so silly! I am much bigger and stronger than you." So Mmutla said boldly, "I will show you that I am stronger." And he gathered a large amount of the tall, rough grass in the field, wove it into a long rope, and took one end of it to Elephant. "Here, take this rope," Mmutla said. "We'll tie it around one of your big front legs. I'll take the other end, go up the little hill over there, and when I say *Pull,* you pull and I'll pull, and we'll see who is the strongest." Elephant laughed again and agreed, quite sure that Mmutla would prove no match for him. Mmutla took the other end of the long rope and ran up the hill. But he didn't stop. He went down the other side and found a big hippo. Running up to the hippo, he spoke confidently, saying, "You look very strong, but I am stronger than you." Hippo laughed and laughed. "Mmutla, you are so silly! That's not possible." Mmutla showed him the end of the rope, saying, "Put this rope around one of your big front legs. I'll take the other end, go the top of that hill, and when I say *Pull,* you pull and I'll pull, and we'll see who is the strongest." Still laughing, Hippo agreed. So the rope went around Hippo's leg, Mmutla ran to the top of the hill and hid in the bushes. "Pull!" he yelled at the top of his voice. Elephant pulled and Hippo pulled—and neither one could budge the other. Mmutla cried, "Stop!" and the two big animals fell with relief. Mmutla ran to Elephant, who said with great respect, " Mmutla, I had no idea you were so strong!" Then he ran to Hippo. "Mmutla, I had no idea you were so strong." He had fooled them both.

Zakes laughed in delight when he finished the tale. Years later, I discovered in my studies that enslaved Africans in the American South told these folk tales among themselves as a form of rebellion, a way of saying that the master thought he had everything under his control, but ultimately he did not. Oppressed people who can laugh at their oppressors and their weaknesses hold some power over their captors, the power of ridicule. Such satire and ridicule have often given oppressed people hope.

CELEBRATIONS

Fourth of July

One year the Americans in Maun celebrated a US Independence Day unlike any other fourth of July any of us had ever experienced. Maun boasted three restaurants. A Frenchman named Bernard ran one called Le Bistro, our favorite. Not long before the three of us had arrived in the country, Bernard had held a contest to determine an advertising slogan for the restaurant. The winning entry, which Bernard had painted in vivid red letters on the outside wall of Le Bistro, seemed distinctly uninspiring: *Ten thousand flies can't be wrong.*

Casting caution aside and defying the unappetizing description, we usually ate there once a week, often with others from the secondary school. As host, Bernard tried mightily to accommodate the tastes of his customers, including the US citizens who lived and worked in and around Maun, a small group of about two dozen Peace Corps volunteers, aid workers, and missionaries. For our first wedding anniversary, Bernard presented us with a special American treat: hamburgers and banana splits. The hamburgers actually looked more like Swedish meat balls, and the banana splits had been constructed from the tiny three-inch-long local bananas topped by an unrecognizable sad substitute for ice cream. But we appreciated the gesture.

By far the most interesting evening at Le Bistro came one fourth of July. Sixteen of the Maun area Americans gathered there to celebrate, sitting at outdoor tables. For his American customers, Bernard had somehow obtained a few fireworks for the event, including Roman candles. At another table not far from our group, four Chinese men, in the area supervising a rice-growing project, sat and watched with curiosity. One of them offered to help us celebrate. So he took a Roman candle, lit it with a match, held it in his right hand, and pointed it toward the sky at an angle, away from the crowd. We all watched and cheered as the sparks flew into the air and out over the grassy area beside Le Bistro. In a burst of international cooperation and fellowship, we celebrated American Independence Day with four Chinese men in a French restaurant in southern Africa. I think I can say with some confidence that such a celebration has never been duplicated.

An African Wedding

The First Day

A different sort of celebration presented itself when the geography teacher Mr. M. Mogapi announced his upcoming wedding. I knew him as a colleague and a tennis player. Carol Schaad and I sometimes had doubles matches against him and Marion. Mr. Mogapi, a solidly built member of the Kalanga tribe, always presented himself to students as a man whose stern disapproval of the world seemed permanently etched on his face, never smiling in their presence. But on the tennis court, he showed another side of himself with flashes of humor. The first time playing against him, I hit the ball out of bounds on my serve, and he quickly responded with a laugh and a joking tone, "Mistake number one!" I soon found that if he reached "Mistake number three," Carol and I had usually lost a game. We all enjoyed those afternoons.

When Mr. Mogapi announced to the school staff the happy news of his upcoming wedding, we all eagerly looked forward to the celebration. Weddings in Botswana combined both Western and African traditions. The entire event, beginning with the formal marriage ceremony itself, lasted not for a mere few hours, but for three days. Africans know how to party.

The bride came from a well-respected Maun family. The couple had an infant child, a sign of a common practice in the male-dominated cultures of southern Africa. Before marrying, the couple had a child together to guarantee that the woman could bear children. Interestingly, among the Zulu in South Africa, people did not even consider a couple married until they had a child. Mr. Mogapi and his bride married in a Roman Catholic ceremony at the Maun Red Cross headquarters, a small, square white building used because no Catholic Church existed in our area. A Ghanaian priest serving in Maun conducted the ceremony, with the bride in a white bridal gown, two attendants also in white, and Mr. Mogapi in a dark suit and tie. At that point, it looked no different from a standard-brand North American wedding.

Afterward, all of us who attended the ceremony formed a long procession of cars and trucks, with people hanging out the windows or piled into the open backs of pick-ups as we wound our way singing through the village to the bride's family compound. People then jumped from the vehicles, forming into two groups. One represented the bride's family and friends, the other representing the groom. The two groups acted out a friendly rivalry, full of laughter and joking, competing to see which could outsing the other.

Some of the school faculty then went home for a while, returning to the compound late in the day to find a large gathering continuing to dance and sing as a group. People raised their hands and waved them back and forth as they danced in a circle, singing songs celebrating and advising the bride. One song included the admonition, "If he ill-treats you, go back to your parents!" It presented quite a spectacle of people enjoying themselves immensely, singing loudly, crowding each other and dancing on the bare ground. From four large tables at various spots set up around the area, all of us ate and relished large quantities of food made available by the bride's family, who obviously had spared no effort in preparation. They provided foods such as seswaa (a kind of beef pounded and cooked so that it became very tender), fried fat cakes, and fruit of all kinds. They spread beef and fatcakes on large platters, the mangoes, papayas, and other fruit in big shallow baskets. We ate well that day, enjoying the happy scene of uninhibited, joyous excitement, everyone caught up in the feeling of a special day.

The Second Day

EATING AND CELEBRATING

The next day the celebration continued at another site. The bride and her two bridesmaids dressed in green for the day. Because Mr. Mogapi came from the Kalanga tribe and lived far from his home area, a Batawana family named Modisa had befriended him, acting along with some of our school colleagues in place of the groom's family. Mr. Modisa offered his family compound as a venue for the day, right across the road from the school campus. The waist-high wall around his compound had been freshly painted with designs and pictures portraying cooking fires, children playing, and other scenes from Tswana life. By midday a large number of celebrants had gathered there, singing, eating great quantities of food, and group dancing. I watched as all ages joined in a large circle to sing songs about the wedding couple. One song proclaimed "Mogapi is the chief of chiefs today!" Other funny songs, with accompanying actions, also filled the air. Children and adults joined in a song of two trains coming together and colliding: the whole group spread out singing in a

huge circle, only to rush toward the center, stomping their feet harder and
harder on the hard, sandy ground the closer they came to one another—
stopping just short of stomping on each other. Smaller children had brief
looks of fear on their faces as people rushed toward them, but the fear
quickly turned to laughter when they realized they were not harmed. I
spent much of the day clapping or laughing, or both.

THE BRIDE'S ARRIVAL RITUAL

Late in the afternoon the bride left the celebration to return to her own
family's compound to prepare for the special ritual of the evening. Everyone else remained at the Modisa home. At dusk, I sat with the married
men and a few women representing the Mogapi family in a small, par-
tially enclosed area in front of one of the four family huts, facing the main
entrance to the compound. We waited for the bride to be brought by her
family to her new home and husband. Traditionally, the bride arrived
with the women of her family in a bridal march unlike anything I had
ever witnessed. Twenty-three women, all wearing shawls, walked single
file on the dirt road through the village, moving very slowly, solemnly.
They turned and entered the husband's family compound through the
opening in the waist-high wall. The arrival, rich in symbolism, included
all the women of the bride's family carrying the bride's possessions. The
mother of the bride entered first, then the bride, followed by an aunt carrying the baby boy, and the other women. The bride's mother wore a rose-
colored shawl. The bride, the baby, and all the other women wore white
shawls, the barest hint of the little boy's black hair visible under the shawl.
Women representing the groom's family stood up to receive all of the
items carried in by the long line of relatives. The bride brought greetings
to the assembled group. Two women took the bride, sitting her down on
a mat on the ground to one side of the crowded compound. The bride sat
with her head down, crying as a sign of her sorrow at leaving her family's
home. The other women of her family then sat on the ground. The slow
walk into the compound indicated respect for the other family as well as
the bride's family's reluctance to give up their daughter.

There at the very midpoint of the joyous celebration of the union
of a husband and wife, a sense of the pain of separation revealed itself in
the slow, reluctant gait of the women and the quiet tears of the bride. The
joy of the new union seemed inseparable from the one family's sense of

loss. This, I thought, is life's reality, and the entire event would have been incomplete without it. Gain and loss, loss and gain at every turning point of life: leaving a past behind, crossing boundaries, open to a new future. I felt honored to be invited to sit with the married men to officially greet the bride and welcome her into this new life.

When everyone had been seated, the mother of the bride spoke first. "We bring you our daughter," she said. "There is not a scratch on her. She is yours now. She brings many good skills and qualities to you. We ask that you treat her well." Several of the listeners in the crowd responded, "We are pleased." A pause, then the bride's mother spoke again. "We have heard that Kalanga men often fail at marriage, so if he does not make a good husband, send her back to us, her family." I could hear women suppressing a laugh at this. Later someone informed me that the comment showed a rather bold bit of cheekiness. Apparently, respected elders could get away with such declarations.

At the end of her short speech, the mother of the bride made the traditional request for departure. "*Ke kopa tsela*," literally, "I'm asking for the road." One of the seated male elders solemnly responded for Mogapi's side, saying, "*Gosiame*," an expression of satisfaction and permission to leave. All the women of the bride's family stood up to leave, leaving the bride there for people to greet. The women departed as they had arrived—slowly, solemnly, in single file.

The Married Men Give Advice

The next step of the evening came when the married men, whom I joined, went to a place at a spot in the open center of the compound, away from the crowd. The wind began blowing and lightning flashed in the sky, and I thought surely we were about to be drenched with rain. But no rain fell. We sat on the ground in a circle with Mr. Mogapi sitting in the middle. The men, each one dressed formally in shirt and tie, spoke in serious tones. Beginning with the eldest, the married men proceeded to give the new husband advice about marriage. Each one spoke earnestly and forcefully, offering the following counsel:

"Do not talk to other people to find out things about your wife's activities, but rather talk with her directly."

"Remember that you have new responsibilities now. No staying out all night."

"Do not neglect your wife."

"You should respect and forgive your wife."

Assuming that everyone would have a chance to offer a word, I mentally prepared to present a statement advising the newly married couple to pay attention and listen carefully to one another. To my surprise (and regret), I did not get the chance. After four men in the circle had given their counsel, suddenly everyone stood up. The advice session had ended. Obviously, I did not know the customs of the evening, so I felt a twinge of disappointment at being denied the chance to offer my own thoughts. The elders then presented Mogapi to his wife, and the day's ceremonies came to an end.

Community and Tradition

The third day, filled with more music and dancing, featured a joyous communal celebration. The strength and beauty of the extended family life gave me a sense of the value and meaning of a culture that focused more on community than the individual. As I had noted before, people in this community helped one another and did not hesitate to request help from others. The feeling of belonging pervaded the community.

It saddened me therefore to discover in later conversations with Batswana that the old traditions of family were breaking down. Traditionally, marriage forged an alliance of families. The extended family worked to keep a marriage together. If a husband mistreated his wife, customarily the wife would to go to her mother-in-law with the problem, saying, "Your son is mistreating me. You need to step in and remedy this." The husband's mother would then call him in and give her son a stern warning about his behavior. If that did not have the desired result, several uncles of the family would give a more severe punishment to the husband. But in recent times, more young people moved away from their home village to larger towns and cities, and thus the strength of the extended family life frayed. The mother-in-law no longer lived close by and therefore could no longer be available. A strong sense of women's inferiority plagued the society, so if the extended family no longer supported women, their marital circumstances could deteriorate badly. This whole system had been breaking down because so many young couples had jobs and lived apart from their parents. The divorce rate had risen, in part because the increase in educational opportunities for women had given them confidence that they could make a living on their own. They were—quite understandably—much less willing to endure an unhappy marriage. This situation resulted in a large percentage of births in the country being to unmarried mothers. I wondered what long-term effects this would have on the country.

Bogadi

Later that week, the two students who met with me for theological education explained the custom of bogadi, or "bride-wealth." They explained to me that foreigners often misunderstand this as a payment made to a family for a bride. Among our local tribe, the Batawana, bogadi is usually two cows, but with some other tribes it is much more, a fact that could raise problems when a person from one tribe married into another. The husband-to-be gives the cattle to the parents of the bride, not as some kind of "payment" for the bride, but actually as an investment. The bride's parents use those cattle, and when the younger couple's first child grows up, he or she can go to the grandparents and claim the bogadi. As Mr. Dikole explained, "It's just like people in the United States starting a fund for a child at birth. Bogadi is an investment for the future, not a bargain made for a bride."

The Grace of Marriage

Elaine and I had entered into a marriage we knew had been strong from the beginning. Our wedding had been a happy celebration, with rousing, overpowering singing filling the church with the supportive joy of family and friends. This African wedding seemed very different, and yet the same, everyone sharing eagerly in the joy of two families and expressing it with their whole heart and soul. Following our wedding ceremony in Pennsylvania, someone had commented to me, smiling in reference to the powerful singing of the crowd, "So, did you invite only people who could sing really well?"

But we still had much to learn about each other. Living in a place where the isolation and lack of distractions gave us plenty of time to come even closer to one another, inevitable pitfalls arose along the way. Marriage is always, after all, two imperfect people stumbling along at first and learning to accept and love each other fully. As a pastor, I knew well that many marriages die because the couple stops taking a long, loving look at one another, failing to see one another's needs and anxieties. We were determined not to have this happen to us.

Over the first year or so in Botswana, the two of us had several times when we realized the need for talking through and clarifying our feelings about our life together. Because from the beginning of our marriage we had always tried to be open, talking freely and thoroughly with each other, Elaine did not hesitate to tell me at one point that she felt we had not been together enough, just the two of us. "Because of my work and my schedule, I feel like I have little time for other friends, while you have much more contact with a variety of people." Recognizing, belatedly, that I had not paid enough attention to her situation, we talked it out and made a vow to be sure to set aside some more definite times for the two of us to be together. We both felt relieved and secure in our openness with each other, knowing that from the very earliest days of our relationship we had been honest and straightforward with one another.

19

Teaching Teachers

LEARNING TO TEACH

Creating Exams

TEACHING A NEW CURRICULUM in almost any subject requires some extra training. So it happened that all of the religious education teachers in the country had many opportunities to attend workshops in our "Developing in Christ" program. I participated in numerous workshops for RE teachers who were learning the new curriculum. This meant six or seven times a year making the long trek south to meet with others in the Gaborone area, where most of the teachers lived and worked. While an arduous trip, it always proved worth it for the insights and new ways of thinking offered. Occasionally Elaine, Sherry, and I would take the trip as an opportunity to visit the Lindfields. Derek and I would go to the workshop, while Elaine and Sherry stayed with Carol and the boys.

But in addition, at the first teachers' conference upon my arrival in the country, the Ministry of Education had appointed me to the national panel for Religious Education. This group oversaw the training and constructed "mock" Junior Certificate exams, practice tests given in the year or so before third-year students took the actual JC exams. Making up the exams and then analyzing the results proved a time-consuming process. I spent many a weekend traveling south to gather together with a most interesting international group of experienced RE teachers.

One especially helpful learning experience for me came at a meeting of the panel mid-October of our first year. After traveling by bus and train to Gaborone, Derek Lindfield picked me up at the train station to take me to Moeding College. The group met there on Saturday and Sunday to analyze a nation-wide exam taken in August by all the Form Two students in Botswana. We also had the task of creating an end-of-year mock JC exam for those same students. The panel consisted of Sisters Therese and Carmel, the two Irish nuns from St. Joseph's College who had provided us with such gracious hospitality in August; Sister Karin, a Dutch nun based in the village of Mahalapye; Derek, the British teacher at Moeding; Caroline, a Motswana from a secondary school in Gaborone; and me. All of the panel except me were experienced RE teachers.

We worked hard all day Saturday from nine a.m. to six p.m., first analyzing the results of the August exam, then writing multiple choice questions for the end-of-year mock J.C. exam. Vigorous and lively discussion filled that day as we examined the computer analysis of the August exam. With the variety of backgrounds of the group, we brought a wide range of ideas and questions to the session, mostly around the issue of how to write valid multiple choice questions. Fortunately, that day we had the help of an excellent resource person who could answer all of our questions, an American serving on contract as director of research and testing for the Ministry of Education. Because I had never seen or examined a computer analysis of multiple choice tests, it surprised me to find out the number of criteria used to determine the validity of a test question. I had no idea how many different factors could be measured, or how they could aid us in a critical evaluation of an exam. A most obvious example concerned the data regarding the number of students who picked the correct answer for each question and the distribution of wrong answers. If, for example, on one question no one at all picked one of the options, then we would know that particular question could not be a valid one because the one option had been eliminated by every student.

Sister Karin, with good humor and wit, began to joke with us all, urging each of us to join in posing one nonsensical answer that no one would ever choose. Laughing, we each contributed one, such as:

"Which of the following did Jesus choose as one of his twelve disciples?

A. Paul

B. Timothy

C. Peter

D. King Herod

Then we returned to our real work. By the end of the day, we had all learned much about guidelines for making up a good exam. We were pleased with ourselves for coming up with what we judged to be a satisfactory list of multiple choice questions. The next morning we spent four hours writing the essay questions for the year-end exam.

Zimbabwe's Experience

A workshop for all teachers in mid-1981 featured a guest from Zimbabwe, a White woman named Audrey Greenshields, a creative and helpful teacher who had been using the new curriculum in the newly racially integrated schools in her country. She showed us clearly how the various parts of the curriculum worked together to reinforce the coherence between African traditions and Christian faith. We were all tremendously heartened to hear that where the course had been introduced in Zimbabwe schools, the lessons about community and friendship had gone a long way toward reconciling Black and White students and helping them to accept one another. For example, students had discussed ways in which they had experienced acceptance or rejection from others, then they had read several stories of Jesus accepting people quite different from himself: Matthew the tax collector, and the woman in Luke 7:36–50 whom others saw as an outcast. Students saw the openness, understanding, and courage of Jesus, then discussed how those qualities helped to bring about true fellowship and community with others. After the bitterness and tragedy of the war, this gave us real hope for the future. Audrey said the only real resistance to the curriculum came from a small number of White teachers.

One evening at supper, Audrey gave us a picture of recent developments in Zimbabwe. Refusing to accept the new circumstances of equal rights for all, at least one third (and probably more) of the Whites were leaving the country. As an example of the attitudes, in the last Whites-only election prior to majority rule, the ruling Rhodesian party had put out an election poster with a picture portraying only the legs of people. The legs showed both Black and White people together in a crowd. Inscribed across the bottom of the poster were the words, "Rhodesia will never accept this!"

Because of the White flight from the country, the new Zimbabwe government had resorted to drastic measures. They issued an order stating that a person could take only a certain limited amount of money out of the country. This produced an odd response on the part of Whites fleeing Zimbabwe. They began buying up all the expensive furniture they could find as a means of shipping money out of the country, so much so that the price of furniture had shot sky-high. The same had happened with the kinds of rare postage stamps that collectors liked to buy. Their price had also risen sharply. The government had passed still another law saying that no automobile more than four years old could be removed from the economy. I marveled at the lengths to which human beings could go when they felt trapped by the sudden loss of power over others. Those leaving were so bitter and desperate that they did whatever they could to retain their goods and escape the prospect of having Black people in charge. I could think only of how severely racism poisons minds and defaces the humanity of both its perpetrators and its victims.

We also discussed some practical problems some schools encountered at a very basic level. Some schools had no Bibles for their students, others lacked worksheets or workbooks for the RE course. A clash of priorities occurred at a few schools where faculty who thought their own subjects more important than religious education had limited RE classes to as little as one period per week. At Maun, I had just two periods for each class per week, inadequate to be sure, but it worked out because we taught the two-year curriculum spread over three years.

Professor Noko

Another session that weekend featured a Botswana University professor, Dr. I. Noko, speaking to us about characteristics of African traditional religion. He made especially interesting points to us regarding traditional religion, explaining it this way: "In Western culture, people think of religion as a suit of clothes one can take off and put on. You can change your religion if you wish, joining another group. In African tradition, religion is more like the skin you walk around in all the time. One can't simply take it off. God is present in the midst of human life, always at work. In our deep sorrow and in our deep happiness we touch God. For Africans, God's salvation traditionally extended only as far as one's own tribe. But in Christian faith, it surprised Africans to hear that the good news of the gospel is that all of us—all tribes and nations—are linked together and saved together." I had sensed that the communal nature of the church and the meaning of salvation resonated more deeply with African culture than with individualistic North Americans, so Dr. Noko's point seemed to me to be on target, confirming what I had thought to be true.

LEARNING BOTSWANA HERITAGE

Visiting Khama's Grave

Leaving Moeding on a Monday—we were on a winter break, so Sherry and I had no school—we drove north on the road toward Francistown. Soon after we started out, we decided to take a side road from the village of Palapye to Serowe, capital of the Bangwato tribe, largest tribe in the country. The former President, Sir Seretse Khama, had been buried there with his ancestors. We wanted to see the graves of Seretse Khama and his grandfather, Khama the Great. But we had no idea how difficult it could be to get permission to visit. Arriving at the tribal headquarters at the kgotla, we parked the car. I found the chief's office and went inside. When I made the request of the man at the desk, a necessity required out of respect for the tribe, the office attendant told me, "You must see the chief for permission. He is meeting with people at the other side of the kgotla area." Leaving Sherry and Elaine in the car, I walked over to the group gathered around the chief. Feeling unsure of the protocols and quite hesitant to interrupt the chief, I stopped at the edge of the gathering and looked around for someone to help me. One man spotted me and noticed my hesitancy. He asked, "What are you seeking?" I answered, "I would like to see the grave of President Khama. Whom should I see for permission?" The man turned, saying "Follow me." He took me to a policeman, who surprised me by interrogating me at some length, questioning my background and my motives. "Who are you? Where do you come from? Why do you want to see the grave?" I had the distinct feeling of great reluctance on his part to allow us to visit the gravesite. But when I explained that I had been teaching in Maun for a year and a half and had great respect for President Khama, his mood softened. "I will send you to the chief. You must get his permission." He called to another man nearby to accompany me, and that one guided me back to the kgotla. My guide walked right up to the chief, interrupting the discussion and presented my request. The chief then motioned to me to come forward.

With a rather solemn look on his face, the chief began to question me all over again. "Where are you from? Why do you want to see the grave? How long have you been in Botswana? Do you know anyone in Serowe? Where have you just been that you're traveling to Serowe?" Finally, after answering those and a few other queries, the chief—rather reluctantly, I thought—gave his permission. "Go siame [Okay]. This man will take you there," pointing to my guide.

We passed the car, where Elaine and Sherry joined us, following our guide. We climbed Thatlayangana Hill, an outcropping overlooking the town. At the top we had a beautiful view of Serowe and the surrounding countryside. Behind a magnificent rock formation seemingly thrown together at awkward angles, sat the great stone memorials over the graves of the Bangwato chiefs: Khama the Great, Khama III, Tshekedi, Sechele I, and Sir Seretse Khama. Each memorial had its own unique style. The one for Seretse Khama stood approximately fifteen feet high, topped by a metal sculpture of a duiker, a small antelope which is the symbol, or *totem*, of the Bangwato. On one side of the stone memorial had been inscribed a biblical quotation, "Righteousness exalteth a Nation." An impressive display of the pride and heritage of the Bangwato, largest tribe in Botswana, the scene on the hill inspired a sense of awe. We could see why access to the gravesite required a demonstration of seriousness and great respect for the heritage. Recalling the stories of Khama the Great traveling to England in the 1890s to persuade the British to maintain the protectorate status of Bechuanaland (the old name for Botswana), we knew how significant his role had been in preventing the country from coming under the control of the people who would later establish apartheid. Seretse Khama, first president of an independent Botswana, had been an honorable leader who insisted on a non-racialist society. We were glad to have the opportunity to work in a nation with such a proud heritage.

ADDITIONAL TRAINING

Kanamo Center

At another weekend conference in May 1982, I joined other RE teachers learning new teaching methods from two Ursuline nuns, Sisters Frances Boston, an Australian, and the Dutch nun, Sister Karin. We met together at the Kanamo Centre in Mahalapye, home to a large group of Ursuline sisters all working in education. *Kanamo* means "a spreading" in Setswana, in this case referring to spreading the gospel as widely as possible. About fifteen of us enjoyed Saturday and Sunday with Karin and Frances, both of whom had creative ideas to share.

Karin shared a simple exercise for younger students about understanding openness to others who are different from one's self: "Have two student volunteers each describe an experience of feeling happy because they were accepted by a group, and then describe a feeling of disappointment because they were rejected by a group. Discuss various kinds of dislikes which can blind us from really seeing another person. Then look at two Gospel stories: the Roman centurion in Matthew 8:5–13 approaching Jesus to request healing for his slave, and the account in Luke of the tax collector Zaccheus. Notice the openness of Jesus toward the two hated representatives of the Rome but also their openness toward Jesus. How does this openness show us something about acceptance of others whom we are inclined to dislike?" Not only did we have fruitful conversation, but the Ursulines offered delicious homemade soups and breads to the group for our main meals.

Sister Frances Teaches

To my good fortune, Frances had a teacher training session in Francistown the following Monday, so Sunday afternoon I had a lift with her in her car instead of having to take the bus. The three-hour drive gave us time for a nonstop conversation. In Africa for the previous twelve years, she worked mostly with primary school teachers in religious education. People held her in high regard for her creative ideas. In a rather remarkable coincidence of mutual acquaintance, I discovered that she had been in Rome not long before on a thirty-day retreat directed by Father Peter Foley, the same Jesuit priest who had been my director on a couple of eight-day retreats in the late seventies at a Jesuit retreat center near Reading, Pennsylvania. It amazed us that we had such connections to one another.

In the early 1980s, Latin American liberation theology had been raising controversy in many Roman Catholic and Protestant circles. I had recently been reading *The Liberation of Theology* by Juan Luis Segundo,[1] a Uruguayan priest who accused the church of callousness toward suffering and oppressed people. I asked Frances for her views, because although I

1. Segundo, *Liberation*, 1976.

had felt some skepticism about some aspects of liberation theology, it had become more obvious to me how much cultural conditioning there is in theology as well as so many other parts of life. To take a simple example, it is easy to talk about loving one's enemies from the comfortable position of a middle-class North American, but an altogether different perspective comes from people who are actually oppressed. Some liberation theologians did not object to the use of violence to bring about a more just society. If a North American like me objected, their response would be, "But you are a privileged White North American who has no experience of real oppression. We're concerned about theological work that accomplishes something and does not simply engage in speculation." Violence and nonviolence could be seen in different ways by people in varying circumstances. I wanted to see if I viewed this fairly or accurately.

Frances had something quite revealing to offer. "What I admire about much of Latin American liberation theology is that there is often an emphasis on the liberation of the self from its inner turmoil and sin as well as liberation from unjust structures." That struck me as an exceptionally constructive and wholistic way of thinking. I thought, "Yes, that's it. Dealing with the whole self is necessary." It occurred to me that North American churches quite often disconnect the inner from the outer liberation, either talking primarily about being "saved" from individual sin or primarily about social justice concerns. The biblical meaning of salvation includes both, I thought. My Australian friend had hit upon that truth.

20

The One Who Has Many Friends Is Not Caught by Darkness on the Road

—African Proverb

ON THE ROAD

The Unexpected Hitchhiker

Traveling any distance in southern Africa proved to be arduous, hot, troublesome, and frequently interrupted either by unexpected breakdowns or delays caused by masses of migrating wildebeest, zebra, or even the occasional elephant.

The most unexpected delay I experienced happened not long after we had bought the jeep for our family. We had sometimes walked into the village to buy our food, so the jeep turned out to be a real boon for us, because it meant that Elaine could use it for trips into the village in emergencies, and I could use it for the occasional trip to Francistown for teachers' conferences. Driving through the village of Nata one day on the way to Francistown, I spotted a young police officer waving vigorously at me from the roadside as I went slowly through the tiny village. I pulled over. He approached the car window with an air of self-importance that seemed exaggerated for one who appeared barely out of his teens. Dressed in what appeared to be a new and neatly-pressed blue uniform, he leaned into the window on the passenger side.

"Can you give me a lift? I have two prisoners for the jail in Francistown, and I have no transport." He sounded annoyed, like a teenager suffering disrespect from his peers.

Stunned at this unusual request, I asked with a nervous laugh, "Prisoners? Are they dangerous?"

"Oh, no, no," he said with a slight smile and shake of his head. He pointed to two men sitting nearby in the shade of a tree. No handcuffs, no chains, clothed in drab brown shirts and shorts, they each also wore an expression midway between sullen and indifferent. A bit reluctantly, I agreed to take the three of them, realizing that the lack of restraints and the youthful inexperience of the officer made it unlikely that I would have two dangerous criminals in the car. So the two prisoners hopped into the back seat, the officer sat in front with me, and we drove off with the young officer continuing to voice displeasure over his plight. Frowning, he said, "I am enforcing the law! I should have the transport required."

A plastic container I carried with me held my provisions for the trip. One never traveled in that part of the world without provisions, because if the car broke down in the middle of the desert, it could be trouble. Wisdom meant having food and drink handy. That day the travel menu featured orange juice and home-made oatmeal cookies, courtesy of Elaine. I offered them to my passengers, which may have been the reason that the officer settled down, the two prisoners stayed silent, and we arrived in Francistown with little conversation and without incident. *Tsamaya ka pula.*

Bus Adventures

On several occasions, I traveled by public bus from Francistown to Maun after attending a teachers' conference in the south. Bus travel in Africa can be an unpredictable adventure for a whole host of reasons involving surprising and sometimes alarming incidents. The usual beginning of the trip to Maun meant getting on the bus about two hours before its scheduled departure in order to get a seat. Giving my small suitcase to one of the two men who operated the bus, I then watched him squeeze the case onto the bus roof with other bags. A steady stream of riders crowded onto the bus carrying big bags, blankets, baskets of food, and sometimes even a live chicken. Often someone boarded the bus and started down the aisle, calling out to all present, "*Dumelang ditsala*" ("Hello, friends").

People cheerfully answered back, a kind of kinship and camaraderie common to a close-knit society. Standard gear for a bus trip consisted of, at a minimum, a warm blanket, a basket of food, a small roll of bathroom tissue, and a plastic jug of water. Food and water were necessary because of the possibility that the bus could break down in the middle of nowhere, with no place to get food for hours. Thus also the blanket, in case the traveler must sleep in the bus if it broke down and had to remain on the road overnight. Last but certainly not least, bathroom tissue could not be forgotten, as no toilet facility existed for stretches of a hundred miles or more.

On one of those bus journeys from Francistown back to Maun, something odd struck me as the bus made its way along the good paved road stretching from Francistown to Nata. Because the entire country of Botswana is almost completely flat, being on a plateau 3300 feet above sea level, the bus always rode along at a steady pace. After about twenty miles, I realized that whenever the driver spotted people waiting some distance ahead, he coasted—rather slowly—to a halt near the waiting passengers. I didn't think anything of this all along the 120 miles to the village of Nata, where we stopped. Everyone got off the bus, and all the people seemed to be taking a rest, sitting or lying on the ground in open areas near the bus. After sitting a while, I became more and more curious about this delay in the trip, so I asked a man sitting nearby, "What are they doing? What are we waiting for?" He replied casually, "They are waiting for a wrench." I looked puzzled, so he added, "To repair the brakes." In other words, we had traveled more than a hundred miles on a crowded bus with no brakes. I felt more than a bit rattled, thinking how dangerous the trip had been thus far, and I hadn't known it. It startled me that no one seemed bothered by this, as though it regularly occurred that a public bus traveled long distances without functioning brakes. No one acted alarmed. No one protested. It seemed simply an ordinary part of life, like carrying a live chicken on the bus, or waiting two hours for the bus to leave.

The man with the wrench finally showed up, two men repaired the brakes, and we set off on the final long stretch of the journey, that difficult 200 miles of road consisting of dirt, sand, and rocks. We had departed Francistown at 1:00 pm. We arrived in Maun at 11:00 pm, the brakes and my somewhat rattled sense of security intact.

On occasions when Elaine, Sherry, and I took the bus, at times people would remark about our family by asking us about other family members at home. Most often, when Elaine answered, "This is our only child," the questioner put on a sad face. In that culture, having many children assured a means of security for aging parents. But once when a woman asked, "Do you have other children?" Elaine replied, "No, this is our only one." The questioner smiled brightly, responding with, "Ah, the family treasure!"

Traveling as a blond-haired, White passenger among Batswana, I occasionally became the subject of other curious, and even surprising observations. A woman sitting behind me on one trip reached up to touch softly the sun-bleached blond hair on my forearm, remarking, "You are just like a lion!" I must say that neither before nor since that day have I ever had a compliment quite like that one.

A Different Kind of Danger

Another quite different and potentially dangerous problem arose on a car trip returning from an RE meeting in Francistown. Right before leaving for Maun, one of our teachers saw me walking and hailed me, asking for a ride back to school. Maapula, a domestic science teacher, had recently been assigned to our school, so I gladly offered her a lift. Starting out in mid-afternoon, we found ourselves on the road, still at least forty miles from Maun, when darkness fell. Out in the desert at night, with no moon and no villages along the way, I could see nothing at all beyond the short stretch of light cast by the headlights. And I mean nothing: our surroundings appeared utterly black, no detectable motion whatsoever, no lights visible anywhere off to either side. It looked downright eerie. More accustomed to this experience than I, Maapula's eyesight seemed superhuman. Every so often she would lightly touch her hand to my arm, saying, "Slow down now." We would move forward more slowly and suddenly I would see several cows lying lazily in the middle of the road. For me, the darkness had entirely obscured them. Her African sensibilities were obviously more heightened than mine, I thought. Had I been driving alone that night, I would have without a doubt had a serious accident, killing a cow or two and very likely damaging the car. Not for the first time did the simple but profound insight strike me that we are more dependent upon others than we realize. I think that is why the strength of community ties in Africa made such a deep impression on me.

21

The One Who Has Many Friends . . . (II)

A SPECIAL PALM SUNDAY

"Hosanna to the Son of David!" Waving palm branches in the air, a large group of our students shouted out the words of Palm Sunday, playing the part of the crowd greeting Jesus entering Jerusalem. Riding on a donkey borrowed from someone in the village, a tall Form Five boy played the part of Jesus. So tall that his feet almost dragged on the ground, he rode so awkwardly I feared that he might easily fall off. But much to my relief, he kept his balance. I watched the students lay their palm branches in front of the donkey as "Jesus" made his way to the dining hall. At the same time, from the opposite direction, a big group of girls came walking from their dormitory singing a rousing popular chorus, "We Are Marching Over to Jerusalem."

With everyone in the best of spirits at the end of first-term 1981 exams, the SU officers and I had organized this Palm Sunday celebration for the beginning of Holy Week. Relieved of their academic burdens, students took great delight in reenacting the familiar tale. Jesus dismounted the donkey, we all sang a song of praise, then everyone entered the building. At the front of the dining hall, several small folding tables had been set up to represent the booths of the moneychangers. Jesus upset the tables and then confronted the Pharisees in their hypocrisy. I stood up dressed in a makeshift costume, introduced myself as James the apostle, and proceeded to tell the story of the events of Holy Week—the Last Supper, the arrest, trial, and crucifixion of Jesus. Several times earlier in the term, I had done a couple of sermons in a similar way, telling a story from the Bible as though I were one of the characters. I found it surprisingly effective; the students had listened quite closely each time. Because classes ended in the middle of the coming week, we would not be together on Easter day, so we ended with a rousing song of praise for Easter. The song of hope made me think of the people in Namibia and South Africa living under the iron grip of apartheid. For the church in those places, surely the hope of the resurrection must have a potent meaning for them, giving them the confidence that the powers which held them captive did not have the last word, providing the hope that no darkness lasts forever. Lifting up the promise of new life, the students' enthusiasm and glorious singing made for an especially fitting climax to the morning.

MOREMI GAME RESERVE

Companions

Elaine, Sherry, and I had completed one full year in our African home, growing increasingly at ease with our surroundings. We welcomed and looked forward to the coming month-long term break. The school term ended on Maundy Thursday, and a special treat awaited us. Only a few of us expatriates remained on campus, all the African teachers having gone to their tribal homes for the term break. On Saturday, the day before Easter, seven of us packed up food, clothing, and camping gear, setting off for a two-day trip to the Moremi Game Reserve. It would be our first time in one of the game parks seeing a wide variety of African wildlife.

Carol Schaad had inherited an ancient, beaten-up Land Rover from her parents, who used it for many years in Angola and for the previous ten years in Botswana. It not only looked beat up and ancient, it had no indication of the miles put on it over all those years. A four-wheel drive vehicle, the Land Rover had a front cab and an open back like a pickup truck. Along with Carol, our other travel companions were Larry the farm manager, Mary Beth, and Torill Solheim, a young Norwegian woman who worked at a government project in Maun teaching crafts to young people unable to complete secondary school. Larry and Mary Beth had met Torill and invited her on the trip. All our gear and four of us rode in the open back and three up front. Out of the whole group, Carol and

Larry were the most experienced in Africa, each of them having picked up the traits of a calm patience and the ability to cope with all manner of difficulties. Having grown up in Angola familiar with African ways, Carol's experience often served us well, whatever the occasion. Ever conscientious in her responsibilities, she never hesitated to cheerfully offer help to those in need or express care for the troubled.

Always considered reliable, and quite knowledgeable both in his agricultural work and anything mechanical, Larry seemed capable of dealing with any situation without panicking. He had all our trust. A careful planner, he had his normal workday well-planned out, from his breakfast routine to his classroom teaching to the supervision of students and garden workers. A kind of slow smile would creep onto his face when he would be about to joke with someone. Others thought of him as sturdy, solid. He rarely ever raised his voice to anyone, his exercise of authority with the students coming through his character and obvious competence.

As we bounced along the rough, bumpy road for the three-hour drive to Moremi, the difficulties began almost immediately. The Land Rover began acting strangely, stopping and starting several times without warning. When it came to a halt and wouldn't start again, Larry got out and poked around until he discovered a bad connection to the accelerator. Somehow he managed to rig it up so it worked again, and we drove on. Arriving at the south gate to Moremi, we saw that the main road into the park had flooded, so we had no choice but to drive a couple of hours farther around the park perimeter to find another route to the campsite. When we finally entered the park, we discovered numerous places on the road with pools of water on them. I use the word "road" loosely, as it appeared as only two parallel ruts in the earth. Some of the pools seemed deeper than others and could have been hiding either rocks or deeper holes in the ground. So Carol, the tallest of our group, jumped out of the Land Rover, threw her sandals into the back, and with her long legs proceeded to walk ahead of us in her bare feet to check if the mud seemed too deep to drive through. We drove slowly behind. Each time she waded all the way through a deep spot, Larry put the vehicle into four-wheel drive and drove right through it, at times with water and mud almost as high as the wheels. The four-wheel drive saved us from getting stuck more than once. I felt thankful for Carol's self-assurance and Larry's good driving.

Animals Roaming

Soon after starting through the park, we spotted our first big sighting: a herd of thirty or forty elephants right alongside the road, the first big herd of elephants we had seen in Botswana and the first ones I had ever seen outside of a zoo. Many of them were taking mud baths. They didn't seem the least bit alarmed by us, but they began to wander off slowly as we passed by. Then we rounded a grove of tall trees, where two enormous giraffes startled us standing only about twenty feet off to the right. Despite their impressive size, they surprised me by seeming quite undisturbed by our presence. We also drove by numerous small groups of impala, the small graceful antelope so abundant in the reserve.

Campsite and Unwelcome Neighbors

In the early 1980s, several of the big game reserves in Botswana had no travel or tourist facilities of any kind—no gas stations, no shops, no restrooms. Nor were any villages nearby. That meant that we had to take everything with us, including extra fuel, drinking water, food, and all our camping gear. Luckily, Carol discovered that clean water ran in a stream near our campsite, where we could fill our water jugs, as well as go swimming. The campsite, an open spot with a few trees close by and a large open field of tall grass next to us, provided a lovely spot where we could relax and enjoy the good weather. A glorious sunrise greeted us each morning with a dazzling golden glow. Each evening we built a good fire and sat around it singing to the accompaniment of Larry's guitar.

One large tent had room for all seven of us. Carol assured those of us with little African experience that we had nothing to fear from animals as long as we slept in a closed tent. The other important safety precaution involved locking up any food in metal containers or in the cab of the Land Rover overnight, otherwise hyenas would come after it. Around sunset on the first evening, Carol and Larry decided to go visit some other campers they had noticed setting up in a grove of trees a bit more than a quarter of a mile away. The two came back after a while, shaking their heads with a pained look on their faces. The tragedy of apartheid had reared its ugly head. The nearby campers were South African Whites with the typecast attitudes, astonished to find that any of us actually liked living in Maun (i.e., with Blacks). One man asked Carol and Larry, "What's it like to live with them?" Taken aback by such an odd and offensive question, they answered, "Like living with neighbors."

Sitting around the fire after dark that first evening, a sudden animal roar sounded off in the distance. A bit dubious about how safe we were, Elaine nervously asked Carol, "Was that a lion?" "No, I don't think so. Might have been a hippo," Carol responded. We had just heard a hippo splashing through water not far from us. Not taking any chances, Elaine got up and announced that she would be going into the tent. The next morning, Carol approached her to say, "That was a lion last night. But he didn't sound hungry!" Elaine did not appear convinced.

Soon after we arose that first morning, a group of about twenty baboons came running through the grass in the field next to us, starting to pass by our campsite looking for food. Larger than I had realized, the baboons reached out with their hands to grab food from trees and other plants. Not shy at all, they stopped to sit on the ground and in a couple of small trees right next to the campsite, watching us as much as we watched them. They looked like a group of theater patrons waiting for the show to begin. Because we had seen almost no other visitors in the game reserve, I had a bit of a quirky thought, imagining a baboon going home later that day saying, "I saw seven humans today, Mom!"

Communion: Worship and Nature

On Easter morning, we wakened early and celebrated a sunrise communion service, using some of my home-made oatmeal bread. Then we set off for a long drive through the game reserve looking for animals. Carol coaxed Sherry into sitting with her up on the roof of the cab so they could be the game-spotters for us. We came upon a small herd of zebra, stopping to watch them frolic. More baboons also appeared at several spots along the way, wandering looking for food. Still farther along, six giraffe came strolling around a grove of trees, surprising us—and them. Numerous impala showed up in various settings throughout the day, so graceful in their high, seemingly slow motion leaps through the air. I kept thinking how fortunate we were to see all these natural wonders, sights that many people paid thousands of dollars to see when coming to expensive safari camps.

In the Okavango, we had to be wary of tsetse flies, carriers of encephalitis, or sleeping sickness. We had to be sure to swat away the big brown flies if they landed on our arms. Tsetse flies were not prevalent in the Maun area, so this was a new danger to Elaine, Sherry, and me. Initially we felt fear, but fortunately, the half-inch long flies were easy to spot and we could brush them off quickly.

Sunday evening as we all sat again around the fire, talking and singing, an overwhelming feeling of peace and contentment came over me, a sense of deep satisfaction with my life and the turn it had taken in coming to southern Africa. I sensed that whatever I did after living in Africa would surely involve enlargening people's worlds, helping them to see beyond the confines of their individual lives. Larry's repertoire included a wide variety of music, from the old gospel hymn "I'll Fly Away" to "Teach Your Children" by Crosby, Stills, and Nash, and Neil Young's "Heart of Gold." We all sang along, enjoying the night air and the valued companionship. In a kind of old-fashioned communication exercise, we shared with one another in a quite open manner the strengths we observed in one another. At one point, Mary Beth turned to me and spoke with real warmth and sensitivity. After all these years, I remember her words exactly. "I want to tell you that I appreciate so much the wisdom and insights you've shown in sermons and discussions. What you've shared has always been very meaningful to me."

I once heard someone on a radio talk show say that although the United States celebrates an Independence Day each year, we really also ought to celebrate a "Dependent on Others" Day. We cannot live without the help and the strengths of others. On the trip to the game reserve, the genuine satisfaction of true and honest friendship gave us a sense of connectedness, binding us together, each one knowing that we could count on one another in any difficulty. As the African proverb has it, "The one who has many friends is not caught by darkness on the road."

Troubles, Surprises, and a Final Treat

On our way out of the park Monday morning, on a road a short way off the main road, we drove through some deep water—and the engine stalled. After several attempts, it still would not start. I started to get a little nervous, because at the time we were in an area far from any village. With his usual calm confidence, Larry knew what to do. He listened for a few minutes, heard the sound of a motor, then ran out to the main road to try to flag down the vehicle going by. He came back a short time later, visibly frustrated and annoyed. The people in the car told him that they were "in a hurry" and did not have time to stop. We were all astonished. Out in the wild as we were, people regarded it unthinkable to refuse a call to help people who were stuck, because they could be stranded in the bush for days. The distinctly unhelpful travelers were the South Africans who had camped near us. They roared off in the direction of the Khwai River, which we knew to be flooding. Finding they couldn't cross, they turned around and came back. I heard them coming and ran out to plead with them a second time for assistance. Once again, they refused to do anything and simply drove off, not even bothering to offer to send someone to help—incredibly rude and unfeeling behavior.

To our good fortune, someone in the group recalled that a safari company called the Khwai River Lodge had its main camp a few miles away from where we sat stranded. Larry and one other of our group hiked to it and came back a little over an hour later with two men in a truck. The Khwai Lodge people brought with them a kind of spray that dried out the wet engine. They sprayed it a few times, and the ancient Land Rover coughed and came to life. Despite our protests, the two men insisted that we not pay them anything. So we set off once again, this time with Carol, Mary Beth, and Sherry sitting on the cab roof to get the last good look at any animals.

Several remarkable sights awaited us. First we spotted a waterbuck running ahead of us, a large antelope with beautiful dark brown fur. Even more exciting, a sable antelope bounded in front of us across the road. One of the most beautiful animals I have ever seen, the sable has sleek black fur and a pair of long horns that curve over toward the back of its neck in a graceful arc. We were awed by the sight. But best of all, and the real highlight of the whole trip, we came upon a big pride of lions who had made a kill and were just finishing their meal: a stout wildebeest. First we spotted a group of young lions and lionesses only forty yards or so off to the lefthand side of the road. Then a short distance farther, we noticed two large males lying under a tree, rolling over and waving their feet in the air, obviously playing and relaxing after a good meal. We stopped the car (but kept the motor running!) and took some pictures. The two big males rolled over again and stretched, almost as though they were showing off. As we moved a bit farther along, we saw two lionesses guarding the remains of the kill. Although they were a little closer to the road, we stopped again (with motor still running). One lioness came to her feet and glared menacingly at us, but we stayed still and she didn't move any closer to us. Someone nervously quipped, "It's a good thing we came along after they finished lunch!" We drove off quite slowly so as not to alarm them. Later on, other people at the school told us that we were quite lucky to see lions that close, an unusual occurrence.

Almost home, about fifteen miles from Maun, the Land Rover failed us once again, losing power and stopping after short distances. We stopped and started several times, until Mary Beth saw another vehicle coming behind us heading toward Maun. Hailing them, she got a lift back to the school to get Kelly Nare to come out with his truck. Elaine, Sherry, and I caught another ride with some hunters who had been up in the game parks for three weeks. They were all Batswana and very kind. One man gave his blanket to Sherry, tucking it around her to keep her warm. I couldn't help but note the stark contrast with the South Africans who had earlier refused to help us in any way.

22

The Circle of Life

BEGINNINGS AND ENDINGS

A Class Celebration

STUDENTS RELISHED THE OPPORTUNITY to celebrate the end of a school year. In mid-November 1981, having completed their two-week, high stress examination period, my Form One homeroom class felt more than ready to party. Two boys and a girl from the class excitedly asked me if they could hold their class party at our house. Elaine approved, and on a Friday morning eight students appeared at the house, carrying various food items and two large round iron cooking pots. More students arrived and everyone pitched in, a few building a fire in the front yard facing the river. It once again impressed me that they could use a single small piece of firewood about two feet long. Made of long-burning mophane wood, that one piece of wood burned for several hours, providing all the fuel needed for cooking meat and rice together in the two pots. As I witnessed so often, the wise use of scarce resources came easily to these students.

It surprised Elaine and me that even though everyone participated in the setup, preparations, and cooking, they all came garbed in their best clothes, the boys in shirts and ties, girls in their finest dresses. Four or five girls crowded into our tiny kitchen, mixing up and cooking delicious fatcakes, doughy bread-like balls in frying pans. Outside, boys and girls cut up large chunks of beef, throwing the meat into a cooking pot with rice and water. Into the other pot went many handfuls of corn meal, water, and sugar to make sweet porridge. A few other students, using a popular concentrate called Citro, mixed up gallons of orange drink. Lots of good cheer and a lively spirit prevailed as they all eagerly cooperated to make the party a success. Groups of four and five sat together, laughing and reminiscing about the past year.

Walking around, I talked with many of them, thanking them for being such hard workers throughout the year. Seeing them enjoying one another and cooperating so well, I felt pleased and satisfied with their sense of responsibility they had shown all year. Just prior to eating, one boy and one girl gave me a formal statement of gratitude on behalf of the class. "Mr. Christensen, our class thanks you for your guidance and for your prayers." Other students affirmed this with applause. It gratified me to have such a satisfying ending to my first full three terms of a school year.

Because we were well into the rainy season, fierce thunderstorms could pop up without much warning. Sure enough, one did, but luckily only after we enjoyed about two hours of time together. When clouds began to gather and an obvious storm loomed, they all quickly cleaned up the yard thoroughly, said goodbye with great appreciation to Elaine and me, and then took the two pots back to clean at the dining hall. Both Elaine and I were greatly impressed by how organized they were, not only in preparing the food and drinks, but also in their careful, thorough cleanup afterward.

Blessed Are the Poor

Just as the last students departed, a heavy, pounding rainstorm hit, filling the campus with mud and rivulets of water in the paths and roadways. By 1:00 pm, the fast-moving storm had passed, and a visitor knocked at the door. Steve Pabalinga had a message for me. "The funeral of the lady who died is at 2:00, and we need you to do it." The woman, from a very poor family who lived by the river just behind the school's garden, had died the day before. Steve and I had gone with the boarding mistress Mma Selema that afternoon to borrow a Land Rover from another neighbor family to pick up the deceased woman's body at the hospital. Being dreadfully poor, the woman's family had no way to get the body from the hospital to the family compound. At the time, I had not known that they were expecting me to conduct the funeral, so when Steve came soon after our class lunch, surprising me with the request, I had less than an hour to prepare for it.

The woman's nephew, a boy named Murunda, often wandered about the school grounds in a half torn-away jersey looking for work or begging. Members of the family dressed in ragged, threadbare clothing. I realized that Steve felt that we at the school needed to help a neighbor family so much in need. We drove out to the family's compound, in a low-lying area near the river, inevitably getting stuck in the deep mud resulting from the big downpour just an hour earlier. Several pickup trucks, a couple of Land Rovers, and a big, open-backed Datsun truck tried to make their way through the mud with me. Every one of the vehicles became stuck in mud at least once on its way into the family compound. Chaos ensued, with nearly a dozen men rushing back and forth between vehicles to push one, then another and another, out of the mud.

Finally, after all the vehicles made it to the area just outside the compound, the drivers all set their vehicles in position to leave for the burial ground. A small enclosure of reeds surrounded the entrance to the hut where the coffin lay. A few people went into the enclosure as two men brought the coffin out, setting it at the hut door. Everyone else gathered outside, and the funeral service began. Speaking solemnly in a quite formal manner, one member of the family acted as host, or master of ceremonies, introducing me as the moruti. I stood at the end of the coffin nearest the hut as my colleague Philip Monnaatsie interpreted for me in Setswana. I spoke briefly on the scripture from John 14: "Let not your hearts be troubled . . . I go to prepare a place for you." Speaking extemporaneously, I made up what I wanted to say on the spur of the moment—something I didn't often do, much preferring to be prepared when speaking to any group.

With the service at an end, I walked out to the compound entrance as family members moved slowly by the coffin to have one last look at their sister. The coffin had thin black cloth covering it, with cloth ties ready to hold the lid on tight. Two women began to cry loudly, leaning on other family members as they passed by the coffin. When they closed and tied the coffin shut, I walked slowly leading the procession as we all walked with the coffin to the cars and trucks. Responsible for leading the way to the cemetery, I had a family member sit with me in my car to direct me. The burial ground lay out in the bush, away from any roads, which made me a bit nervous about driving over rough territory. We drove along a sand track, my guide pointing the way. We would drive a short way, the man would point and say suddenly, "Turn here," often indicating thick areas of brush and small trees that looked impenetrable. Driving through and over numerous places of tangled shrubbery, bushes, and trees, all the while I hoped that nothing would damage the underside of the car.

Arriving finally at the burial ground, the people congregated around the open grave. Several men lifted the coffin from a truck and passed it to two men standing in the grave, who placed it in position. They climbed out of the hole, and the master of ceremonies turned to ask me a question. "May I conduct the burial service?" I noticed that he had a Setswana worship book, so I readily agreed. As he said the words, "Ashes to ashes, dust to dust, earth to earth," he and I each threw a handful of sand onto the coffin. Other men of the family then began shoveling sand into the grave while everyone joined in singing hymns. Two men at a time used the two available shovels. They worked at it for a time, then two more would take the job, continuing until the grave had been filled. As the sand fell onto the coffin, the two women who had broken out crying earlier did so again. Four other women took the two aside and sat down on the ground with them to console them.

As I watched the men shoveling the sand into the grave, I recognized that there must be a sense of finality and common loss when many people take part in filling the grave. Glancing at the faces gathered at the gravesite, it seemed to me that more than a few of the people were thinking, "They'll do the same to me one day." Family members began to leave, each one coming to me, shaking my hand and expressing their appreciation for my presence, some with wordless smiles, others with warm words of thanks. I thanked Philip and Steve for their good help, then made my way back to the main road by following other vehicles. Otherwise, I would surely have gotten lost.

A Completed Circle

All the way home, events of the entire day ran through my mind, as I thought of the wholeness of life I had experienced. The day began with a vibrant, lively gathering of youth celebrating a marker along the way to adulthood, and it ended with an acknowledgment of a life lived and the finality of death. It seemed to me that I had carried out a pastor's work through the whole circle of life in that one day. The youth demonstrated potential and a hope for the future of the nation. They had no certainty about what the future might hold for them, but it seemed full of promise. The poverty-stricken family, even with a quite different sense of uncertainty, showed a solidarity that sustains people even in the poorest and most desperate of circumstances. Finally, Steve Pabalinga had helped me to see once again that aiding one another is not a burden, but a communal responsibility, and that the connections we find with one another are what save us from fear, despair, and hopelessness.

23

The One Who Stumbles, Falls Forward

—African Proverb

SHERRY'S SCHOOLING

In the Village

EARLY IN OUR TIME in Botswana, Elaine discovered an English Medium
Primary school in Maun that could take Sherry as a Standard Seven student. Since they used English as the medium of instruction, it seemed
like a good fit for her. Sherry attended the school for the 1981 school year,
glad to be out of the house and meeting other children. Initially, she had
to overcome her shyness—and the experience of numerous other students expressing their fascination with her hair and her pale skin. They
wanted to touch her hair, a distinct discomfort for a shy eleven-year-old.
But she made at least two friends in her class: Tracy, a Motswana from the
village, and Shraddah, daughter of an Indian teacher at our school. At the
end of the year, Sherry came out at the top of her class with a first-class
pass in all her Standard Seven examinations. That meant that she qualified for a place in the first year at Maun Secondary School.

Knowing that the coveted places in any secondary school were hard
to come by, I felt a little uneasy about Sherry taking a spot in our school
in place of a Motswana child. I thought perhaps others might think
this unfair. So I consulted Philip Monnaatsie, whom I often relied on
for advice and counsel. Highly respected by others on the staff, Philip
had always been straightforward and helpful to me. After expressing my

concern to him, he answered with grace and wisdom, assuring me that people accepted this situation as normal. "You and Elaine are providing a great service to the school and to our nation. No one begrudges Sherry a place in the school. It's fine!" I felt relieved and could rest easy after this expression of gracious African hospitality.

Secondary School

Sherry entered our school in January 1982, happily joining her friends Tracy and Shraddah, who had also been admitted into the first year class. Including her Dutch friend Neeltje, Sherry had thus made friends with girls from three separate continents. Tracy and Sherry shared a four-by-eight foot garden plot for their Agriculture class with Larry Kies. She still had some problems with other students teasing or harassing her at times, but she learned to be bolder in dealing with them in her own way.

One afternoon after she had joined the school tennis team, the boys' and girls' teams were practicing together. Their coach, Carol Schaad, had left the practice for a short time, so one of the boys took her absence as an opportunity to annoy Sherry with teasing and some hair-pulling. Sherry grabbed one of his arms, pulling it up behind him and holding him tightly in an armlock, a wrestling move learned from her Uncle David back in Pennsylvania. Mightily surprised that a girl could do this to him, the boy didn't know what to do. When Sherry finally released him, the other boys teased him unmercifully for being bested by a girl. He apparently felt embarrassed and humiliated. Sherry did not tell Elaine and me about this until some months later, ending her description of the incident with, "Don't worry. He's never bothered me again." I never worried about her standing up for herself after that.

Although Sherry attended the Form One class in our school during the 1982 school year, Elaine worked with her on home schooling materials from the United States for eighth-grade English and math. We wanted Sherry to be completely ready to enter ninth grade when we returned home. At times it proved to be an ordeal for both of them. Sometimes, tears flowed when both Sherry and Elaine became frustrated by a seeming inability to explain or understand math problems, especially word problems, such as, "If a car left point A traveling at fifty mph . . ." But Elaine met this challenge with her usual determination and perseverance. All the effort paid off, as they finished the coursework in both English and math early in 1983. Sherry would be ready to enter ninth grade when we returned home. All three of us were pleased and relieved.

In an attempt to be creative, Elaine began using the acronym CLIMB for the home school: the Christensen Learning Institute of Maun, Botswana. Hearing the proposal, Sherry responded by rolling her eyes. Inspired by another idea, Elaine once proposed with a straight face that she and Sherry should create a school yearbook for CLIMB. The cover photo would be Sherry standing on a ladder reading a book. Sherry responded with a grimace of disapproval and another eye roll. The yearbook never materialized.

OBSTACLES IN NATURE

Although Sherry had academic obstacles to overcome, the natural world also presented problems. For part of each year, we had to use mosquito netting over our beds at night to protect from the danger of mosquitoes bearing malaria. We had also been provided chloroquine pills to take regularly once a week as an additional preventive measure. The mosquito netting hung from a central point in each bedroom ceiling, draping down all around the bed and tucked in on all sides.

But mosquitoes were not the only threat. One evening, after we had been in bed and were almost asleep, Sherry called out, "Mom!" Elaine answered, "What's wrong?" "There's a bat on my mosquito net!" Elaine turned to me saying, "Rich, go help her." I went off to the rescue, stumbling a bit as I stepped out of bed to put on my slippers. Grabbing a long-handled broom from the hallway, I went to face the enemy—the bat, not Sherry. When I flipped the light on, Sherry and I could see the netting lying loose on one side—she must have gotten out of bed after the net had been placed—and that the bat hung, not on the outside but on the inside of the net, right at the top where the netting gathered to its narrowest near the ceiling. Startled, Sherry quickly scrambled out of the bed as I held up just enough of the netting to allow her escape. We quickly tucked it back in so the bat could not make his escape. While Sherry ran to the other bedroom and stayed with Elaine, I began poking at the bat with the broomstick, knocking it from its perch. Pulling up the netting on one side, I swatted at the bat to get him out. But when it came from under the netting, it flitted hastily around the room and out into the hall, evading all attempts to catch it. Elaine helped me look, but we lost track of it after a search, so we decided we would let it be for the night and went back to bed.

In the morning, Elaine had a surprise when she found the bat clinging to the side of the blender on the kitchen counter. Disconcerted by the sight, she called out to me, "Rich, you have to come here!" I came and captured it with a towel, opened the screen door, and threw it out of the kitchen. Later that morning, Elaine related the tale of Sherry, the mosquito netting, the bat, and its capture to Ketoni, one of the secretaries in the school office. Ketoni asked, "How big was it?" Elaine replied, "Oh, it wasn't very big." Ketoni then surprised Elaine with the response, "Oh, the big ones are really good! You cook them for a couple of days and they taste good." When Elaine related this comment to me, we agreed that we had made the right choice setting the bat free.

ELAINE'S DETERMINATION

Money Troubles

Along with her efforts teaching Sherry, Elaine also showed her determination and perseverance in her work as the school treasurer. At the end of September in 1981, she had gone through several months of struggle with the job because the school finances were not in good shape. The government had not sent as much money for the students' food as the school expected by mid-year. At the time, it cost over 50,000 Pula a year to feed all the students, and she needed at least that much to pay all the bills and have the accounts balanced by the end of the year. I could tell it worried her. Fortunately, she managed to put off some payments for a short time and finally received the government subsidy which made the accounts come out right. This became another reason for her to work to get a Botswana citizen to be hired and take over as treasurer in the following year. Needing to do the work on the eighth-grade English and math with Sherry added to her motivation to have a new treasurer.

Resignation and Resistance

Early in 1982, she attempted to carry out her plan. She wrote a letter of resignation, explaining her intention to work with a newly hired person throughout the third and final year of our assignment. But to Elaine's great surprise and dismay—or rather, disgust—the American principal called her into his office to inform her that, in his view, this move amounted to dereliction of her duty. He told her that he had written a letter to the UCC Board for World Ministries in New York saying that she had "abandoned her responsibilities as a missionary." He recommended that the UCC Board reprimand her and insist that she do her job. Elaine tried to explain patiently to him her sensible rationale for her actions, but he wanted to hear none of it. He refused to see that she had chosen the wise path of working herself out of a job and arranging for a person native to Botswana to assume the work. Remaining adamant that Elaine had failed at her assigned task, he sent the letter to New York.

A few months later, the principal retired and left Botswana, never having made mention of any directive from New York. Confident that she had done the right thing, Elaine felt sure that the mission board would see her actions as appropriate and wise. The American missionary Bishop Ralph Dodge, the last White Methodist bishop in Zimbabwe and a founder of Maun Secondary School, had written some years before about this very issue.[1] He insisted that by failing to turn over more control and resources to indigenous churches, American and European missionary projects were doomed to go the way of colonial governments. All attitudes and practices of White superiority needed to be utterly rejected. Elaine understood this and agreed. Exactly as she had suspected, no reprimand letter from New York ever came. Admiring her for her courage and persistence, I viewed the whole matter as one of many illustrations of her strength of character.

1. Dodge, *Unpopular Missionary*, 160.

24

Beauty Will Save the World

—Dostoyevsky[1]

END OF TERM TASKS AND REFLECTIONS

Finishing the Term with Hopes for the Future

Toward the end of the first term of the 1982 school year, Elaine and I came to the same conclusion: we needed a vacation. Both of us realized that we were getting mentally tired. Since Sherry had the same break, we planned a lengthy trip to Zimbabwe. We planned to camp along the way, visit Victoria Falls, drive through the massive Wankie game reserve, and spend a day or two in Bulawayo, Zimbabwe's second largest city.

By April 7, the final day of the term, I had almost finished grading the massive pile of 325 student exams. I had forty left to grade. A tedious task as always, the work took four more days to complete all the grading, record the grades, and make any comments regarding students' progress or difficulties. A single, all-too-brief space on each student's record provided this comment opportunity. Seeing the remarks of other teachers on the records, I noticed that most teachers took this commenting task seriously, a few others not so much. One of our colleagues had the habit of writing exactly the same blunt (and most unhelpful) comment on many of his students' records: "Wasting time and money."

With my heavy task of marking done, I then tackled another job, one assigned to me by the Ministry of Education. Because a few of the

1. Dostoevsky. *Idiot*, 432.

189

nation's secondary schools were still phasing out the old RE Bible Knowledge curriculum, the Ministry had asked me the year before to compose and grade the old national Junior Certificate exam in Bible Knowledge (still used in a few schools) for 1981 and 1982. Writing the exam each year—an all-essay exam with numerous options for students—took me three full days. I couldn't repeat the same exam two years in a row, so each year presented a daunting task. In essence, the exam involved memorization of many Bible stories and teachings rather than understanding and applying them, which meant that the newer curriculum we had begun to use seemed much more fruitful and effective for the students as well as more fun for the teacher.

As I finished the task, carefully wrapping the exam in thick paper and material to ensure its security, the thought struck me that I had been in the role of a teacher for two full years, something I had never expected. With a feeling of real satisfaction, I realized how much I loved teaching. A flash of memory came to me of an almost-forgotten conversation with my college academic adviser many years before. When I asked him to write a recommendation letter for me for admission to seminary, he responded, "I'll be glad to do that for you. I do know, however, that frequently when students are thinking of seminary, what they really want is to be a teacher." I dismissed the thought at the time, but sitting with my packet of exams in front of me on the table, I realized he had discerned for me my true calling. Surely I had more to learn, but it struck me that I had come to recognize some real strengths. I could relate to the students well and get them to talk in class. Illustrating the lessons with stories from history and my own personal experience seemed to bring out students' enthusiasm, curiosity, and understanding. Half a world away from home, I had found success and a calling in that African setting.

By the middle of the second year in Maun, I had become so enthralled with teaching that I decided to seek a PhD in church history and teach in a theological school. An article I had written, entitled "Reflections on African Community," had been featured in December 1981 by the national magazine, the *Christian Century*—my first published writing.[2] After contacting Dr. Bard Thompson, a noted church historian at Drew Theological School in New Jersey, inquiring about study there, I received a reply strongly encouraging me to apply for doctoral study at Drew.

---

2. Christensen, *Reflections*, 1325.

A Helpful Friend

While discussing this dream of mine with others in our weekly Bible study group, someone asked if I knew the German language, a skill I would surely need for doctoral study, especially in Protestant Reformation studies. Marion then surprised me with a kind offer. "I'd be glad to give you some lessons," she said. "I've studied German quite a lot and lived in Austria for a several years." I happily accepted, so the following Sunday afternoon she arrived at our house to begin with a series of tasks for me. Sitting down in a chair facing me, she started by giving me a number of verbs to learn, then explaining pronouns and word order. She seemed quite eager to teach me, saying, "It will be good for me to review it all."

In previous months, Marion had come to our house occasionally to play a game of chess with me. A few days after my first German lesson, Elaine suggested that for the next one, we invite Marion to have dinner with us. She readily agreed, arriving at our door the next Wednesday, armed with a good appetite and several pages of vocabulary for me to learn. Elaine and I had both been concerned about her because Carol (one of her housemates) had informed us that Marion had been in poor spirits the previous week or two, staying in her room in the evenings rather than being out talking with the others. So after my lesson I walked her down the short lane to her house, asking her along the way if anything troubled her. "No," she replied, "I feel quite good, especially since Karl wrote me recently," referring to a German who had taught in Maun two years before. We talked a bit more, but I didn't press her any further, then she went into the house.

The next day Carol told Elaine that Marion had come in the night before in high spirits, sitting down with Carol and another teacher to talk for quite a while. Carol thought it likely that teaching me German would be really good for Marion. The news made us glad. We knew that Marion had a bit of a cynical streak and appeared at times to reject others' care for her, often acting suspicious of other people's motives and seeing the negative in others. On the other hand, she did serve as a valuable asset to the school, generously giving time after the regular school day to help her science students with extra chemistry experiments.

ZIMBABWE

Starting North

The Russian author Dostoyevsky once wrote that "beauty will save the world." Upon seeing the magnificence of Victoria Falls in the recently war-torn Zimbabwe, I thought he could be right. We traveled to western Zimbabwe in mid-April, soon after the beginning of the dry season. We invited Marion to come with us, along with a new Peace Corps teacher named Edith Young. We packed our Chevy Nomad tightly with two tents, assorted camping gear, food, clothing, and the five of us. A short while before we left, we said our fond goodbyes to Mary Beth. She had finished her three-year term as a missionary for the Board for World Ministries, having done excellent work as an English teacher as well as becoming a good and trusted friend. Always conscientious and compassionate, her competence and sense of dedication had been obvious and valuable to the school. She readied herself to set out on her way home, and we were sad to see her go. The school constantly experienced many comings and goings, with so many people being on short-term assignments or contracts. Saying goodbye had become a frequent activity for us. With hugs all around, we wished her well and set off on our respective journeys, Mary Beth south to Gaborone, us north toward the border with Zimbabwe.

Traveling with us in their car were the Jains, an Indian family working in Maun. Mrs. Jain taught English at our school, while her husband worked for the government offices for the Northwest District. They had two daughters, the older being Sherry's friend Shraddah. We set out on the road to the northeast, driving 200 kilometers to the tiny village of Gweta, where we were given overnight lodging by a kind British couple who owned a small shop and ran the telecommunications link for that area. The next day we took the long trip north to the Chobe River and Chobe National Park, the game reserve along the river bank. It turned out that we were fortunate to have two vehicles. Only a few kilometers down the road, the Jains had a flat tire—and discovered a broken jack in their trunk. So we all stopped, I dug under a stack of equipment to find our car's jack, pulled it out, and we changed the tire. It would not be the only time we were all grateful for companions on the road.

Camping at the Chobe River

The Chobe River bordered the section of Namibia known as the Caprivi Strip. Soon after entering the park close to sundown, an enormous bull elephant ran across the road directly in front of the car, startling us with its speed. Because April marked the beginning of the dry season, nothing would stop the thirsty big bull from his rush to the riverside. Collective sighs of relief came from each of us, knowing that if we had arrived at the spot just a few seconds earlier, we would have likely been bowled over and suffered serious injuries. After starting up again, two fierce wild dogs, some of the most vicious creatures in southern Africa, ran ahead of us on the road for a short way. Their sharp teeth and strong jaws made a small number of these animals capable of taking down a wildebeest for food.

Soon we stopped to camp at an inviting open spot off to the side of the road. The Jains had already found another campsite in a different section of the park. We were pleased to find a beautiful spot for ourselves, with the unusual (to us!) sight of a wide, deep flowing river close by. Petite monkeys moved all around us in the nearby trees, and the sounds of elephants and other creatures filled the evening air. Just as we had observed on our earlier venture to Moremi, large baboons sat in the low branches in the trees nearby, still and silent, watching our every move as we set up camp. Some of the smaller monkeys scampered around the area occasionally like mischievous children, looking for snacks to grab and trying to sneak off with them.

Camping in southern Africa required some special equipment. Most people carried with them sturdy metal boxes with secure, tight-fitting lids, necessary because animals searching for food during the night had to be prevented from stealing it. The metal containers were called "hyena boxes," after the most notorious night-time thieves and scavengers. Our food containers were not quite as sturdy as they needed to be, so we quickly realized that we had to keep all the food locked securely overnight in the Nomad.

Marion had brought a small tent for her and Edith, so they set that up while Elaine, Sherry, and I pitched the new tent we had bought recently. Before it got completely dark, we drove around the park for a short while, seeing quite a few elephants and almost being trampled again twice when huge elephants charged out onto the road in front of us. After the second near-collision, we thought it wiser to go back to the campsite and settle down.

Edith Young, a soft-spoken New England woman in her fifties, had decided in retirement to offer her services as an English teacher somewhere that had a teacher shortage. She came to Botswana with the Peace Corps and became a welcome addition to the faculty. We were happy to give her the opportunity to travel. Marion had been in Africa for some time, teaching science at a girls' secondary school in South Africa before arriving in Maun. She planned to go with us to Victoria Falls and then go off on her own to visit Harare, the capital city.

As we sat by the fire in the evening air, Edith suddenly said, "Oh, look!" She pointed to the Nomad. On the hood where we had carelessly left two pears, a monkey sat there happily munching on one of them. The moment I rose to chase him off, he quickly scampered away with his prize. Monday morning we packed up all our belongings and drove across the border into Zimbabwe. It had been exactly two years since the seven-year war for independence had come mercifully to an end and majority rule had become a reality. Several of our students in Maun had fled from the chaos and agony of the fighting, traveling only at night to evade the Rhodesian security forces and then finding refuge in Botswana. We knew their stories and were aware of the immense sadness and profound relief of the people when the war finally ended. We agonized over many of the stories of danger, torture, and killing. I recalled Barbara Moyo, who fled the war at night through lion country to reach Botswana, praying the twenty-third Psalm the entire way. For years prior to liberation, 5.5 million Shona and Ndebele people (the two predominant tribes) had been under the strict control of 250,000 Whites, descendants of British colonizers who had named the country Rhodesia. Traveling there as we were, we all felt a sense of wonder and real relief that we were able to move around the country without the threat of war. This later turned out to be a mistake.

Mosi-Oa-Tunya

Traveling for our first time in the country, known for its lush green hills, forests and wildlife, we were eager to see its reputed beauty and the post-war circumstances of the people. Some distance from the town of Victoria Falls, we could hear the steady roar of the falls. At first we did not identify the sound, but as we came closer and the sound grew louder and louder, we were in awe of the power of the falls. We stayed at a lovely campground, the five of us occupying two small rondavels, round cottages with thatched roofs. Early in the afternoon, we walked the short hike to see the falls.

The ancient African name for the falls is Mosi-oa-tunya, or *the smoke that thunders.* It is an apt description. The Zambezi River runs through Zambia into Zimbabwe, becoming a mile-wide torrent of water by the time it arrives at Victoria Falls. The falls are higher than Niagara, water crashing over the edge of a deep but narrow gorge more than 350 feet to the riverbed below. Because of the narrowness of the gorge and the enormous impact of that much water cascading into it, huge plumes of spray flew upward into the air, rising higher than the level of the river above. A pathway ran all along the midway point of the opposite wall of the gorge so that visitors can see the falls up close and be overwhelmed by their beauty and power. All along the way, the spray frequently flew up into the air and came down on us like rain, soaking us thoroughly as we walked the path. The first time it hit us, we laughed at the sudden drenching on the warm day. It caught us several more times as we wandered down the path and back. As the afternoon went on, high in the spray above us the sun's rays began to create the most lovely and vivid rainbows. Double rainbows formed several times, creating a magnificent sight, overwhelmingly beautiful. The sight dazzled us all. It remains to this day the most astonishing and magnificent natural scene I have ever experienced, a heartstopping, beautiful sight.

"Ugliness has the capacity to destroy life; beauty has the power to save the world." I thought of this quotation from Dostoyevsky, who knew personally more than a little about suffering and evil. When faced with the beauty and magnificence of the falls, I felt a jarring sense of dissonance knowing that in the same country people had so recently and tragically endured the brutal ugliness of war. Perhaps it may not be at all obvious that beauty could save the world. But the war had ended, and I had recently heard from an RE teacher from Zimbabwe that the very RE curriculum we used in Botswana had been instrumental in reconciling Black and White students in the newly-integrated schools in Zimbabwe. When a new community comes into being, unexpected creativity can arise in surprising ways. Adversaries can become friends, people open their eyes to new possibilities, and creativity can emerge from the mix. The beauty of reconciliation and the new sign of community seemed to me a hopeful sign in that still-uncertain nation.

Back at the end of the falls nearest the old Victoria Falls Hotel, we could walk across a bridge that overlooked a section of the falls called the Devil's Cataract, where gushing water seemed to leap over large rocks and then spread out like a huge fountain bubbling over and then dropping into the gorge. On the other side of the bridge stood a statue of David Livingstone, the first European to see the falls. In later years, the statue became a source of contention because of its obvious reminder of British colonialism.

We enjoyed the evening braai (South African lingo for barbecue) at the restaurant on the terrace at the front of the old Victoria Falls Hotel. A very relaxing place, it featured good food and a wide veranda overlooking a beautiful view of the terrace and falls. Part of one day Sherry spent with the Jains visiting a crocodile camp, then she returned to enjoy the falls with us. We stayed at the campground nearby for two nights, mesmerized each day by the splendor of the falls. Marion then departed for her own trip to Harare to the northeast, and the rest of us re-joined the Jain family, who had been staying elsewhere for a short time. We all set off on the road southeast for the Wankie game reserve, located some sixty miles along the road to Bulawayo, the second-largest city in the country.

Travel Trouble

Twice on that stretch of road, we were stopped at roadblocks by soldiers of the Zimbabwe army checking cars for weapons. They were trying to catch dissident rebel soldiers of the minority Ndebele tribe (who had opposed Robert Mugabe's Shona people) known to be in that area. Obviously the reconciliation had not gone well everywhere. Even though the soldiers were very polite to us, the experience gave us all an uneasy feeling.

Driving through that area of Zimbabwe, with its lush, thick wooded surroundings, we remarked on the great difference between this land and the sparse, open spaces of the Kalahari Desert. At a point on the good paved road about eight miles from the town of Wankie, I suddenly felt an alarming bumping. Thinking it meant a flat tire, I pulled off the road and stopped immediately to check it out. When I looked, no flat tire. Then Elaine pointed to the right rear tire. Four of the five bolts holding the tire onto the axle were missing, so that the wheel had almost completely come off, being held on by one remaining bolt. We thought we were in real trouble, fearing that perhaps we would not be able to get it repaired because the bolts had actually been sheared off. To our great relief, the Jains, who had been ahead of us some distance on the road, realized that we were not anywhere close behind them. They turned back and after a few minutes driving found us. We decided that I would go into the town of Wankie with them to find a garage. With Mr. and Mrs. Jain and their two children, only one of us could fit in their car. Elaine, Sherry, and Edith stayed with our car in the midday heat, having no idea how long it might take for me to return. They rigged up a bit of shelter from the sun by unfolding a bed sheet and attaching one end to the roof and another corner to the open side door. Then they took turns sitting under the sheet, swatting at the constant barrage of insects in the warm air. A stone collector, Lainie took advantage of the delay by seeking and discovering several colorful stones she had never seen before.

In Wankie, we quickly found a garage, a busy place run by three White Zimbabweans, brothers with a long Greek name I cannot recall now. When I explained our breakdown, one of the brothers said, "You'll have to wait about an hour until we finish some work. Then we'll take a tow truck out." So I waited. I noticed that the owners spoke easily with their Black employees in fluent Sindebele, the language of the dominant Ndebele people of that area of Zimbabwe. I knew that at least one-third of the Whites had fled Zimbabwe for South Africa when the war ended and majority rule began, so I thought that this might possibly be one of the small glimmers of hope for the future.

After saying our grateful goodbyes to the Jains, who were setting off for another part of the country, I waited almost an hour. Then one of the brothers motioned to me to follow him, and we both climbed into the cab of the big tow truck. By the time we made it back to our car, it had been almost a two-hour wait for Elaine, Sherry, and Edith. I worried about them sitting there in the heat of midday. No traffic at all had passed their way during their wait, as the end of the war had yet to bring much of a tourist trade back. Mightily relieved to see us (and to escape the insects), they quickly took down their shade sheet. With the tow in place, we all got into the roomy cab of the truck and made our way back to the garage in Wankie. We had no choice but to stay in an expensive hotel for the night, making it necessary for us to send a telegram to request a wire transfer of money sent from Maun. Elaine did note one bright spot—in the hotel restaurant, she had what she called the most delicious rice pudding she had ever eaten.

The next morning we walked down the street to the garage. To our great relief and delight, we found the car fixed. The mechanic had somehow removed all of the pieces of the bolts and replaced them, using extra washers to be sure the new bolts would be tightly secured. We thought ourselves quite fortunate that we were able to get it fixed at all. Not only that, but the charge for towing and all the repairs came to just $48 (Zimbabwe). To say that we were greatly relieved would be a vast understatement.

Talking with one of the owners, the chief mechanic who had done the work with another employee, I asked him how long he had lived in the country. He replied with a smile, "Born here." When I commented, "Zimbabwe is certainly a beautiful country," he responded, "There's no place like it on earth." Perhaps another small indication of hope for the future of the new nation, I thought at the time, although I knew well that many Whites still remaining in the country had much more negative attitudes toward majority rule.

Game Viewing

Resuming our journey, we backtracked a short distance to the entrance to the Wankie Game Reserve. A thoroughly beautiful, well-kept park, famous for its wide variety of wildlife, the reserve featured a paved road running for over sixty miles right through the middle of its grounds. Numerous dirt side roads stretched out from the paved road into all areas of the park for game-viewing. At the main camp, little round thatched-roof chalets rented for $4.00 (Zimbabwe) a night, two people to each chalet. Edith and Sherry took one, and Elaine and I another. The price pleasantly surprised us, each chalet being equipped with running water, two beds, and a refrigerator. As an added bonus, a park attendant came at each mealtime if we asked, bringing wood and preparing a fire for us in the outdoor cooking spot. A store on the campground sold various kinds of food and supplies.

The first afternoon we drove out through a section of the park, spotting a small herd of elephants at a waterhole, some zebra, and several types of antelope, including a waterbuck, a sturdy bushbuck, and numerous graceful impala. We also encountered two enormous giraffes, a warthog, and a hippopotamus lumbering across the road not far ahead of us. At one point, as we rounded a wide bend in the road, four rhinoceroses blocked the roadway completely. Hesitant to get very close, we stopped, waiting until they moved before we thought it safe to drive on. Rhinos are notoriously unpredictable, so we had no intention of provoking them.

In two days there, we took several long drives around the park. On a Friday evening, the last time we went out to view animals, about eighteen miles from the main camp, we came upon a special viewing platform near a waterhole. It stood at least fifteen feet high, with a wooden stairway to the flat viewing platform. We were the only people there. As we arrived, three adult elephants drank from the waterhole. Upon climbing to the top, we began to take photos. But after only a few minutes, a herd of at least forty elephants marched over a hill nearby and surrounded the waterhole. Awed by the impressive sight, we kept snapping pictures as the elephants moved around. We had never before seen that many elephants together in one place. Sherry and Elaine spotted a baby elephant who we estimated couldn't have been more than a week old.

Bulawayo and an Odd Birthday

Reluctantly, we left Wankie the next day, a Saturday, and drove to Bulawayo, camping in a lovely park in that city of 300,000 people. We loved the city—beautiful, clean, and well-kept, with wide streets lined with lovely bright blue-flowering jacaranda trees. Completely forgetting the southern African practice of closing all businesses for the weekend at noon on Saturdays, we searched and searched for a nice place to eat, because that day I celebrated my thirty-seventh birthday. But we could find nothing until we spotted a rather dismal-looking takeout restaurant with the peculiar name The American Fried Rooster. It seemed to be the only place open in the entire city. In spite of it not being the most desirable of birthday dinners, we decided to purchase some chicken and eat it in the car. Then we returned to the campground to spend a comfortable night. Sunday we visited the national museum, and then poked around the big downtown shopping area on Monday morning.

We loved Zimbabwe, and found the people very friendly and open. We left there hoping that the war-torn country had finally found peace. We left Bulawayo Monday afternoon, stopping to enjoy the gracious hospitality of our friends Tony and Betsy Jones in Francistown, then made the long trek home to Maun the next morning.

Home and Tragic News

Four months later, sitting at the supper table in Maun, we heard a report that the US embassy in Zimbabwe had issued a recommendation that American tourists not travel either by car or rail between Bulawayo and Victoria Falls because of the danger of dissident soldiers attacking and/or kidnapping people. The same evening we heard that report, a BBC World News bulletin came on the radio saying that six British and Australian tourists in Zimbabwe had recently been kidnapped near Wankie, most likely by the dissident members of the same smaller opposition army that had been a rival to the triumphant group of Robert Mugabe. We remembered the military checkpoints we had encountered and suddenly realized that those six tourists had been traveling on the same stretch of road outside of Wankie where we had broken down.

At this news, Elaine and I grabbed each other's hands, and a shiver went through us, a combination of fright and relief simultaneously. We knew very well that if something like this had happened to Elaine, Sherry, and Edith after I had left them for two hours on the road with the hobbled vehicle, the horror would have been unspeakable. At the time, we had thought the war for Zimbabwe ended, despite having been stopped at the military checkpoints. We had, naively, not given much thought to the threat from hostile dissidents. But we were wrong. The threat had been quite real.

The six tourists were never seen again.

25

The Road to Freedom Is Full of Thorns and Fire, Yet Happy Is the One Who Follows It

—AFRICAN PROVERB

A HISTORY OF TRAGIC CONSEQUENCES

Background

SOME OF THE MOST momentous decisions in history carry within them the seeds of their own destruction. The institution of African slavery tore millions of Black Africans from their families and their heritage, resulting in tragic divisions and destructive racism. South Africa's institution of apartheid, the system of rigid segregation of the races, guaranteed from the beginning the result of poisonous division and rebellion, resting as it did on fear and an extraordinary ignorance among Whites regarding the vast majority of the population.

South Africa presented a strange paradox in the 1980s. White citizens enjoyed one of the highest standards of living in the world, the economy being built on cheap Black labor. Large numbers of Blacks lived in poor, crowded townships with no paved roads, inadequate medical care, and high unemployment. A place of extraordinary beauty had been coupled with the ugly, rigid oppression of apartheid, the strict separation of the races held firmly in place by a vast and ruthless security system.

The nineteenth-century roots of this oppressive system lay in the worship of the Dutch Reformed Church, church of the Afrikaners, descendants of seventeenth-century Dutch settlers on the Cape of Good Hope. Even though baptism brought Black and White alike into the church, by the 1850s racial prejudice had become so entrenched that Black members faced an edict to sit in the back of the church and receive the Lord's Supper last. In a further act of segregation, because of many Whites refusing to worship with Blacks, the church decided to permit separate services of the Lord's Supper. This led to the splitting of the church into separate bodies for White, Colored (mixed race), and Black people.

That tragic denial of the unity of the body of Christ led to the theological justification for the movement resulting in strict separation of the races in virtually all aspects of South African society—the apartheid system that made South Africa a pariah in much of the world. The National Party, Afrikaners who claimed that the Bible supported racial segregation, came to power in 1948. They embedded apartheid in the whole legal structure of the country, forbidding even marriage to a person of a different race. Separate schools were mandatory. Businesses had separate White and non-White entrances. The government created the concept of "separate development," setting up so-called "homelands" for each tribal group in the society. Laws passed in Parliament reserved the major portion of land for Whites. The notorious Group Areas Act of Parliament designated small regions of the poorest land as the Black homelands, each one with a population smaller than the total White population of the whole nation. In the well-worn political strategy of divide and rule, the government thus set tribe against tribe, making each one dependent upon the government and in competition with one another.

Like nineteenth-century American slave holders, Afrikaners manufactured elaborate biblical and theological defenses of racial superiority, tying those defenses together with a fierce opposition to the threat of atheistic communism. They claimed, for example, that the tower of Babel story in Genesis indicated that God willed that people of different races be separated and spread over the whole earth. Any opponent of apartheid became accused of supporting communism, deemed a threat to both the religious and social structures of South African society.

Non-Whites were forced by law to carry the hated pass, called by the people a "dompass", a term with a meaning exactly as it sounds. The pass designated where the bearer had permission to live and work. Because the Black homelands lacked economic strength and employment opportunities, thousands simply moved elsewhere and worked illegally. They moved to areas near cities to find employment, illegally occupying barren land and building pitiable homes out of scrap metal, old fencing, mud, and wood. They lived there in a situation of mind-bending uncertainty. On the one hand, the government grudgingly accepted the illegal housing because cheap labor made businesses more profitable. But when traveling almost anywhere, workers could easily be arrested for violations of the pass laws. In the 1980s, South Africa averaged more than 200,000 arrests annually for pass law violations as the government attempted to control where people could live, work, and travel. In that era, apartheid appeared both paradoxical and tragic, a demeaning and violently oppressive system supported by the Afrikaner Nationalist Party and the Dutch Reformed Church leadership.

Refusing to See

The Afrikaners appeared to me as a group of people with no foresight at all, digging a hole so deep that they were unable to climb out, and then continuing to dig deeper. It all seemed so senseless to me, an extraordinarily graphic illustration of the obstinacy of a people utterly convinced of their own righteousness and superiority. Afrikaners seemed totally unaware that a different path could be possible. They lived with a kind of blindness, a refusal to see other people as human beings with the same hopes, dreams, and desires as anyone else.

Botswana President Seretse Khama once encountered a South African government official at a diplomatic reception in another country. Khama had a reputation as a leader who commanded respect and could work well with others. The South African posed this observation to President Khama: "If we had more Blacks like you in South Africa, we would have far fewer problems." Khama looked the man directly in the eye and replied, "There are many, if you would only look."

In South Africa, Blacks and their poor living conditions were out of sight of most Whites. Whites were barred by law from staying overnight in a Black township. Blacks, with few exceptions, could not live in designated White areas. What could this possibly produce, I thought, except an inevitable uprising? Certainly I could not be alone in thinking this. More than a few people assumed that the whole system plunged headlong toward a violent and bloody end.

FIRST VISIT

Surgery and Apartheid Face-to-Face

Our first visit to South Africa occurred when Elaine needed surgery unavailable in Botswana. The mission board instructed us to go to Johannesburg, so we arranged through church contacts to stay with Rev. Peter
and Barbara Anderson, a pastor and his wife who lived in Kensington, a
White area of the city. Peter served as pastor to separate White and Black
congregations, both churches members of the United Congregational
Church of Southern Africa. Peter told me that in the Black congregation,
everything had to be translated into Zulu, Xhosa, and Sotho, because all
three languages were represented in the congregation. It made for very
long worship services. He also participated in another Christian charismatic group that was racially mixed and lively in its worship, a small sign
of reconciliation in the midst of apartheid.

Peter, his English wife Barbara, and their two children were gracious hosts. Each morning at seven, before she went to school, their
eleven-year-old daughter Susie brought cups of tea to our bedroom.
Either Peter or Barbara drove us wherever we needed, all the while attempting to explain the intricacies of South African society. Noticing the
thick walls with broken shards of glass embedded on top built around
so many homes in the White neighborhood, I commented on how high
they looked to me. Responding with a tinge of bitterness and resignation,
Barbara said, "Yes, and they're getting higher."

Elaine went for surgery to a medical clinic for Whites only in the
posh area of Sandton in another part of the city. The doctors were all
White, the aides and janitors all Black. When Elaine spoke with the
doctor, he surprised her by saying that there would be no charge for the
surgery. They treated missionaries for free. The Board for World Ministries would have paid the costs, so we were pleased to be able to spare
the Board the expense. But it gave us a small glimpse into the privileges
Whites enjoyed in South Africa.

While Elaine recuperated from the surgery, Peter Anderson invited
me to a Sunday evening Bible study group with eight White parishioners.
The group, all South Africans of English background (that is, not from
the Dutch Reformed Church of the Afrikaners), tried to justify the apartheid system to their foreign visitor. One member casually explained to
me, "Oh, it'll be a hundred years before the Blacks are ready to vote. They

need to be better educated." I hesitated to get into a confrontation, realizing how thoroughly the culture in which we are formed is ingrained in all of us. So I remained silent, listening. But I felt dumbstruck, suddenly confronted with nineteenth-century ghosts making spurious, discredited arguments from long ago. Quite similar arguments had been made by North American slave owners in an attempt to prove that Blacks were better off under slavery. I could not stop thinking that these people sitting with me in the Andersons' dining room surely must have had nineteenth-century English working-class ancestors who had been denied the right to vote with the very same argument. "Look how ingrained the racism is in this society," I thought. I listened, hesitant to confront them directly because they seemed so clearly entrenched in their societal norms. They likely would have viewed me as a strange, uninformed, and naive foreigner with no real understanding of their situation. I failed to raise any meaningful challenge to them that night. But witnessing this racism embedded so deeply, I did begin to perceive more acutely than ever before how the racism in America arising from slavery had embedded itself in American culture.

Reflection

Not until months later did I think more about that evening Bible study and remember my own upbringing. Born in 1945, I grew up as part of a generation aware of the dangerous and deadly consequences of racism and war. But it took me a long time to see the attitudes that were embedded in my own life, a long time to recognize that one of the most destructive enemies we can have is our own narrow-mindedness and lack of vision.

Growing up in Baltimore in the 1950s and early 1960s oblivious to the systemic racism rampant in the city, I had little awareness of the situation until the last couple of years of high school. Only then did I discover that movie theaters, restaurants, and public amusement parks in the city banned my African-American teammates on the high school track team. Living in a security blanket of absence of information, I had been clueless about this for a long time. Never mentioned by anyone around me, the mindset and circumstances of racial segregation were not only ingrained in the society. They also lay within myself. I came to recognize this very slowly.

August 28, 1963, I sat in my living room in Baltimore, Maryland, watching on television as Dr. Martin Luther King Jr. delivered his famous "I Have A Dream" speech a few short miles from my home. The day before I had called the local office of the Congress of Racial Equality to reserve a seat on their bus heading to the March on Washington. But to my great disappointment, my Dad had other ideas. He refused to let me go. Rumors of expected violence linked to the march ran through the news. "There's going to be trouble there," he said. Being introverted and not much of a rebel at age eighteen, I reluctantly stayed home.

When I think about my feelings that day and on into my early adult years, I recall vividly the stirrings in my mind and heart, feelings of yearning, uneasiness, and uncertainty that I could not articulate at the time. Earlier that summer, a "Whites-only" amusement park in Baltimore had been the scene of a protest march met by angry Whites, who spit upon the marchers and tossed firecrackers at them. The civil rights movement filled the newscasts that spring and summer. I now know that as I listened to Dr. King, the feelings arising in me went something like this: "Oh my God! I have to become a different person, someone who can face these challenges with more courage and creativity. And I don't know how to do that." Many of my contemporaries in the year 1963 had the vague soul-disturbing feeling of not knowing where to turn.

A few months later on a November afternoon in my first year of college, someone came up to me as I walked to a two o'clock math class and said, "Have you heard the news? The President's been shot." It seemed in the days after Kennedy's assassination that the whole world had undergone a seismic shift. I wrote in my journal that night, "something unbelievable happened today." Tragically, I doubt if anyone would write anything like that today. The Kennedy assassination acted as my generation's 9/11. It shook up everything. The world seemed very different. That unarticulated uneasiness grabbed hold of me again. It took a long time for me to break out of the bonds of tentativeness and introversion and find my own voice.

A few years later in the summer of 1971, I had taken the position of assistant pastor and minister to students in the town of State College, the central Pennsylvania home of Penn State University. It proved to be a time of life, energy, and uncertainty for many, including me. The campus had experienced several anti-war protests and incidents of racial conflict over the two previous years. I had over a number of years given frequent expression to my self-righteous liberal contempt for the racism I saw as obvious in others. I lived, to put it plainly, almost totally blind to my own ingrained racism.

Until I met Bob Simmons, and came to grips with a powerful lesson about racism in the United States.

In the late sixties and early seventies at Penn State, the student body numbered almost thirty thousand. Only 300 were African-American. The Black Student Union on campus, well-organized and filled with a fierce determination, challenged racism on the campus and in the local community. During the 1971 summer term, someone had the idea of holding evening group discussions on race in a large student activity center. The BSU and several campus ministry staff people arranged for small, racially mixed groups of twelve to fifteen students to be formed, each one moderated by two co-leaders, one African-American and one Caucasian. A young Black student named Bob Simmons and I co-lead one of the groups.

Large numbers of students showed up for the evening. We did some group exercises to help us understand prejudice and its effects in our lives. The BSU members gave the rest of us an education about the Black experience in America: how it felt to be put down in many ways, to be ignored in classes, to see Whites stiffen with anxiety and fear when Blacks walked nearby, what it felt like to be dismissed as less important than others. Then we began the discussion groups. Bob, a BSU vice-president, sat with me as co-moderator of our group. In another group immediately to our right, the BSU member began his group's session by launching quickly into a real tongue-lashing of the White students in his group, indicting them for their conscious and unconscious racism. He gestured forcefully, like a prosecutor listing heinous criminal acts. In our group, Bob sat quietly, but with an intense look about him. He leaned forward slightly, head cocked a bit to the left, hand against his cheek, listening carefully. At a pause in the conversation, he finally spoke, with a tone of voice and a look on his face communicating a sense that we were about to hear the unvarnished truth, truth that we needed to hear. Pointing his finger one by one at each White person in the group, he said, "Don't let anybody ever tell you that you are responsible for slavery. You're not! But I'm telling you that if you perpetuate the attitudes of the slaveholders, then you are just as guilty as they were."

I remember almost nothing of the rest of the discussion that evening. But I had heard something I needed to hear and have never forgotten. Memories, long ignored, came back to me. Some years before, watching the summer Olympics on television, I had noticed three African-American male athletes competing in one of the track events. The thought that had entered my mind at the time went like this: "Where are all the real Americans? Aren't there any in this event?" That is, why no White people? But how could I have thought this? I couldn't be racist—or so I had believed. Shocked at this revealing memory of my own prejudice, for the first time I had a beginning realization of the pervasiveness of racism. Bob Simmons had driven home to me how deep-rooted racism could be in myself as well as the wider society.

Blindness Prevails

The South Africans I encountered in the Andersons' Johannesburg kitchen were so immersed in the apartheid system that they had convinced themselves of their superiority, accepting the givenness of their circumstances. But I had grown up in segregated Baltimore, unable to recognize the tragic racism in my own hometown or in myself. My life had been embedded in my own culture, just as those South Africans were surrounded by and embedded in theirs. I started to understand that to refuse to see things as they really are can be one of the worst forms of blindness. The tragedy is that sometimes that kind of blindness has no expiration date.

To many of the students in Botswana, I and other Whites represented the tragic and bitter history of colonialism and the racism which accompanied it. I came to realize that racism had to be battled not only in apartheid South Africa or in American society, but within myself as well. I recalled again the common African saying: *To be a human being is to know that by carrying one brick you can contribute to the building of the world*. I had to learn to teach in such a way as to uphold the human dignity of every person. Although having much to learn, I wanted to be able to carry my one brick. My education continued in Botswana and in later visits to South Africa.

26

The Light Shines in the Darkness . . .

TRAVEL TO THE ASSEMBLY

Delegate and Driver

MY SECOND VISIT TO South Africa occurred as a result of an entirely unexpected invitation. In mid-1982, the Rev. Meshach Serema, general secretary of the Botswana Synod of the United Congregational Church of Southern Africa, delighted me by appointing me as an official Synod delegate to the annual Assembly of the UCCSA, scheduled for the second week in July in Kimberley, South Africa. But upon visiting the UCCSA office in Gaborone in mid-June just prior to an RE committee meeting, I discovered that I had an additional assignment. When I walked into the office to check out details for the Assembly with Jean Fischer, the Synod secretary, she surprised me by announcing that I had been appointed driver of one of the mini-buses carrying some of the delegates. So that I could be sure of my responsibility, she explained that the last time she took a trip to South Africa with Whites and Blacks in a bus together, the police stopped them and searched the bus. She had no need to say what I immediately realized—that I needed to be extraordinarily careful driving to make sure the police had no obvious cause to harass us.

The UCCSA, a multi-racial denomination, had members in five countries: Mozambique, Zimbabwe, Namibia, Botswana, and South Africa. Intrigued to think that I would be in the midst of people entangled in the struggles for justice and survival in that region of Africa, I looked forward eagerly to the trip. Fourteen other Batswana delegates and I would make up the delegation from our Synod. Because the Assembly had been scheduled during our school's second term, I arranged for my colleague Peter Mudiwa to take over my classes for the time I would be away. I then spent almost a week in the evenings preparing the lesson plans for Peter to use.

The Long Discomfort

Early on Wednesday, July 7, I set out on my journey. The plan involved an all-day bus trip from Maun to Francistown, then the overnight train to Gaborone, where I would meet Rev. Serema. Travelers could not always count on the bus to arrive in Francistown in time for the one overnight train, so I had given myself two full days for the trek to Gaborone. If I missed the Wednesday evening train, I would have a twenty-four-hour wait for the next evening's train. The delegation did not plan to leave the capital city until Friday morning, the ninth, so either way, I would arrive in time.

The best-laid travel plans in Africa often get sidetracked, and it started for me at the very beginning of the journey. Elaine drove me to the departure point for the daily Maun to Francistown bus, normally scheduled for a 7:30 am departure. However, we discovered that day that the bus had broken down. No bus would be going to Francistown that day. Elaine and I then drove around Maun seeking transportation for me. After about forty-five minutes of searching, success—the government's district council office informed me that one of their large, open, flat-bed trucks would be leaving "soon." In that part of the world, "soon" could mean twenty minutes, or four hours. They instructed me to wait on the main road which ran past the gate of the secondary school, and the truck driver would stop there for me.

Elaine drove me back to the school, dropping me off at the gate about 8:40. I sat on my suitcase, holding a small cushion I had brought with me and waited at the side of the road. The truck finally came at 10:40. Piled haphazardly on its long flat bed were huge boxes, wooden crates, several large metal cooking pots, four mattresses, two men, and a woman. Two male drivers sat up front, sharing the driving. No room for me up front, so I had no choice but to sit on the open back. One of the men on the back reached down to take my suitcase and then gave me a hand to pull me up onto the truck. Seeing almost nowhere to sit that looked inviting, I moved around to the middle section of the flatbed, where the mattresses were tied together, lying on their sides. I perched on a big suitcase, leaning against the mattresses, with my cushion underneath me. I soon became very thankful for that cushion. Having nothing to hold onto, I didn't want to think about what could happen if the truck were in an accident.

I had also brought along a pullover knit hat, which I immediately pulled down over my head as far as possible to save my head and ears from a severe sunburn. When the truck started moving, I found that I had a Hobson's choice: I could face to the rear and get a sunburned face, or I could face front and get wind burn. I chose the wind, which stung more than it should have because the drivers raced across the desert at an incredible rate of speed, arriving at our destination in six hours. The drive normally took eight. Six hours at high speeds bouncing around on a rough road took a toll on my side and back, and I have been forever grateful that I've never had to travel like that again.

On the bright side, we arrived in Francistown about ninety minutes before the train departed for Gaborone, plenty of time for me to get something eat and buy my ticket. I had a decent sleeping berth on the train, but my sore back gave me a rough night of fitful sleep. At 5:30 am when the train pulled into the Gaborone station, I staggered out of the station, suffering from exhaustion and a pounding headache. I caught a taxi to the hotel in the central mall. Spotting nothing open—not the hotel, no shop—for two hours I sat on a bench outside the hotel because I had nowhere to go. Feeling about as miserable as could be, I dragged my suitcase up to the UCCSA office at the other end of the mall, only to discover the main building door locked. Luckily, after a few more minutes, someone came to unlock the door, whereupon I went straight to the restroom and almost vomited. Meshach Serema had just come into his office, took one look at me, and drove me to his home for the obligatory cup of tea. He then drove me to my host home for the overnight stay before we began our long drive to Kimberley.

Unexpected Kindness

To my great surprise, my hosts were the Mokama family, the Attorney General of Botswana, his wife, and young son. Mr. Mokama, a prominent member of the UCCSA, lived in a beautiful home between the Chinese embassy and the home of Botswana's President. I felt a bit overwhelmed, having had no idea that I'd be staying at such a fancy place.

They kindly offered me a delicious breakfast of egg, toast, cereal, and tea, and then let me collapse in the guest room bed for two hours. It felt wonderful. The soft bed became a marvelously comfortable contrast with the painful discomfort of the previous twenty-four hours.

ON TO SOUTH AFRICA

On the Road in South Africa

The next morning, Meshach Serema collected me from my Shangri-La, taking me to the meeting place for the traveling delegation headed for South Africa. Fifteen of us left Gaborone about 9:30 for the trip to Kimberley. Martin Morolong, a pastor in the group and one of the tutors for the Botswana Theological Training Program, drove a mini-bus filled with most of the delegation. I drove Meshach's Toyota Hi-Lux pickup with all the luggage in the back. I, a White man, prepared to enter apartheid South Africa with fourteen Black colleagues. It dawned on me along the way that Rev. Serema had most likely asked me to be a driver because a White man would have far less chance of being hassled by South African police.

My fellow travelers had warned me of the possibility that border police might search the vehicles and ask a great many questions, but I really didn't have any idea what else to expect when we crossed the border. To my surprise and relief, no drama occurred at the border post. We entered by way of Bophutatswana, the so-called "homeland" for Setswana speaking people in South Africa. Only Black officers were on duty. No one searched our vehicles. No one asked us more than a simple question about our destination. We passed through with ease. Meshach then made it clear that I had to stick strictly within the speed limit. We drove almost 600 kilometers that day, stopping briefly for lunch in Mafeking, Bophutatswana's capital. I spotted a familiar sight and pulled right in to it—a Kentucky Fried Chicken. I hadn't seen one in a long time.

Embedded Racism

Arriving in Kimberley around 7:00 pm, we promptly got lost in the maze of a big city. Martin finally figured out the proper route, and we arrived at the home of Rev. Solomons, a leader of the Colored (mixed-race) community who had made housing arrangements for us in the homes of church members. No other possibilities existed for overnight accommodations. No hotel would take us. I realized that housing all of the delegates to the Assembly must have been an elaborate and vexing chore. I walked into Rev. Solomons' home, trailing several of my Batswana colleagues. After a few words of greeting, the pastor turned to me with what seemed to me an odd question. "Are you alone?" he said. Puzzled, I somewhat hesitantly responded, "No, I'm with my fellow delegates here." With a trace of exasperation in his voice, Rev. Solomons said, "No, no. I mean, are you the only White?"

Suddenly I became acutely aware of the fact that race determined everything in South Africa. Racial division had been planted so deeply in the society that these categories pervaded almost every circumstance. To an outsider like me, this seemed tragic, sad, and almost incomprehensible. By law, my fellow travelers from Botswana had to stay in the Black township outside the city, but I as a White could not legally lodge there overnight. So I couldn't stay with them. I drove the Hi-Lux with the luggage to the Black township, dropped off their bags, left my fellow delegates there, and drove back to the Solomons home. The pastor had arranged for me to stay with a Mr. and Mrs. Corns, one of his church families in the Colored neighborhood of Kimberley. Strangely enough, I had a roommate for the week—a Black pastor from Capetown named Edgar Bukashe. Edgar came from the Xhosa people, that tribe and the Zulu being the two largest in the country. I say "strangely" because it made no sense at all to me. As a White, I couldn't stay in the Black township overnight, but a Black pastor and I could stay with a Colored family in the city. Edgar explained to me that the church had most likely obtained special permission for our stay from the local authorities. "What a crazy country," I thought.

Race consciousness dominated life in South Africa. Every person had a classification, one of four possible: White, Black, Colored, or Indian. Blacks usually lived in townships outside the cities, the townships having no paved roads with small houses and shacks. Coloreds and Indians lived in their own separate areas in the city. Whites usually lived in more plush neighborhoods in their areas.

Gracious Hosts

The Corns family, very kind people with a very small house, showed us gracious hospitality right from the start. As soon as we arrived, the parents and the two sons quickly began to move several chairs and a table out of the room they had planned for us. They dragged beds and other furniture into the room, then put up a blanket over the open doorway for our privacy. After a sound sleep that night, we awakened on Saturday morning to the sound of Mrs. Corns knocking on our door frame shortly after 8 AM, holding a tray of tea for her guests. She had brought this to us just prior to leaving for her job for the day. Edgar and I enjoyed our tea and stayed in our beds a bit longer, then crawled out from under our piles of blankets somewhat reluctantly when we were summoned to a huge breakfast of eggs, mounds of sausage, bread, and more tea. We were in no hurry—the UCCSA Assembly did not begin until late that afternoon.

Sitting at breakfast, I asked Mr. Corns if, by chance, he might know of a shoe store close by. I thought I should take the opportunity while in South Africa to find a good pair of shoes. My host smiled and said, "I'm a shoe clerk." Without further comment he picked up the telephone, calling someone he knew who might be able to get me a pair of shoes at factory price. No luck. So he sent me with one of his sons to search for shoes. At the first place we visited, I found quite a nice pair of comfortable brown shoes for a 33 percent discount. African hospitality continued to impress.

AT THE ANNUAL ASSEMBLY

The Gospel of Reconciliation

The Assembly's opening session began late Saturday afternoon at St. Cyprian's Anglican Cathedral, an extraordinarily beautiful stone structure with a notice on the carved wooden doors that read, "Being a Christian Church, this Church is color-blind." Meeting in the cathedral's large auditorium, a racially mixed fellowship of almost 200 people gathered together from five countries in southern Africa. I discovered that the accents of some of the Colored pastors grated on my ears and caused me to experience an initial visceral dislike of them. Embarrassed at my reaction, I realized once again how easily prejudice could arise and how quickly superficial matters could divide people.

The opening business session began with a brief constituting statement and a prayer in the Afrikaans language. The Rev. Joe Wing, Secretary of the UCCSA, proceeded to the order of business with that year's moderator, Rev. Andrew Julies, presiding. I found it oddly comforting to see that the same kinds of administrative hassles, parliamentary procedure arguments, amendments to amendments, and stacks of documents are universal at church gatherings. ("You will find this report on the pink page marked 2B in the green folder.") As an experienced church conference attendee from North America, I felt right at home. One bit of British influence I appreciated came twice each day the Assembly held sessions. No matter how heated the discussion became, or how incomplete the business of the body, promptly at 11:00 am and 4:00 pm the moderator would halt the proceedings with the announcement, "It's time for tea." I admired their priorities; nothing had priority over teatime.

That first evening the Assembly celebrated the Lord's Supper together. We heard a powerful sermon from Andrew Julies preaching on the fourth chapter of Exodus. Moses, responding to God after God has told him to lead the Israelites out of Israel, objects: "Suppose the Israelites do not believe me? What shall I do if they say that you did not appear to me?" God replies, "What is that in your hand?" The text records that the staff Moses held became a snake, and God instructs Moses to use that sign to prove to the people that the Lord has sent him. The preacher went on to say that we in the present moment should not lament our meager resources or apparent lack of power, because that showed a lack of faith. "We hold something in our hands and hearts, the Word of God, which is a weapon more powerful than any other." He cited the example of the feeding of the five thousand in the Gospels, when Jesus showed the disciples that what little they had would be enough. He cited the story of Elisha the prophet in 2 Kings, when Elisha and his servant were surrounded by the Syrian army. Elisha prayed, "Lord, open his eyes that he may see." The servant's eyes were opened and he saw the Lord's chariots of fire all around. Elisha spoke, saying, "Those who are with us are more than those who are with them."

Faith and courage spoke there in the midst of the power and dominance of the South African government's apartheid policies. Moving and inspiring preaching, the words of the sermon called earthly powers into question and spoke with hope for Christians and others openly opposed to the government and the tragedy of its policies.

During the worship, just prior to the Lord's Supper, the moderator and secretary called special guests before the whole Assembly to greet them. I didn't know that I would be called up front, but they read out my name, had me come forward, and introduced me to the Assembly with a warm embrace from Andrew Julies.

Worship included hymns in three languages: English, Afrikaans, and Setswana. At the close of worship, just after the benediction, the Bible, the communion vessels, and the offerings were taken from the altar and carried out of the cathedral at the head of a procession of the whole body, a symbol of the fact that the church entered the world with its true strength and nourishment. It served as a way to proclaim, "The resources of the church may seem meager, but they are enough: the Word of God's grace and reconciliation, the elements of bread and wine, and the gifts of the people."

Leaving for our hosts' home, my Xhosa roommate Edgar and I proceeded to get thoroughly lost once more in the maze of downtown Kimberley. No GPS being available in those days, it took us a while to find our way back to the house, but we finally made it back to the right place about 10:00 pm.

More Powerful Preaching

Sunday morning Edgar and I attended worship at St. Joseph's UCCSA, Rev. Solomons' congregation. We lost our way (again!), so arrived a bit late. We slid into a pew in the back of the sanctuary just in time to hear an extraordinarily powerful sermon by a White South African, Dr. John DeGruchy. A well-respected professor at the University of Capetown and former Moderator of the UCCSA, DeGruchy stood in the pulpit, a tall man with a dark brown beard. He spoke of names and their importance. "Some names strike fear in people's hearts," he said, "while others make us smile when we think of someone we love or admire." His text was Phil 2:5–11: because of the crucifixion "God has highly exalted [Jesus] and given him the name that is above every name." He told the story of Andrew Melville, one of the sixteenth-century Scottish reformers, preaching before King James of Scotland. "Your majesty," Melville had said, "There are two kings in Scotland, King James and King Jesus, and King Jesus is higher than King James." There is a power higher than the government, De Gruchy said, "the God who spoke to Moses, the God who showed himself to us in Jesus Christ, a God who wants people to be free. It is the task of Christians to say that the nation is not God. It is the task of Christians to say that there is a name which is higher than the name of any nation." It struck me forcefully that an enormous difference lay between the hearing of the word in apartheid South Africa and hearing the same text expounded in the United States of America. In the South African context, this word from the preacher spoke in a powerful way to people caught in the rigid oppressiveness of apartheid. A feeling arose in me I had never felt before, a feeling of witnessing an enormous shift, a sign of hope and assurance that the apartheid system could not endure. Knowing that many people had been arrested by the security police simply for protesting verbally in public, I couldn't help but speculate that DeGruchy must have been aware of the line that could not be crossed in public speaking.

Edgar Teaches Me

Back at the Corns home that afternoon, my education about South Africa continued in a talk with Edgar about some facts of life in the country. We each sat on our beds as he explained some of the circumstances of Black life in South Africa. "My son is a qualified accountant," he said. "Not long ago he had a job interview with a firm in Capetown." The young man had taken a test, had the interview, and seemed to have excellent results. The White interviewer then gave him the news. "Your results are very good, but we're sorry we can't hire you. We have no office you can work in." Edgar then said, "In plain words, he meant that they had no employees who were willing to work with a Black man." I thought how his son might have reacted: did he feel humiliated, or did he react with anger and disgust, or perhaps stoically, knowing how commonly this situation occurred? Edgar further explained that Blacks could not legally qualify for many jobs, so some Blacks would break the law by changing their names from African tribal names to those sounding like Colored family names. But in Edgar's words, "I could not do that, and I would not even let my own son do that. I'm a Black man, and I'm proud to be Black. I must suffer with my people." He said this with a sense of firmness rather than resignation, a sense of endurance rather than submission. I remarked to him at one point, "Color dominates everything." Edgar quickly responded, "You've got it—exactly."

The Witness of Bishop Desmond Tutu

That evening I witnessed still another demonstration of the faith, hope, and confidence of Christians in that troubled land. At the Kimberley city hall, a large congregation of worshipers from the surrounding area joined together for a joyful and inspiring evening worship. The Anglican Bishop Desmond Tutu preached the sermon. Not long before that evening, his passport had been revoked by the government, largely because as head of the South African Council of Churches, he acted as a spokesman for many opponents of apartheid. He took as his theme the meaning of worship. Tutu read the texts of warning about false worship and fasting in Isa 58, and the great message of reconciliation from Eph 2:11–22. "The church exists," he said, "not for like-minded people to meet together, not for the purpose of getting everyone into a frazzle doing good works, nor for mysticism, but for God." He declared that if we do not come away from our worship of God with more sensitivity to those who suffer, then our worship is false and corrupt. "How can we remain unmoved," he said, "when people are uprooted from their homes and dumped like rubbish into areas where people starve and children drink water because they have nothing else with which to fill their stomachs?"

I admired Bishop Tutu, not only because of his courage in openly opposing government policies and practices, but also because of his fearlessness and sense of humor. His faith burned brightly in his refusal to speak of people as enemies, insisting that even the president of South Africa (who had publically attacked Tutu harshly numerous times) lived under God's grace and mercy.

At the close of worship, a candle-lighting ceremony followed. Depicting Christ as the world's light, representatives of every region and synod lit their candles from the central candle, representing the Light of the World. As each candle-bearer returned to his or her region/synod with the lighted candle, each group invoked God's help with the prayer,

> Come, Holy Spirit, Fill the hearts of your faithful people,
> And kindle in us the light of your love.

Worshipers then carried the lighted candles, symbols of the undying flame of God's love, in procession out of the city hall into the streets to the strains of the old hymn:

> Clear before us through the darkness
> Gleams and burns the shining light[1]

After the evening worship, Edgar and I went out to the car. As we passed the back of the building, we came upon Bishop Tutu and his secretary. Edgar and the bishop greeted one another in Xhosa, their common heritage. Edgar introduced me to both the bishop and the secretary. Tutu, a man short in stature but with a big heart full of courage and love, along with a hearty laugh, shook my hand and greeted me with a genuine warmth. He made a point of giving a great deal of credit to his associate, saying to us, "She runs the diocese while I'm running off elsewhere." Just two years later, Desmond Tutu would be awarded the Nobel Peace Prize for 1984.

A Good Spirit Prevails

The delegates at the Assembly, while having deep and sometimes contentious discussions on the struggles of the church and the society, demonstrated their own forthrightness and courage, all leavened with a sense of humor. They reminded me of an experience as a chaplain in the emergency room of a city hospital many years earlier where I had witnessed medical staff joking with one another in between frantic action to treat drug overdoses, heart attacks, and knife wounds. Like doctors and nurses in the emergency room, the Assembly held on to a sense of humor in the midst of the violence, insecurity, and chaos swirling around them. One afternoon the Assembly heard a report from the churches of Mozambique, living in terribly difficult circumstances: dire poverty, high unemployment, food shortages everywhere, no soap, sugar, or bread to be had. Many pastors had not been paid for more than six months. The churches there made a request, not for food aid, but for donations to purchase donkeys for their pastors. Rugged terrain in parts of the country made it impossible for pastors to travel to many villages by car, so the donkeys were a necessity for pastoral care. Delegates began popping up at various spots in the Assembly Hall to offer money for donkeys. "There's

---

1. Ingemann, *Pilgrim Hymnal*, 387.

one in the second row," said the moderator as a delegate rose to offer as-sistance. "And there's an ass over there. And another ass in the fifth row!"

In another bit of whimsy, a pastor sitting by me in the session told me the tale of one of the Zulu pastors who had once been in a Synod meeting listening to another pastor pray in Setswana. When the prayer ended, he turned to the Setswana speaker, asking, "Do you really think God understands that language?" To which Rev. Joe Wing, the UCCSA Secretary, interjected, "Oh, don't worry. I think heaven will be like the United Nations—simultaneous translation, only with better results!"

Fear Intervenes

During a scheduled lengthy afternoon break one day, I had a chance to wander around the city of Kimberley. Walking in a busy shopping area, I saw a demonstration of the kind of power that the police exercised. I wit-nessed a White police officer grabbing a young Black boy who appeared to be about twelve years old, handling him roughly. Holding him in a tight grip on the boy's upper arm, the officer picked him up, threw him into the back of a police van, and slammed the door. When the officer turned to look around him, his eyes and facial expression struck me. He had an angry look that spoke volumes. I could read in that face, "I've got you and we're going to keep you under control!" His eyes flashed a look of anger mixed with fear. Knowing that many of the opponents of apartheid had lost their fear of the government, I suddenly realized that the fear had been transferred to the apartheid regime. The thought struck me that no system based on the attempt to induce fear could survive for long. In that startling display of fear and anger, in that single face, I thought I observed the beginning of the end of apartheid. A little more than eight years later, the government released Nelson Mandela from jail, and free and fair elections brought majority rule to South Africa. It may be the only time in my life I ever accurately predicted the future.

My Education Continues

After that experience at the shopping area, I stopped at a gas station to fill the tank. A Black attendant stood ready to pump the gas for me. He addressed me as "Boss," always speaking the word with a smile and an underlying tone of mockery. "Sure, Boss, I'll fill it up for you. Thanks,

Boss." He could tell from my accent and from the Botswana license plate that I did not live in South Africa. I felt annoyed and uneasy about being addressed this way, so I blurted out, "Oh no, I'm not a boss." As soon as the words left my mouth, I knew they were utterly senseless. I could not have felt more foolish—what a stupid thing to say! I could not change my standing in that society. I stood there, without question, as a "boss" in that circumstance, no more able to withdraw from my position as a White man in that society than the attendant could escape from his embattled and grim situation.

I felt I had been slapped hard on the side of the head, suddenly realizing that no matter what I might think, or how I viewed myself, I held within myself a phony self-righteousness. I dwelt there as a White man in the apartheid society. I couldn't shed my identity. Moreover, to imagine that I could ever fully understand what it meant to be a Black person, in that society or in my own back home in the United States, would be impossible. I had privileges that Blacks and other people of color did not have in South Africa. I could enter places non-Whites could not. I had a US passport and a visa that allowed me to travel anywhere I wished in the country, while millions of Blacks were forced to carry passes with them restricting where they could live or travel. In reality, "boss" accurately characterized me. My identity as a White man placed me in a superior position, no matter my noble ideals of racial equality, no matter how much I wanted to deny it. To protest that I didn't actually have that status could not have been more absurd. The man ignored my statement, kept sarcastically calling me "Boss" as he finished filling the tank. Slowly I learned to see the world a bit more clearly.

For my students back in Botswana, living in a democracy had given them a kind of confidence. They knew their democracy to be a reality. They were free of the oppression that still existed in Namibia and South Africa. They knew they would not be arrested simply for being Black and in the wrong place. The South Africans I met in Kimberley also held onto a real confidence, a confidence rooted in their faith that the apartheid system did not have the last word, that the oppressors finally had no power.

The Power of Faith

Over and over again at the Assembly, the courage and inner strength of so many people left me in awe. I met people who had been jailed, sometimes for months in solitary confinement, still holding on to a firm assurance that God brings down the powerful and delivers the captives. It felt like being an eyewitness to extraordinary historical events, one of the remarkable times in history when seemingly powerless people stood up to what appeared to be impossible odds. I sat in the midst of people far braver and bolder than I had ever been in my sheltered life. The feeling gripped me that I witnessed what faith and courage really meant.

In the next few days, I spent much time at the Assembly asking questions and listening to other Assembly delegates, hoping to learn as much as possible about the lives and the faith of the people. I wanted to know how pastors coped with the poverty and cruel injustices that they faced every day.

In conversation with two young Black pastors, I learned more of the destructiveness of the government's homelands policy. The two told me of the tragedy of people being dumped in the Ciskei homeland without any work available, with no roots or contacts to rely upon because they had never lived there before. Because the Ciskei, one of the two homelands set aside for Xhosa people, lacked economic opportunity, many people dwelt there with no hope and no realistic future. As I had already noted, this seemed stunningly absurd to me. People with no hope either fall into despair or fierce anger, a recipe for unrest and rebellion.

Several pastors explained something called the Internal Security Act to me. Under that law, the government could detain anyone indefinitely without bringing any charges against the person and without ever bringing him or her to trial. People held under this act were often kept in solitary confinement. Christians held like this kept their strength up by being comforted and sustained by the words from Ps 46, "Be still and know that I am God," and by Jesus' promise in Matt 28, "I am with you always, even to the end of the age."

One morning at the opening devotions, a Zulu pastor read the passages from Isa 52–53 regarding the suffering servant of God. The pastor commented that the text had a certain connotation to many South Africans who spend their lives in servant jobs. "My people don't want to hear this Scripture. They're tired of being servants." Once again I saw how the Scriptures could speak so pointedly in a context different from my own experience. The words of the prophets about the oppression of workers and the message of the Psalms about the destruction of evil had a very different meaning and feel for me at that moment in South Africa, a meaning quite apart from the experience of so many Christians in other rich nations.

Talking at teatime one day with a Zulu pastor recently released from prison, the Rev. Ben Dlu-Dla, I heard one more account of the cruel consequences of apartheid. The people of his small town in an area in the southeast near the city of Durban had been informed sometime before by the government that they had to move from homes they had occupied for several generations to a barren area six miles farther away from Durban—where all the jobs were. Their living space had been declared a "White area" under the terms of the Group Areas Act, and the government had told the Zulu people they could no longer live there. So they would have to move from their own homes, where families had dwelt for generations, and move to a place requiring a much longer trip to any employment. Not only that, they would have to pay rent for the new homes that the government had built for them, houses that were inadequate for larger families. Pastor Dlu-Dla and several other ministers from the town had called large town meetings with their people to discuss what to do. He stood up to speak at one point and told the crowd to defy the government. "You tell the government that these are your homes and you're not moving. Tell them that your pastor told you not to move!" He said that the church provided real strength to people ordered to relocate. Another pastor, the Rev. Ben Ngidi, had also publicly opposed the government's orders to move and had been arrested and jailed for three months.

The faith and bravery of the people I met gave me hope that the tyranny of the present moment never has the last word. With grace and courage, so many Christians I met in South Africa faced their tragic circumstances with a determination and faith that I had seen only once before—in the US struggle for civil rights in the 1960s. I remembered the words of John Lewis, head of the Student Non-Violent Coordinating Committee, opening a speech in 1963 with the words, "I'm John Lewis. I'm twenty-three years old and I've been arrested twenty-three times."

New Light Emerging

Other signs of light and hope had emerged in South Africa. Many Christians and others worked for reconciliation and change. Even in the NGK (Nederduits Gereformeerde Kerk, or Dutch Reformed Church of the Afrikaners who supported the government), signs of hope had arisen.

Two months before our Assembly, 123 ministers of the NGK had signed a public statement calling for reconciliation between the races and an end to laws concerning race classification and group areas. Such laws, the statement declared, "cannot be defended on the basis of the Bible." Upon its release, the leaders of the NGK vigorously denounced the signers, calling them communist sympathizers—an entirely predictable reaction.

I felt an extraordinary disconnect between my experience at the Assembly and the actions of my own American government. Under President Reagan, the United States had in the early months of 1982 protested vigorously against the police state tactics used by the Soviet Union to subdue and deny human rights to the people of Poland, who were using strikes and other means of protest at the time under the leadership of Lech Walesa and the Solidarity trade union. At the same time the Reagan administration vigorously supported and encouraged the government of South Africa because of its strong anti-communist stance, even though South Africa used the very same police state tactics to deny the rights and dignity of 80 percent of its people. Hypocrisy ran rampant, I thought. It is one thing to read about incidents in the rest of the world, but another to actually see what occurred, and what I saw clearly showed real ugliness and tragedy. Throughout the week-long Assembly, I wavered between the feeling of awe I experienced being with these people of great faith, and feeling at times like an extra on the set of a really dreadful movie, having no power to change either the plot or the screenplay.

Controversy

The most controversial act of the UCCSA Assembly involved a proposed suspension of a dialogue with the NGK. Both churches were members of the World Alliance of Reformed Churches, an international ecumenical group. The NGK and the UCCSA had been engaged in theological dialogue over a period of several years. But many UCCSA members had been increasingly frustrated by the NGK's continuing refusal to discuss the injustices of apartheid. Black pastors at the Assembly pushed a resolution stating that "we [the UCCSA] will have no dialogue with the NGK unless they state officially that apartheid is a sin and a heresy." Several pastors explained to me that the NGK had been interested in dialogue with other churches of the Reformed family for the sole purpose of convincing the World Alliance that they were really in friendly contact with their sister churches. That is, they were trying desperately to preserve their good standing in the world ecumenical movement.

Initially, I thought that the resolution seemed misguided—honest dialogue does not mean talking only with those with whom you agree. Doug Bax, a well-respected White pastor and theologian, stood up during the tense debate over the resolution to say, "We can't refuse to dialogue with people because we think they're so sinful. We're all in the same boat. If God had refused to dialogue with us because we were so sinful, where would we be? The question is, how can we best affect the Dutch Reformed Church, by keeping in contact, or not keeping in contact?" That struck me as a sensible argument, and when the resolution came up for a vote, I voted "no" on the motion to suspend the dialogue. The motion passed by a vote of sixty-nine to fifty-five.

Later I realized that, as an American visitor—and outsider to the whole debate—I had no true understanding of what so many people had endured for so long. I eventually understood the vote. After all, I had not been one of those who had been knocking my head for years against the stone wall of Afrikaner intransigence.

More Light and Calls for Justice

Other occasional sparks of light shone forth in my time there. Talking with Edgar late one night, I heard a tale about his experience teaching Xhosa to a group of police officers of the Capetown area. The police chief had asked Edgar to teach his officers some Xhosa phrases so they could better communicate with some motorists. Many of the police officers were White Afrikaners who had been ordered by the chief to attend the classes. At first, Edgar explained to me, most of them sat back with their arms folded, obviously resisting the class experience. They made it clear that they were present only because they had been ordered to be. But as Edgar went further into the language, he noticed that the men became more and more interested, even to the point of beginning to show some love for the language. They began to ask Edgar questions about attitudes in the Black community. He told me he had a chance to explain some things to them in a gentle way—no doubt an enlightening experience. At the end of the course, the class presented Edgar with a beautiful pen set as a gift of thanks. Yes, it seemed a small thing in the whole context of South African life, but it struck me as another small ray of hope of reconciliation in that divided country. Edgar then made a striking observation. "People from outside cannot change South Africa, it has to be the younger people of South Africa who have a real hope."

The closing worship for the week featured the Rev. Margaret Constable, a member of the Colored community and newly-elected Moderator of the UCCSA, preaching on the Gospel text about the church from Matthew, "The gates of hell will not prevail against it." Once again, a Scripture text sounded far different in apartheid South Africa than it would have at home in the United States. The Assembly had passed numerous resolutions speaking out against the practices of the government. As an official delegate, I joined in the call to the government to reject detention without trial, deplored the forced removal of people, and expressed support for pastors who solemnized interracial marriages (then forbidden by the Prohibition of Mixed Marriages Act). The feeling grew stronger through the week that I had been set into the midst of a revolution, a time when the mighty were being called to account, and the captives set free.

I thought of the startling New Testament text in the sixteenth chapter of Acts, when Paul and Silas set a slave girl free from an evil spirit. Her owners, furious because the demon-possessed slave had made money for them, had Paul and Silas severely beaten and tossed in jail. At midnight, the text relates, while the other prisoners listened to the chained-up missionaries singing hymns, an earthquake struck, knocking off everyone's chains and throwing open wide the prison doors. The Roman jailer, seeing the doors open, logically assumed that the prisoners had all escaped. Despairing, and knowing he would be held accountable by the imperial authorities, he grabbed a sword preparing to kill himself. Paul called out for him to stop: "We are all here." The jailer became a Christian when he saw that Paul, the prisoner, felt more free than he, the jailer.

Paul and Silas, Desmond Tutu and Ben Dlu-Dla, each of whom had been captive to powerful forces, were more free than their captors. Knowing Rome to be an unforgiving master, the Roman jailer stood ready to kill himself because he thought his prisoners had escaped. Desmond and Ben, whom the South African government believed they had under government control, had a trust in another master who had set them free from fear. It all hit me as an extraordinary demonstration of the faith that casts off fear like shedding an old ragged coat that had fallen to pieces and no longer held together. Desmond and Ben, along with many others, lived in faith and joy because they knew that the government did not have the last word.

Reflection and Dissonance

In South Africa, I learned that experience itself is not the best teacher; reflection on experience is. I could see in Desmond Tutu, Edgar Bukashe, Margaret Constable, John DeGruchy, and others the same grace at work as it had been in Martin Luther King Jr. Dr. King had insisted on loving his enemies, a radical act in defiance of usual human practice. I realized that they all knew that the act of baptism is a radically countercultural act, because it puts us into relationship with people whom we would not choose on our own. The grace of God in Jesus Christ overcomes the highest barriers and reconciles us to one another because it is a radical act of hospitality that opens us to the gifts of other people. For Christians, to refuse to see others who differ from us as the revelation of the face of God is a denial of the faith. As the Setswana proverb puts it, "A human being is a human being because of others." We cannot live fully without those who are different from us. I returned home knowing I could never let go of this lesson.

On my way home to Maun after the Assembly, I had a jarring experience at the railway station in Gaborone. Meshach Serema had dropped me off there after making the long drive back to Gaborone from Kimberley. Standing in the crowd of travelers, Blacks and Whites together waiting to get their seat assignments, I overheard a conversation between two young White men a few feet away from me. They spoke English, talking in normal voice tones so that anyone around them could easily hear them. In what struck me as a startling and offensive comment, one said to the other, "I hope I get assigned a compartment with some White people, so I have someone to talk to." No one paid attention to the comment—at least not visibly—but I felt like I had whiplash, bouncing from a setting of defiant, courageous witness against apartheid to a casual expression of its tragic consequences. Painful for me to hear, but at the same time I couldn't imagine that many people in the crowd around them did not have a visceral reaction of sheer disgust. Once more I witnessed the chasm between people produced by the apartheid system.

AUTHORITARIANISM AND RACISM

Zambia Visitors

At home during the term break in August, we had visitors from another type of authoritarian regime. American missionaries would occasionally show up with no advance notice, knowing that other mission folks would provide hospitality. We had been told to expect this. Others could not contact us ahead of time, given the lack of telephone lines and the uncertainty of postal service. But it never felt burdensome because of the inevitable interesting stories they had to share. Another UCC missionary, teaching at a girls' secondary school in Zambia, appeared at our door late one morning with her son, visiting from America. Peggy served as a teacher and chaplain at her school, and her son Cliff had recently arrived for a visit. The United Church of Zambia sponsored the school, which featured something that sounded like a real luxury to us—a swimming pool.

They arrived with some rather disturbing news about the situation in Zambia. The government had put forth a plan to begin teaching "scientific socialism" (i.e., Marxism) in the schools. Zambia's churches adamantly opposed the proposal and had been trying to fight it. However, the strong influence of the communist Eastern European bloc nations, who provided much of Zambia's economic support, seemed to be dominant. Peggy explained that the government intended that scientific socialism would eventually replace religious education in the schools. She said that they still had good reason to hope that the opposition would be vocal enough to stop this from happening, and that President Kenneth Kaunda had been losing a lot of support because nothing much had improved in his seventeen years in power. With a rather weary expression, Peggy described the authoritarian nature of Kaunda's rule. "Whenever Kaunda comes to town, all the students are trotted out in front of the school and strictly instructed to wave as he passes by. Earlier this year, one of our teachers was arrested after a Kaunda appearance when she refused to wave as he went by in his motorcade." Elaine and I felt grateful that we lived in a functioning democracy, an unusual phenomenon in Africa at that time.

Recognizing Racism

After lunch our two guests went off to wander around the village. A bit later Peggy and Cliff returned later from their sightseeing, saying that they wanted to take a canoe ride into the Okavango delta the next day. Elaine couldn't go because of pending tasks in the treasurer's office, so Sherry and I readily agreed to go along. In the morning we went to the Okavango River Lodge, a safari camp in the delta, where they offered all-day canoe trips up river from the lodge. The lodge rented out long, slender boats called mokoros, each boat carved out of a single tree trunk. A twelve-year-old boy went with us as a guide, using a long, thick pole to push the mokoro through the water. He stood straight up in the front of the canoe, the four of us seated in a single line behind him. The boy's strength and endurance surprised me, poling for four people in a canoe trip that eventually covered eight hours.

As we rode smoothly along the calm, clear waters, we passed two-foot-wide lily pads scattered over the water's surface. Tall grasses, nourished by the waters, lined the sides of the river channel. Magnificent bird life abounded—blacksmith plover, lilac-breasted roller, and numerous other species. Fish eagles soared high overhead with keen eyes on the water. An occasional crocodile could be seen slithering out of the water into the grass along the way. At two places where the channel opened to a wider expanse of water, we could see some silent, motionless hippos almost completely submerged. The guide had to be especially careful at those points, since a hippo could rise suddenly out of the water and easily upset a canoe. Once a few impala performed their graceful leaps close to us on the right side of the river.

I had noticed back at the lodge that the woman in charge had given our young guide a tin of beef, presumably for his lunch. But when we stopped for lunch, sitting on an open spot next to the water, he never opened the tin. We had food for ourselves, so we shared some of our food with him. It didn't occur to us until later that he may have been in the habit of saving the tin for his family.

Okavango river channels are serpentine, winding around in various directions so that it is usually impossible to see very far ahead. Later on the way back, we came to a wide spot in the river that gave us a longer view of the water ahead. Spotting two fishermen in a mokoro some distance from us on the river, I made a thoughtless, senseless move. Foolishly, I began to focus my camera on them. The older man in the other boat immediately began yelling angrily at me. I felt more than embarrassed, quickly lowering the camera, realizing that I acted no differently from any other insensitive White tourist who viewed local people only as sightseeing objects. After feeling superior to, and judgmental toward, the two White men at the Gaborone train station who expressed the wish for White travel companions, I once again faced the reality of my own false sense of moral superiority. Trying to insist that I should not be called "boss" in South Africa, reacting negatively to Colored accents at the Assembly in Kimberley, insulting the people in the mokoro in the Okavango—all made me disturbingly aware me of the embedded prejudice stubbornly remaining in my life.

Returning to the lodge, we paid the P11 fee for the day's use of the canoe. Then we watched with disgust as the woman in charge gave our guide the miserly sum of P2.50 for his eight hours of work poling a canoe with four other people in it. Less than the minimum wage at the time, the amount seemed pitiful. I walked quickly to catch the boy as he left and gave him more money as an extra tip. The outing had opened my eyes a little farther.

27

... And the Darkness Will
Not Overcome It

CHRISTMAS TRAVEL

Another Long Trek South

ALMOST ENTIRELY COVERED WITH beautiful fresh daisies, the altar in
the Anglican Church of Uitenhage appeared especially lovely on that
1982 Christmas Eve. Warm summer December weather in South Africa
looked and felt quite different from the cold and snow of a Pennsylvania
Christmas. Near the Indian Ocean at the tip of South Africa, Uitenhage
in the Eastern Cape province served as home base for UCC missionaries
Jack and Lou Ann Parsons. Talented, energetic, and experienced, the two
had worked for many years as Christian Education consultants for the
United Congregational Church of Southern Africa. At the annual Assembly in July earlier in the year, Lou Ann had cheerfully insisted that Elaine,
Sherry, and I come as their guests for two weeks at the school year's end
so we could all celebrate Christmas together. Their warm hospitality had
made us feel very much at home. And the sight of fresh daisies in December made for an especially joyful celebration of the Lord's Supper
that evening.

Before we departed for South Africa, I spent ten days early in December marking over 200 RE examinations from the small number of

secondary schools still using the old Bible Knowledge exams for the Junior Certificate. Contracted for the task by the Ministry of Education, I had written the exam and had the task of marking them all, a job made particularly tedious by the fact that the exams were in essay form. Because of the heat—110 °F—I took all the papers out on the screened-in porch. With our cat Peanut stretched out on the table next to the pile of exams, I spent almost ten hours a day grading. Peanut disturbed neither me nor the exam papers, much to my satisfaction.

Finally finished, I sealed all the exams into the special packaging sent by the Ministry and took the bundle to the post office. Then back home the three of us happily packed up our car and set out on the long drive to the southernmost coast of the continent. The trip took five days, stopping to visit the Jones family in Francistown, Jack and Chris Purves in Gaborone, and Peter and Barbara Anderson in Johannesburg the first three nights along the way.

At the overnight visit with the Purveses, we were shocked to hear the news that Richard Kashweka, one of our top former students and leader of the Scripture Union, had been arrested and imprisoned for stealing a large amount of cash from his employer, Air Botswana. Somehow having gotten himself into a difficult financial situation, he had succumbed to the temptation upon finding the money on one of the planes. Christine had been visiting him in prison every Friday, as well as checking regularly on his wife. Christine told us that Richard, having agonized over his guilt, made the best of a bad situation, spending time helping other prisoners study for their JC exams, conducting Bible study with others, and tending the prison garden. We found this to be a sad, yet hopeful account of repentance and possibility.

After the overnight in Johannesburg, we still had two days and 600 miles to go. From Johannesburg to Bloemfontein and then on to Uitenhage, we encountered gorgeous scenery, including the stark beauty of the Great Karoo, a vast semi-arid area with seemingly endless plains, jagged hills, and intriguing rock formations. Beautiful campgrounds dotted the landscape, often in or near a town. But again and again when we stopped, we saw businesses with separate entrances for Whites and non-Whites, the campgrounds always for Whites only, and no indication that Blacks lived in areas farther removed from the sight of tourists.

A Warm Welcome to Tragic Circumstances

When we arrived at the Parsons home, tired but pleased to be there, Jack and Lou Ann welcomed us with warm hugs and even warmer cups of tea. Jack and Lou Ann, both in their fifties, had been in South Africa for close to twenty years at the time, and we were fortunate to have such experienced guides to the tragic contradictions of the country. Tall and blond-going-gray, Jack had a laid-back manner about him, with an easy smile that masked his fierce, determined opposition to apartheid. Lou Ann, curly-headed and energetic, gave the impression of a strong-willed woman who always had the ability to cope with any situation. We arrived at a time when the Black and Colored population of Uitenhage had quite recently been upended and placed in great distress by the government's Group Areas Act. Many Colored and Black families had been forced to move from long-time residences to a different location because their land had been newly-designated as a White area. This resulted in many people having to rise an hour earlier each work day because of the longer distance they had to travel to jobs in the cities of Uitenhage and Port Elizabeth. Not only families, but churches and businesses had to move, all forced to leave their old buildings behind—with no compensation from the government.

Jack took us one day to visit the new Dale Street United Congregational Church, a Colored congregation required to abandon the big church where they had worshiped for many years and build a new church in a different area. They had no choice but to move their families and their church building. The government had declared their previous site a "White" area, and they could do nothing to protest it.

As we walked into the church building, we noticed immediately a big plaque on one wall dedicating the building to a former pastor "and to all those hurt by the Group Areas Act." On another wall hung a banner with the words "The kingdom of God." Underneath the words, two symbolic portrayals showed their sense of the meaning of God's action in the world: the scales of justice and a length of chain broken in two, representing the chains of oppression being broken. The pastor, the Rev. Allen Hendrickse, held the position of leader of the Labor Party, the Colored political force in the country. The Colored parliament, set up by the government in another attempt to divide the opponents of apartheid, had little power, but Rev. Hendrickse leveraged whatever he could to help his community. Since he worked through the system to get things done, other anti-apartheid activists sometimes accused him of being co-opted by the government to be a supporter of its policies. With a combination of realism and strong conviction, he explained his position to us, saying, "You can't shout at these Afrikaners. They won't listen if you just shout at them. So I talk and negotiate and do what I can. There is a housing shortage in the Colored community, so I went to Pretoria [the capital] to talk to the government minister responsible for housing and came back with money for several hundred houses."

I thought at that moment, "He's in a difficult position, because to some people he looks like a sell-out and to others he looks like a leader." It made me think of the old political dilemma of ideology vs. compromise with the system. In Pennsylvania a few years prior to this, I participated in a prison visitation program at one of the Pennsylvania state penitentiaries, going once a week over a period of a year with four other men to meet with a group of inmates. An anti-incarceration activist who lived nearby once reprimanded me harshly for doing this, insisting that taking part in an in-prison program meant that I had been "co-opted by the system." I recalled being startled by the vehemence of his objection. Answering him, I had replied, "But *in prison* is where the inmates are. If I can have some positive effect by meeting with them, I will. It doesn't mean that I do nothing else to promote criminal justice reform." Jack Parsons had told me that Rev. Hendrickse had been arrested by the government before, so I knew that the pastor had no fear of opposing the government by speaking out against apartheid.

Jack himself had been picked up and interrogated by the security police several times. They usually asked him whom he knew among church leaders active in anti-government protests, and whether or not he received any money from organizations the government considered subversive. Lou Ann told me later that two police officers once came to the house while Jack attended a church conference, barging in and searching all the files and drawers in his study. They insisted that Lou Ann stay with them and watch them. Then they would be sure that she could swear that they had not planted anything incriminating in the study. She laughed about it, saying, "The only problem they caused was that, after they left, I discovered that our dog had made a mess on a rug in another room while I was stuck in the study!" Jack and Lou Ann had been in the country so long that it seemed obvious to me that they knew what lines in the society they could and couldn't cross. They knew how to be careful in an atmosphere where the security police tried to smother any dissent or opposition to government policies.

This came clearer to me one day when Jack drove me around to see some of the living conditions in Uitenhage. Whites often lived in beautiful homes, while Blacks most often lived in cramped quarters. Black townships usually were composed of small, square block houses, or shanty huts made of wood, corrugated metal, wire, and whatever else they could find. He drove me past shanty towns with appalling conditions, houses packed tightly together, no sanitary facilities. One of these places sat at the bottom of the long hill from the Parsons' house in an area designated as "Black" under the Group Areas Act. Jack said that people who lived in those miserable conditions had jobs, or under the pass laws they wouldn't be allowed to live there. "But the government makes absolutely no provision for housing, so they must scrape together places like these."

Viewing the overcrowded, chaotic scene in front of me, I felt both a deep sorrow for the residents and a real anger at my own US government's support for the people responsible for imposing these despicable conditions on so many members of their society. Under Reagan, the United States supported the apartheid government as a bulwark against communism, when South Africa actually acted more as a bulwark of racism condemned by most of the world. Apartheid raised up a fierce resentment and rage in the oppressed groups, a situation that seemed so clearly to lead to an inevitable violent outburst.

While in the car, I had taken only a few pictures of housing in both Black and White areas. Jack said to me, "We have to be a bit careful about taking pictures. The government doesn't want people taking pictures of poor conditions and showing them to people outside the country." He pointed to a UCCSA church in the midst of the shanties, saying, "If anybody asks, we'll say we were photographing that church building." It dawned on me that I couldn't send the camera film to Johannesburg to be processed as usual, because it could be confiscated. I recalled that some people had the experience of photographs taken in South Africa not being returned. South Africans certainly had to be wary of matters and actions that I would never have considered.

One gray, windy afternoon, the Parsons drove us to Jeffreys' Bay, just southwest of Uitenhage on the Indian Ocean. Few people were out that day, but Sherry and Elaine enjoyed searching the beach for seashells, which were found in abundance. Elaine had gathered a good collection when we began walking back to the car. Taking a slightly different route up the beach, we passed a sign we hadn't seen. It read, "This beach is for the use of White persons only." As I had noticed in Kimberly back in July, the ugliness of apartheid loomed wherever we turned.

Disconnect with Reality

As White people visiting South Africa, it would have been easy to develop a great deal of admiration for the country. Beautiful campgrounds, excellent highways, and lovely scenery marked our entire trip south through the nation. But passing movie theaters with ticket lines made up of Whites only, and seeing only White people at large shopping areas gave us a jarring sense of disconnect with reality. We knew very well that the White population made up just five and a half million of the almost thirty million people in the country. The government deliberately put Black townships out of sight, often completely outside the cities, creating a nuisance, as I noted, for many people to travel a distance to places of work. A strong feeling grew in us that the whole situation could not possibly endure.

That disconnect with reality stayed with us almost everywhere we went. The only time we observed a more public display of Black life and African tribal tradition came one afternoon driving along the main highway between Uitenhage and Port Elizabeth. At one point we passed a large open area along the highway where a couple of dozen small shacks, apparently made of thatch and branches woven together, had been constructed. Several dozen Black teenage males, bodies painted white with clay, sat or walked around the area. Lou Ann gave us the explanation. "This is the initiation camp for young Xhosa males. Over the long Christmas holiday, they do their month of training then go through the rite of initiation into manhood. The bodies are painted white as part of the purification rites. When the initiation period is over, the young men burn the huts. Among the Xhosa, if a boy does not go through initiation, he is not considered a man and has little status in the tribe. The ritual is considered very important by the Xhosa people, but interestingly, hasn't been practiced so much by the Zulu." Xhosa and Zulu, the two largest tribes in the country, both possessed a strong sense of identity and political clout. I reflected on this powerful force of tribal identity held by the Xhosa youth we observed and the sense of strength this gave them, something that could not be denied or taken away even by a brutal, oppressive government.

Driving farther, we visited Port Elizabeth, where less than two weeks before the Black township had held a memorial service for thirty people killed by the South African army in a raid on Maseru, capital of the independent nation of Lesotho. The raid had been condemned by most of the rest of the world as arrogant, cruel, and illegal. Many Black communities around the country had held memorial services for the dead. Lou Ann said that at the event in Port Elizabeth, the police had set up roadblocks into the Black township, arresting a number of Whites who attended, charging them with entering a Black township without a permit. They fined each one thirty Rand—the South African currency. Lou Ann commented, "It was just a tactic of harassment, because the police don't normally pay any attention to such minor violations of the law."

The summer weather at Christmas time presented another kind of disconnect to us. One day when visiting a large shopping mall, we noticed that the doors into the mall and the walls inside had decorations on them exactly as we would have normally seen in the United States, including Santa Claus, reindeer, and sleigh—and snowflakes. As we began to go to the exit, I saw the snowflakes and sleigh on the glass door and had a split-second reaction in my mind: "Oh, it's cold, I don't have a winter coat on!" Then I laughed, realizing how my mind had played a trick on me. I wasn't in North America after all. We went home with the Parsons and later that evening attended the joyous Christmas Eve communion with the fresh daisies, the sure sign of warm weather.

THE LIGHT AND THE DARKNESS

Christmas Joy

All the time at the Parsons' home, we felt pampered and entirely at ease. The Parsons had two adopted children who were at the time in college in the United States, so they had plenty of room for us to stay in their big home. In a treat for Sherry, Jack introduced her to music she had never heard, playing the 1960s Simon and Garfunkel album *Parsley, Sage, Rosemary, and Thyme*. When our hosts discovered that we had no telephone available to us in Maun, they insisted that we use their phone to call our families at home in the United States to wish them "Merry Christmas." A generous hostess, Lou Ann had a habit of passing around a bowl of snacks as appetizers before a meal, including many kinds of snack foods we could never find available in Maun. An excellent cook, she introduced us to new recipes we had never seen. A few days before Christmas, we enjoyed a South African Malay item called sosatis, small chunks of lamb, onions, and apricots alternately arranged on each of several wooden skewers, covered with an herb sauce, then cooked on a barbecue. On Christmas day, Lou Ann surprised us (because we now knew her to be such a good cook) by admitting that she had never before cooked a turkey. But since we and the Hitchcocks were invited for Christmas dinner, she decided to bake her first turkey for the whole group of Christmas guests.

On Christmas day, all seven of us sat in the Parsons' living room offering gifts to one another, trading stories of Christmases past, and thoroughly enjoying the company. Sitting in the midst of smiles, laughter, and stories told, I could see that Sherry felt at ease, obviously appreciating and respecting these adults who were witnesses to a kind of courage and strength she admired. Having just turned thirteen, her education about the world had expanded in ways that I hoped had been leading her to realize the truth of the African proverb, "A person is a person because of others." Life is a web of relationships which hold us and support us in life-giving ways. Jack, Lou Ann, and the Hitchcocks treated her as an equal, never talking down to her, always including her in the conversation. Watching the scene, I felt a satisfying sense of joy and gratefulness. Even in the midst of the pain and struggle of the nation, we were heartened by the faith and witness of the people we had encountered. As John's Gospel puts it, "The light shines in the darkness, and the darkness has not overcome it."

The Ugly Darkness of Oppression

At the Border Post

After the enlightening and enjoyable visit with Jack and Lou Ann, the three of us began to make our way back to Botswana. Leaving the coastal region of Uitenhage and Port Elizabeth, we drove on the excellent main highways over 600 miles in one long day to arrive in the Johannesburg area, stopping at a campground for the night. Our time in South Africa had made clearer than ever the stark contrast between the lives of Blacks and Whites in that rigidly segregated society. For Whites traveling through the country, it seemed like an idyllic place—we had seen lovely beaches, marvelous scenery, and could easily find comfortable campgrounds. Each one featured excellent sanitary facilities and grass-covered campsites, the one drawback being that each family spot seemed rather small. We could drive almost anywhere we wanted, with the troubling knowledge that the campgrounds, beaches, and other facilities were completely unavailable to Black or mixed-race people. Neatly painted wooden signs indicating *Whites only* appeared frequently over doorways in the towns and cities along the route. We had that eerie feeling of unreality staying at a campground and seeing nothing but White faces, knowing that Whites were such a small minority. The Black townships in the country, like the one I saw in Uitenhage, were mostly crowded shacks or shanties pushed up against one another in order to squeeze in as many people as possible on the small amount of land allotted. Usually no paved roads ran through the townships. In White areas, good paved roads and larger houses were common. As one of our British missionary friends in Botswana once put it, "South Africa is the most desirable, beautiful place in the world to live if you're White and have no conscience."

Leaving the campground the next morning we took the road north, planning to reach Gaborone that evening. Upon arrival at the border with Botswana, Sherry quickly but quietly observed that about a half dozen Afrikaner soldiers in full combat dress, rifles slung over their shoulders, were stationed at the border post. "And look at that big dog with them." Two soldiers had tight grips on the leash of a large German shepherd guard dog, a menacing greeting to be sure. I stopped the car and said hello to one of the soldiers, who asked gruffly for our passports and travel visa. He then asked where we had been, and I replied, "Visiting friends in Uitenhage." On the travel visa I had recorded my occupation as "Teacher" because I knew that "Missionary" might have drawn closer scrutiny. We were well aware that several foreign missionaries had been expelled from South Africa in the previous two years for speaking out against apartheid. The guard then asked, "Did you obtain any books or magazines in South Africa?" I replied, "Yes, we bought a few religious books in a bookstore in Port Elizabeth." His no-nonsense response: "Show me." No fooling around with this fellow. He grabbed a large roll of paper which had long lists of publications banned by the South African government, ready to check anything we had against the list.

The box that held the books sat right behind the back seat of the jeep. I crawled between the seats to the back and looked down over the box. Pulling the brown cardboard flap up, I picked up the first three books in the pile: John Howard Yoder's *The Politics of Jesus* , C. S. Lewis's *The Screwtape Letters,* and a book on spiritual life by historian Richard Lovelace. But I saw immediately that the next item in the pile could be a problem. A pamphlet published by the South African Council of Churches entitled *An Empty Table? Churches and the Ciskei Future,* it described the so-called homeland for Blacks where the government forced many Xhosa people to live. Although I knew it did not fall under the classification of banned literature, anything from the SACC would set off alarm bells in the guard's head. The anti-apartheid leader, Bishop Desmond Tutu, served as president of the Council of Churches, and the pamphlet featured serious criticism of the government policy. If the guard saw the pamphlet, I instinctively knew he would quite likely insist upon searching everything in the car. Knowing that the guard stood alongside the jeep's front window, I realized that he could not see exactly what I did with my hands. So I pulled up the corners of several more items in the box and slid the SACC pamphlet underneath them. I closed the flap of the box and turned to get back to the driver's seat, handing him the first three books.

Sherry and Elaine had stepped out of the jeep, a somewhat apprehensive Sherry standing close to her mother while the soldier went around to the front passenger seat to sit and examine the books. As he sat down he also spotted a Nancy Drew book of Sherry's on a seat and picked that up. He looked through all the books briefly, pausing longer over the Nancy Drew and the C. S. Lewis books. He seemed puzzled by Nancy Drew, paging through it more than the others. He also did not seem to know what to think about *The Screwtape Letters.* I remember having the strange feeling that any government with that much fear of the printed word had to be in serious trouble.

Finished with his reading, he insisted upon looking under the seats and examining a couple of our packed bags. But he never went around the back to look in the boxes there. After another minute or two of inspection, the guards opened the border gate and waved us through. As we drove across the border into Botswana, we had the satisfying feeling of relief of once again being in a free country.

Ugliness Reveals Itself Further

We headed for the Purveses' house in Gaborone, eager to see them again and report on our trip. After a couple of hours' drive, we left the variegated landscape of South Africa, driving into the flat, sandy Botswana country-side. Finally arriving in Gaborone, we found the Purves' house and told them about our experience at the border post. To our great surprise, Jack and Chris told us that just one week previously, two young Mennonite couples returning to Botswana through the same border post were detained by the guards for having a banned pamphlet. At the time, Mennonites were already under suspicion because their missionaries had been expelled from South Africa a few years before. The two couples had a valid travel visa to drive through South Africa to a conference in Lesotho, the small independent country surrounded by South Africa. But they had a twelve-hour, single-entry visa; that is, they were allowed to enter and leave South Africa one time, and could spend a maximum of twelve hours in the country. The drive from the Botswana border to Lesotho took eight hours. Easy to see how much the South African government distrusted and despised Mennonites. In contrast, we had a twelve-month, multiple-entry visa, meaning that we could come and go from South Africa as many times as we wished over a period of twelve months.

The young couples did not know that the banned list included the pamphlet they had. Upon spotting it in the car, the guards immediately took the two couples into an office, phoned the nearest security police office in Zeerust, a town about sixty miles away, and waited. Two state security police officers drove for an hour to get to the border post for an interrogation session. The security people kept the two couples for four hours, asking them questions about where they obtained the pamphlet, what they did in Lesotho, who they were working for, who their Mennonite colleagues were in Botswana. One police officer cursed and yelled at them for quite some time, telling them that the Mennonites in Botswana they had mentioned were communists. Then the police separated the young couples, putting the men in one room and the women in another, interrogating them and continuing to put them under considerable strain and distress. The police kept the four so long that the border post closed for the night, forcing the couples to stay on the South African side of the border overnight before they could leave the country. I knew right away how relieved and happy they must have been the next morning to cross the border into a free country.

Chris and Jack also told us the tale of a British family, friends who had been living for a time in South Africa. Their two children, who attended a White school, were taken one day to an office at the school and interrogated by police about what they had heard at an Anglican Church gathering featuring Bishop Tutu. The two children were seven and nine years old. I thought once again how tragic it must be for people to live under the circumstances of such fear and repression, and how ghastly that those in authority felt so threatened that they would interrogate small children. The obvious fear of losing control had a tight grip on those in power. But I knew that the light still burned brightly, and the darkness had not overcome it.

28

Too Many Bends on a Footpath Do Not Prevent One from Reaching One's Destination

—African Proverb

RICHARD

At Maun Secondary School, Richard Kashweka had always been a leader and example to others. He often intervened to aid other students in difficulty and offered comments in Scripture Union meetings which showed his thoughtful Christian faith. Well-respected by everyone, his act of theft from the airline certainly stunned everyone. Not long before his Cambridge exams were to begin, his mother became ill, which, along with other problems, prevented him from completing the exams. That prompted him to take the job with Air Botswana. When sentenced to a multi-year term in prison, he met his fate with a determination to redeem himself and a constructive attitude, giving himself immediately to helping other prisoners by teaching them and leading Bible studies. He also began to study on his own in preparation for retaking his Cambridge exams when the authorities released him from prison after he served a three-year term.

I found out years later that after his release, he did pass his Cambridge exams and began to work, eventually becoming the director of a human rights project in Kasane in northern Botswana. He also became the owner and host of a safari lodge in that area. His determination and

perseverance to overcome his grievous blunder earlier in life gave me a
sense of the hope and possibility of redemption and renewal.

MOJADI

Nationwide regulations for schools included at least one rule which
I found troubling and unfair. If a school girl became pregnant, the authorities subjected her to dismissal from school and forbade her from re-
entering school for a period of one year. And she could not return to the
same school. The punishment for the boy who impregnated her? Not a
thing. Certainly the possibility existed that someone other than a student
could have been guilty and no perpetrator identified, but the regulation
seemed unfair to me.

When Mojadi Kwerepe, one of our student leaders, became pregnant and failed to return to school in September for the third term of
the 1982 year, a combination of frustration and sadness for her hit me. I
discovered that she had been dismissed from school. Not even her father,
the member of Parliament for our area, could have waived the ruling. At
the time, it appeared that her future prospects in life had been drastically
cut short, much to the dismay of everyone who knew her.

Only a couple of weeks into the term, a Form Three student named
Obuile had to be sent home for a different reason. Because he had not
yet paid his school fees, and could not take his Junior Certificate exams
that November unless he paid them, the principal had to insist that he
go home to obtain the money. After he traveled the long distance home
to Kasane in the north, we waited three weeks and he had not returned.
I worried about him because it probably meant that he couldn't find the
money. Knowing that he had a good chance of passing the JC exams, I
thought about how to get in touch with him, realizing that without telephone service the quickest way would be to send him a telegram urging
him to return to Maun right away. "Somehow," I thought, "we could find
scholarship money to help him." I immediately went to the post office to
send the telegram.

Walking into the post office, I found it crowded, three lines of
people waiting for tellers to serve them. Numerous others stood writing
at the several stand-up desks available. Finding the shortest line, I waited
only a few minutes before arranging for the telegram. Glancing around,
I saw Mojadi writing something at a stand-up desk. I hesitated for just

a brief moment, unsure about what I could say to her. But I went up to her, greeted her, trying to say that we hoped and prayed for her good health and that we had not forgotten her. Obviously ill at ease, she would not look at me directly. Although she replied that she felt well, her lip trembled and I could tell that she fought to hold back tears. I had such an agonizing pain for her because she looked ashamed and depressed. I could only imagine that she must have felt that the world had crashed in on her, that she might never get back into school and so had much less of a future than she once hoped. Struggling to find words for her, I sensed that at that moment surrounded by other people in such a public place, I felt constrained in what I could say. I expressed the hope that she would take good care of herself and then left the post office. A combination of anger at the system and sorrow for Mojadi remained with me for a long time. I berated myself for not being more helpful.

More than thirty years after being in Africa, I had a surprising encounter with two former Maun students at a conference in New Jersey, Dr. Bernard Bulawayo and Dr. Morrison Sinvula. They told me many tales of the students from our three years at the school. To my great delight, one especially heartwarming story concerned Mojadi. She had her baby, then went back to complete her secondary school at a different school. After obtaining a BA degree from the University of Botswana, she earned a Master's degree in business and economics at the University of Stellenbosch in South Africa and eventually worked her way up to become an important official in one of the big banks of Botswana. More recently, she left that position to become an official for the Non-bank Financial Institutions Regulatory Authority of Botswana. She leads the team that regulates among others, the stock exchange, investment companies, and securities brokers. Her evident hard work, resilience, and determination filled me with admiration for her persistence. Thrilled at hearing this excellent news, I felt greatly heartened, vividly recalling that last time that I had seen her at such a low point in her life. It is a story of triumph, faith, and perseverance I will never forget.

NCHUNGA

On term break in August 1982, we had a surprise visitor: our former student and friend Nchunga Nchunga. After receiving a first-class pass on his Cambridge exams in 1981 at the end of Form Five—a feat very few students accomplished—he had entered the national community service program called Tirelo Sechaba (lit., service to the country). For the previous several months, he had been working far up in northern Botswana in the village of Etsha, teaching Standard Four in a primary school and working at the local clinic. He looked well, confirming that he had been enjoying the work. Having to learn Mbukushu, the language of 90 percent of the people of the area, had been a big challenge for him. He said, "The first day I arrived, people began to speak to me in Mbukushu. I did not know Mbukushu." We asked, "So what did you do?" With just a hint of a grin, he replied, "I remained silent."

He found a total of five students in his Standard Four class, which at first seemed ideal. But he quickly discovered a significant barrier: the children knew neither English nor Setswana. Because they needed both languages for the later schooling, he had no option but to teach the children both. He began with English, and then after a while started on Setswana. It seemed to me an overwhelming challenge, but he appeared quite cheerful and up to the task. We were happy to see him, knowing that he had begun his adult journey in good spirits and in creative work. He departed for Etsha after a two-hour visit and some snacks. Many years later, Nchunga Nchunga earned a law degree from the University of Edinburgh and served as an attorney for the Botswana government.

BATLHALEFHI

The first time I encountered Batlhalefhi Moeletsi, one of the top students at the school, I watched him as he participated in a debate against another school. Only a Form Two at the time, he impressed me with clever and effective use of argument. Attending the debate with me, Chris Purves turned to me at one point to comment, "Can you imagine—he's just a Form Two!" He seemed to have a bright future ahead of him. The name Batlhalefhi means "the cleverest (or wisest) ones."

One Friday early in March the next year, now in Form Three, Batlhalefhi suffered from a sudden, violent fit in the dormitory. The boarding master sent him to the hospital, where a doctor gave him a sedative. I had heard that he had endured painful boils under his arms, and initially I thought that he had reacted to some injections given him to heal the boils. Saturday he slept most of the day, and then upon waking, he began lashing out at people around him. Molapo, the head boy that year, found me and asked me to get Batlhalefhi to the hospital. We called on Mary Beth, his class teacher, to come along. She wisely found the Zimbabwean teacher Kelly Nare to help convince Batlhalefhi to go. As one respected by students, Kelly persuaded him, fortunately without much trouble. When we arrived, the nurse on duty gave Batlhalefhi some valium and had him stay and sleep at the hospital that night.

When he awoke Sunday morning, he remembered nothing at all of what had happened. He came back to school that afternoon, but just to be sure we were covering all the possibilities, I took him to see the Motswana psychiatric nurse Monday morning. That way I could be sure that someone who knew the mindset and attitudes of the culture would be able to deal with potential issues. We were fortunate in Maun to have a keenly perceptive man in that position who would likely deal effectively with the problem. After a talk with him, Batlhalefhi came back to campus, but he went back again in the afternoon. The nurse and the other medical staff had decided to keep him in the hospital for a couple of days.

Talking with the church deacon Mr. Dikole at our weekly meeting for the theological training, I learned that malaria often causes a high fever and makes a person delirious. That seemed to be a possible answer. We also worried that Batlhalefhi might believe that he had been the target of a bewitching spell. After returning from the hospital later in the week, another kind of strange malady struck him. A couple of students from the dorm came to our door to say that Batlhalefhi had begun "feeling badly again." Carol Schaad went with me and the two students to check on him. We found him lying in a lower bunk bed with his head turned to the left, looking ill at ease and obviously scared. In a slightly trembling voice, he said to us, "My neck is stiff and I can't move it." Thinking more than ever that he may have thought himself bewitched, we put him in the Nomad and took him back to the hospital. All students were keenly aware of the possibility that relatives of a good student could be jealous because their own child had not received a spot in secondary school; they could pay a traditional doctor to cast a spell on the successful student. I thought that Batlhalefhi might have this fear. Whatever had happened, he felt much better after another two days in the hospital, returning to school a few days before students had mid-term exams.

My Form Three Religious Education class had been focused on authority and its proper uses in church and society. One question which the national RE panel had chosen for that term's exam read like this: "Give an example of someone in authority who uses his authority to serve others."

On his exam paper, Batlhalefhi wrote this answer: "A teacher, e.g., Rev. Christensen. A teacher (Rev. Christensen) serves students. When the students have problems they go to see him and he takes his time explaining until the students understand—that is service." Upon reading that, I had a keen sense of gratitude for this opportunity I had been granted to teach.

Sometime that term, Batlhalefhi had begun attending the evening Scripture Union chapel prayer services. In his RE class, he began to raise questions about some aspects of Christian faith as we discussed the teachings in the curriculum. One day in class he asked me a pointed and perceptive question about the passage in the Gospel, "How hard it is for a rich man to enter the kingdom of heaven." He read the passage out loud, then said bluntly, "That must have no meaning today, because many churches have rich people who keep themselves apart from poor people. Did Jesus really mean that?" He had obviously zeroed in on the glaring inconsistency between Jesus and his supposed followers. I must admit that I did not have a very good answer for him. He saw the hypocrisy clearly. I simply said that most Christians fail in many ways in following Jesus, and that if someone claims to be a Christian and shows no concern for the poor and suffering, that person has neither read the Bible very well nor taken Jesus seriously.

A few weeks later in the same class, Batlhalefhi offered another comment about Christians which showed again how he had a knack for zeroing in on the obvious: "If it's true that Christians are to care for their neighbors and be concerned about justice, then Christians everywhere ought to get together and work for that. Right?" Yes, that ought to be obvious, but it has been sadly omitted from many Christians' thinking. Disunity among Christians is always a scandal and ought to be regarded as such. It harms the effectiveness of Christian witness and hinders genuine care for the world.

The next year, in Form Four, Batlhalefhi had Mary Beth as his English teacher. She also served as his class teacher. At the close of one school day, she met me on the path just outside our house with a big grin on her face. Always the conscientious teacher, Mary Beth often made it a point of emphasis to have her students pronounce words clearly and correctly. One day in the classroom, Batlhalefhi said *gonna* for *going to*, and Mary Beth quickly corrected him. "Remember, it's *going to*." Batlhalefhi quickly responded, "But Rev. Christensen says *gonna*!" They had me, obviously a certified bad example! Mary Beth couldn't resist telling me, laughing as she did so.

During his Form Four year, Batlhalefhi had occasional bouts with health problems, so Jack and Chris Purves invited him to stay in Gaborone for the August term break. They arranged for him to undergo a variety of medical tests. Strangely enough, the tests uncovered a malady involving a surplus of red blood cells. Part of the treatment included being bled once a month, which sounded to me more like eighteenth-century medical practice than anything modern. But the doctors knew what they were doing.

Batlhalefhi had begun attending the evening Scripture Union meetings in the chapel. One evening he surprised me with a comment about discouraged people who are inclined to say that there is no God. He smiled and said, "But, you know, they still use the expression, 'My God!'" He went on to say, "If we are depressed and discouraged, God is present for us in our minds and hearts, and he will not abandon us."

One Saturday afternoon, Carol Schaad had a conversation with Batlhalefhi which showed his growing sense of Christian faith. He mentioned to Carol that the love and fellowship of Christians had impressed him, so Carol asked him, "What do you think will happen when you're out of school and away from the fellowship?" Referring to the former student leader who had been convicted of robbery, Batlhalefi quickly responded, "Well, look at Richard. He got into trouble and is in jail, but we are praying for him every day. That shows that the fellowship is still there."

Thankfully, the treatments he received turned out to be helpful. But then in early January, Batlhalefhi became infected with bilharzia, a nasty parasite found in some rivers. Fortunately, it could be cured with some medication. He felt quite ill until he took the pills, but then he had to be very careful to be sure he would not be re-infected. Because first term had not begun, Elaine and I went looking for him to see how he felt. We found him looking more discouraged than we had ever seen him. He explained about the bilharzia, and then he told us more bad news. The small hut in Maun where he had been staying burned to the ground the day before we saw him. Almost everything he owned—most of his clothes, all of his books and notes from Form Four, and his blanket—all burned. He said, "I cried like a baby" when he and a friend came back to the hut and found it burning. Terribly disheartened—especially by the loss of the notes, which he needed for his Cambridge exams at the end of Form Five—he looked so discouraged that we took him back to our house and sat him down while we gathered together some of my extra clothes, a blanket, and a toothbrush. He commented that having so few possessions and losing them did not seem so bad when he realized how much worse it could have been if he owned much more. He said that despite being terribly discouraged, the whole situation made him think again of Richard, the former Maun student still in prison. With deep feeling, Batlhalefhi remarked, "There he is, with nothing, in a difficult situation that he can't escape, but he's making the best of it—doing bible study with others, teaching other prisoners so they can pass their Junior Certificate exams, studying on his own to take the Cambridge exams, as well as working on tending the prison vegetable garden. It's inspiring!" That's when we knew that Batlhalefhi would move on with confidence and hope.

In March 1983, as we were preparing to leave Botswana for home, Batlhalefhi became sick once again. Elaine and I tried to look after him, making sure that he made it to his doctor visits. On our final Saturday in Maun, he came to visit us one last time. I had gone out on an errand, so he talked with Elaine for quite a while, telling her that he could never forget people who "saved my life," as he put it. Telling her his plans, he said that he thought he would like to become a doctor now with all that experience with what it meant to be sick. I remembered that back in Form Two, his ambition had been to be a soldier in the Botswana Defense Force.

But he changed his mind after that. Years later, after having earned law degrees from the University of Botswana and Harvard University, Batlhalefhi became a prominent lawyer in Gaborone. He is one of many Maun Secondary School graduates from the 1980s who have gone on to make meaningful contributions to their country.

29

Farewells and a Final Adventure

GOODBYE TO STUDENTS

IN MID-NOVEMBER AT THE end of the 1982 school year, I decided to tell my Form Two classes that our family would be leaving for home during the next year. When I told one section, a collective groan arose from the classroom. Several students called out at once, "When?" "In March," I answered, "at the end of the first term." An anguished cry came from a boy named Gideon, "We will be emaciated!" He obviously meant to express his dismay, but I didn't catch his meaning at first. Thinking it possible that he had tried to use a fancy word and chose one that seemed a bit off-target, I asked, "What do you mean by that?" His heartfelt reply came quickly, "Because you are a good teacher!" Thanking him, I suggested to them that perhaps some day one of them would get a scholarship for study in the United States "You should be sure to inform me so that I can see you. I live about four hours' drive from New York City." Gaewe Morapedi quickly raised his hand to ask, "How much does a taxi cost from New York to your house?" "Gaewe," I said, "If I know that you're coming, I will drive to New York and get you!"

Later that day another boy explained to me that Gideon knew exactly what the word "emaciated" meant. He used the expression to say that they would be thin and deprived when I left, as though a beloved parent who had provided good nourishment for them had left. They would be unhappy and not eat, thus becoming "emaciated." A more touching and satisfying student evaluation would be hard to find.

On the first day of the 1983 school year, I reluctantly turned over my Form Three homeroom class to Dwayne Stewart, a new British RE teacher. He took over until a recent University of Botswana graduate would arrive. As I introduced him to the class, I turned to the students, saying, "I want to hear news in December that all of you passed your J.C. exams!" Then going on to the next class, I walked into the classroom of Form Five Bible Knowledge students to let them know of my family's departure the end of March. In unison, four or five students called out, "Why?" Upon telling them I would be going home, they asked, "To America?" "Yes," I replied. "But can't you extend your contract?" So I told them my plans. "I'm going back to school." To which one young man immediately retorted, "But you're too old to go to school!" I smiled and said, "You're never too old to go to school."

SHERRY'S DESERT ADVENTURE

"She'll be a lot happier to see you when she comes back."

With a smile, the school's principal George Fleshman made this observation as Elaine and I watched Sherry, a bit of an uncertain look on her face, in the group of fifty students crowded onto the back of a large truck. With the rainy season over on a dry, sunny day in late February, the group had scrambled onto the truck to leave for a weekend sports trip. A conscientious leader who always exuded an air of authority, George eagerly showed his support, giving the students a thumbs-up and then clapping for them as they were about to depart. Groups of students gathered around the back and sides of the truck, waving and shouting their support to their classmates. Sherry, a member of the tennis team along with four of the Batswana students and her Dutch friend Neeltje, had been reluctant to go on earlier trips, but this time she had made the effort to put aside her shyness and decided to participate.

With no television, movie theaters, amusement parks, or shopping malls, students created their own entertainment. Organized school sports teams served as a primary form of recreation. As in almost every other nation in the world except for the United States, soccer captured the most interest. Our boys' team, coached by the Zimbabwean math teacher Kelly Nare, had a reputation as one of the best in the country. Netball, a favorite girls' sport, also drew a lot of attention. Similar to basketball, but with no dribbling (impossible on the rough, sandy ground), netball featured quick, clever passing and shooting the ball into a net. Ten years before, Peace Corps volunteers had introduced softball to the nation. A girls' team and a boys' team competed with other schools. Other sports included tennis, volleyball, and chess. I assisted Kelly in coaching the chess players. Sherry enjoyed playing tennis with guidance and coaching from our American faculty colleagues Carol and Susan.

Once or twice a year after the rainy season concluded, the school scheduled a weekend sports trip. Along with the sports teams, the school's debate team joined the trip. Other schools would reciprocate and bring their teams to Maun. All the schools traveled the same way, loading approximately fifty to sixty students onto an open-back flatbed truck. It had horizontal steel bars set close together along the sides, but no covering. Students often stood for the entire trip because they were packed in so closely. Upon first hearing about this mode of travel, I thought, "Whoa! That sounds really dangerous!" In fact, It could be not only dangerous, but disastrous. If a truck full of young people had an accident with another vehicle, or became stuck in deep sand and attempted to turn, it easily fell on its side, throwing students roughly onto the hard ground, resulting in many injuries. A girl from Francistown Secondary School had died in just such an accident the year before.

On that Friday afternoon in late February 1983, Sherry and the other students departed with the school teams for a trip to Ghanzi, located in a remote area of the Kalahari Desert more than 150 miles west of Maun. Elaine and I watched as the truck pulled away, waving to Sherry and the others as they peered through the bars from half-way back in the truck. Because they were headed out into the desert on the single, barely-used road between Maun and Ghanzi, we knew they had little or no chance of an accident with another vehicle. In that part of the country, if a driver passed more than two cars in a full day's driving, it qualified as a busy road. Although Elaine and I were certainly leery about the crowded truck, we had great confidence in Kelly and Boikanyo, the two teachers accompanying the group. Well-respected and experienced with sports trips, they would make sure that the driver stayed alert and drove carefully. So despite the mode of travel and the potential danger, we were not overly worried. The trip should have taken about three hours.

Shortly after nine o'clock the next morning, the one telephone on campus rang in the principal's house. The Ghanzi school principal had a question: "Where are your students? They haven't arrived yet." Carol came rushing to tell us this alarming news. Fear formed a tight knot in my stomach and wouldn't loosen. It eased only slightly when one of the other teachers said, "Oh, they probably broke down. We should hear word of them soon." But Elaine and I didn't know what to think. The cruelty of uncertainty can be harsh, and it held us in its grip. We wandered the campus, talking briefly with others, exchanging expressions of sympathy and encouragement. We wavered between anticipating disaster and thinking that the truck had simply broken down. Maybe they were all stranded in the desert, safe but hungry. The agony and helpless feeling of not being able to do anything weighed heavily on us. As the morning dragged on, the weight got heavier. Thinking the worst, Elaine and I wandered around with the unspoken word between us: if we lost Sherry, our lives would be devastated.

Another teacher suddenly had an idea, suggesting that we contact an American missionary couple who had recently arrived in Maun. For their assignment—the husband worked as a dentist—they had a small airplane to reach more remote villages out in the bush. One of the staff members rushed to their home to request that they fly toward Ghanzi to locate the truck. He came back a short while later, a combination of incredulity and disgust on his face. The extraordinary, disturbing response of the plane owner had been, "No, I'm sorry. We only use the plane for missions of mercy." This greatly distressed and disappointed those of us so concerned about our students.

Saddened and dismayed by this display of indifference, we had no alternative but to wait for any reassuring word of the lost travelers. Finally, after nearly two hours of anxiety and nervous waiting, Boikanyo appeared to tell us what had happened. First he arranged for another truck to go pick up the stranded students and staff, then before leaving, he briefly explained to us what had occurred. Friday afternoon, about seventy-five miles from Maun, the truck had broken down. The left front wheel had caught fire and the truck screeched to a sudden stop. Momentum caused the students to fall forward against one another, but fortunately no injuries resulted. Using most of the drinking water they carried with them, several students and teachers doused the flames and extinguished the fire. But they quickly regretted their first impulse, realizing that they should have used sand from the side of the road to put out the fire. No one had been hurt, but they sat stranded in a particularly remote area of the Kalahari, with little food and even less water.

On such an isolated road, they had little hope or expectation of anyone driving by. Kelly, Boikanyo, and a few students had set out on foot northward toward the village of Sehitwa, arriving about 10:00 pm. Getting a ride in a small pickup truck back to the stranded school group, they could bring little with them except a container of rather salty water. Tired and very thirsty, the students had built a fire and were getting ready to sleep on the ground. They had kept as close as they possibly could to the fire, because the threat from wild animals loomed as a possible danger. A few students slept in the truck. Sherry sensed that the others knew what they were doing by building the fire, so she pushed aside her fears and slept on the ground. She told us later, "I wasn't afraid." Several other students said to her confidently, "Your father will find us!" Out in the desert with no artificial light anywhere, the clear night sky shone brilliant with thousands of stars, but somehow I doubted that the night beauty had held anyone's attention.

After obtaining a truck of adequate size, Boikanyo left to pick up the group and bring them home. They arrived back in Maun about 8:00 Saturday evening, all of them hot, tired, dusty, and hungry. As soon as she spotted us, Sherry came running up to us, saying as she hugged us both, "I thought I'd never see you again!" We held her tightly to us without words. We could not imagine a sweeter family reunion than ours that evening. Happily, none of the travelers had been harmed, and our family had been made whole again. And George had been even more right than he realized.

LAST DAYS IN MAUN

A few weeks before we departed for home, the school received good news from the 1982 Cambridge examination results. It especially pleased me that forty-seven of my fifty-three senior students in Bible knowledge had passed the Cambridge exam, a highly satisfying outcome and considerably better than the 1981 results.

Those final weeks before our departure included numerous farewell dinners with other staff plus a party for Elaine and me hosted by my former Form Two class two days before we left Maun. The students planned a program including a couple of short speeches, then a small group sang a song, "Farewell to You." Tjingovera read a Bible verse, asking everyone to bow their heads in a moment of silent prayer for our safe travel. Then they brought out several big cakes and fruit punch, eagerly shared by all. We were quite touched by their warm expression of appreciation.

Our last day in Maun, March 30, 1983, Elaine, Sherry and I gathered for one last time at the 7:00 am morning assembly, where a singing group from the Scripture Union stood on the podium singing a song of good-bye to us. Tseleng, a Form Five student who had recently been elected chairman of Scripture Union, gave a short speech thanking us for our service to the school. Later in the day, many of the teachers came to the small Maun airport to see us off, with Larry bringing a large supply of M&M's that he passed around for all to enjoy. Because two other passengers had seats, and because we three had all six of our suitcases to take on the cramped little five-passenger plane, the airport officials decided they needed to weigh each passenger and all luggage to be sure the plane could stand all that weight. After the weigh-in, they pronounced it a close call, but they let us all board the plane, luggage included. The cramped space meant that each of us sat with suitcases under our outstretched legs for the two-hour flight to Gaborone, uncomfortable to be sure, but better than carting luggage onto an overnight train.

Off to Gaborone, then Johannesburg, a flight to Nairobi, and then arrival in England, where the Lindfields hosted us in their Sussex home for a week before we crossed the ocean to home.

30

The One Who Never Leaves Home Thinks Mother Is the Best Cook

—AFRICAN PROVERB

RELATIONSHIPS BRING LIFE

Family Ties

WHETHER MAKING SIMPLE GIFTS for one another, sitting down for a modest supper, joining in the beautiful singing of the students, or walking outside under an utterly clear sky filled with stars, we relished the simple life we found in Maun. It provided the space Elaine and I needed for our love to unfold more completely. Away from the rapid roller coaster ride of a middle-class American life, our household had the best, most complete opportunity to be transformed into a family.

In our last month in Botswana, we sat at the supper table one evening talking about our most cherished memories of our time in Africa. Elaine and I spoke of friendships made, warm hospitality, the creativity of the people, and the beauty of the land. We turned to Sherry, waiting for her impressions. She paused a moment, then spoke. "Well, Rich and I have become better friends." Numerous experiences of feeling fulfilled and gratified came to me living in Africa, but none warmed my heart like this one.

A sudden flash of memory struck me that evening. At the age of twelve, I almost drowned. Swimming in a river north of Baltimore with a group of Boy Scouts, I drifted a bit too far out into the middle of the river, where a swifter current began to carry me away. A sense of complete, utter helplessness overwhelmed me, frightened me and made me too scared even to shout. My skinny twelve-year-old body had no chance to fight the current. I remember feeling like a toothpick on an ocean wave. One of the adult leaders ran a short way downriver, jumped in, and proved capable of catching me as I came by, pulling me to safety.

When remembering all that I have seen and experienced since that day, and the life I would have missed had I not been rescued, every day seems to me a gift beyond measure. The many occasions of experiencing a vivid sense of being fully alive—walking with Elaine on calm, clear evenings, observing students coming to a flash of inspiration, sitting around a campfire to the music of Larry's guitar, seeing up close the real faith and courage of opponents of the apartheid system—all showed me that meaning is found in connections, real openness to one another, refusal to abandon one another, refusal to abandon hope for the future.

Seeing Rightly

Relationships constitute our lives—not achievements, not wealth, not reputation. The Setswana proverb has it right: *A person is a person because of others*. To be rich in relationships, to have the experience of belonging to one another, that is true wealth. As a boy growing up in the Reformed tradition of Protestantism, I learned from the Heidelberg Catechism that "I am not my own, but belong, body and soul, in life and in death, to my faithful Savior Jesus Christ." African Christians clearly know that they belong to one another in Christ. Such belonging is not limiting or restrictive, but freeing. It is a lie that Christian faith has to do only with individual salvation. Freedom in Christ is not freedom from one another, but freedom for one another. Salvation embraces that belonging. God promised to make you free; God never promised to make you independent. That's what Christian faith reveals. In Africa I learned to see this in a fuller and richer way.

Sometimes it takes a long time to see what surrounds you always. When I witnessed South Africa apartheid's systematic racism, the inhumanity, cruelty, and poisonous division it produced revolted me. But in my own life experience, the racism of American society had been all around me and ingrained in me growing up. Living through the 1960s civil rights era, I still lived in real blindness to racism's pervasiveness.

Only in Africa did I arrive at a fuller understanding of my own persistent and unacknowledged racism. Coming to understand that racism is never eradicated completely, I realized that only constant vigilance and vigorous resistance can combat it. Racism remains embedded, and I can resist it only with an acute self-awareness. Whites who think that they can understand the Black experience are naive. After a long time, I have come to understand that a White person trying to fully grasp what it is to be Black is like trying to embrace a shadow on a wall. If I have learned to see myself more clearly, I owe it to the variety of my life experiences, the joy of teaching, and the love of Elaine.

BACK HOME

Supermarket and the Power of Affluence

Soon after we returned home in 1983, Elaine and I went to a large supermarket with a list to restock our shelves. Taking a shopping cart, we started down a long aisle where breakfast cereals lined the shelves. Faced with the rows and rows of multiple varieties, we stopped, looked at one another, and said what we were both thinking, "We have to get out of here." The display overwhelmed us, assaulting our senses. It startled us to realize how much. After the three years in an African village, it proved too much for us to bear. We returned our empty cart to the storefront, put it in the lineup of grocery carts by the door, and drove home.

The cereals aisle showed me how much I had taken the affluence of my North American life for granted. It reminded me how easy it can be to accept the myriad ways we are immersed in our own cultural setting, how easy to accept the circumstances of prejudice, affluence, and self-righteousness. Before the African experience, I had looked with a kind of self-righteous contempt on people immersed in a materialistic lifestyle. But returning home from Botswana, I knew I dwelt in the same trap as they did, and I realized that any feelings of superiority I had could never be justified. Years later I learned of the ancient Christian monks who went into the deserts of north Africa to escape from the pressures of society in order to examine their own sinfulness. The monks wisely realized that if they were surrounded by people who shared their same level of greed, there could be no recognition of their own level of greediness.

Coming home, seeing the cereals aisle in the supermarket, I realized something I had never understood before. Real freedom has nothing to do with having choices. It has more to do with how much one is willing to give up, something I had recognized in Nelson Mandela. In that cereals aisle, the sheer number of choices proved to be too overwhelming for us to bear. We had lived for three years in a pared-down, simple lifestyle, with a vastly diminished set of choices of food and entertainment. There in the cereals aisle, we saw what affluence meant, and it did not mean "freedom" or "a better life."

I had to go to Africa to realize the influence of affluence, how great the differences were between my own middle class life and the lives of the world's poor, including the poor in the United States who so often remain invisible—or unnoticed—by others. Seemingly simple matters such as the availability of food, clean water from a spigot, and easy access to health care were realities for me but not for vast numbers of the world's people, and I could never take them for granted again.

Back home in Pennsylvania, we frequently encountered people who posed the following question to us: "What are the people like over there?" The underlying tone of voice nearly always implied, "How odd and different are those foreigners?" Elaine, so often wiser than I, had the best answer. She always responded simply, "They're no different from us. They want to have decent food and shelter. They want what's best for their children. They want to be satisfied with their work. They're just like us."

Affluence had so clouded my life that I had never realized the deep riches, remarkable resiliency, and great creativity of those who did not possess an abundance of things or the abundance of choices of an affluent culture. The simplicity of life in Botswana made me much more able to slow down, to be still and actually see the world more fully, savoring every day as a gift. To this day I believe that anyone not regularly overcome by the presence of beauty in the world, or by the sheer wonder of another human being, is simply not paying attention. Beauty springs up even in the midst of ugliness. Warmth and hospitality arise in unexpected places. Hope can appear even in the most despairing of circumstances. "The light shines in the darkness, and the darkness has not overcome it." Another word for this is resurrection.

The One Who Never Leaves Home

An African proverb wisely states, "The one who never leaves home thinks Mother is the best cook." We suffer from a failure of imagination in our day. So many people have lost the ability to imagine the lives of others or to see the world as they do. Most of us live with people like us, talk with people like us, and have little notion of what it must be like to live in another culture, another neighborhood, or another thought-world. Dwelling for a time in an African culture taught us something about our common humanity, taught us to imagine others as our neighbors, and thus be open to them.

Africa became for me a source of endless fascination. The clash of cultures can result in a larger vision and greater self-understanding. My world became much larger and infinitely more interesting. Learning to see that the world is indeed larger than I knew, I felt a deep longing to learn more and dig into the roots of the modern world, and so in the late 1980's embarked on a PhD program in church history. It became for me a way of discovering how the world came to be as it is today. I always hoped to help students to see new worlds and to appreciate the wonder and variety of the one all around us.

In the summer of 2003, some twenty years after returning from Africa, Elaine and I spent a week at the Chautauqua Institution in upstate New York, a rather idyllic vacation spot featuring concerts, lectures, art, and music. By coincidence, we encountered Pennsylvania friends from thirty years before. Jeanne and Ernie had known me when I served as a pastor and were well aware of my African experience. Jeanne had broken her glasses. Trying to be helpful, I set about engaging in a repair job involving a set of tweezers, a piece of wire, and a rubber band trying to hold the pieces together. Ernie came out onto the porch where I worked, watching what I did for a moment. Then smiling, he asked in jest, "Now, what is your vocation again?" Before I could respond, Jeanne answered on my behalf, "He helps people to see."

Bibliography

Christensen, Richard. "Reflections on African Community." *Christian Century*, December 16, 1981.

Dodge, Ralph E. *The Unpopular Missionary*. Ada, MI: Revell, 1964.

Dostoevsky, Fyodr. *The Idiot*. http://www.literaturepage.com/read/theidiot-432.html.

"I Am Prepared to Die." https://www.nelsonmandela.org/news/entry/I-am-prepared-to-die.

Ingemann, Bernard. *The Pilgrim Hymnal*. Boston: Pilgrim, 1958.

Mbiti, J., et al. *Christian Living Today*. London: Cassell & Collier Macmillan, 1975.

Segundo, Juan Luis. *The Liberation of Theology*. Maryknoll, NY: Orbis, 1976.

Twain, Mark. *The Innocents Abroad*. New York: Random House, 2003.